CW00951569

Stacey Duguid is a journalist and fashion editor. She frequently writes for the *Telegraph*, *The Times* and the *Sunday Times Style*. In 2004, Stacey joined British *ELLE* as Executive Fashion Editor and during this time, wrote the award-winning column, 'Mademoiselle, Confessions of an *ELLE* Girl'. Featuring on the back cover of *ELLE* for over half a decade, the column was a fictionalised version of her life as a single woman living in London. While heavily pregnant with her second child, she resigned the position and began freelancing for Matches Fashion, Net-A-Porter and many more fashion retailers. In the months that followed her marital breakdown, she poured her broken heart into 'The Midlife Dating Diaries', a column that ran for two years in the *Saturday Telegraph*. Leaving the *Telegraph* to write this book (and thereby not leaving bed for several months), growing tired of being in meetings where people chirp, 'we can churn out seventy blogs using AI', Duguid is currently gently stewing in a career-crisis casserole dish of her own making. Future career options include renting herself out as an Emily Blunt lookalike. Or selling her knickers online.

In Pursuit of
Happiness

STACEY DUGUID

PIATKUS

PIATKUS

First published in Great Britain in 2023 by Piatkus

1 3 5 7 9 10 8 6 4 2

A CIP catalogue record for this book
is available from the British Library.

ISBN: 978-0-349-43519-0

Typeset in Garamond by M Rules
Printed and bound in Great Britain by
Clays Ltd, Elcograf S.p.A.

Papers used by Piatkus are from well-managed forests
and other responsible sources.

Piatkus
An imprint of
Little, Brown Book Group
Carmelite House
50 Victoria Embankment
London EC4Y 0DZ

An Hachette UK Company
www.hachette.co.uk

www.littlebrown.co.uk

**Note: Some names and identifying details have been
changed to protect individuals mentioned in this book.**

To Mum and her mum, to Kim, Sara, Jill, Claire, Kate Spicer, Nicole and Natalie for our precious school years.

To countless strangers met via Instagram in the dead of night, I wrote this book for you.

In memory of Rory.

Contents

PART 2
Marriage

PART 5
Mayhem

Introduction

Life Memo – URGENT, Please Read

To: Stacey Duguid
Subject: Life plan
From: The Life Department
Date: Before you hit thirty-five, preferably around the age of twenty-six
Re: Mating (finding The One), Marriage (floofy white dress incoming), Motherhood (it'll be fucking brilliant), Money (you'll have plenty of it), Mayhem (you didn't see that one coming . . .)

Dear Stacey,

It's the Life Department here.

Now, call us terribly organised, but we thought we'd give you a quick heads-up as to what's coming your way. We have a few tips 'n' tricks on how you might best deal with this mad ole thing called life, but, as you make your way through the decades, the way in which you respond to things will be entirely unique to you (code for: book therapy immediately).

So, here goes!

WITH REGARDS TO MATING: Everything you learnt from watching Walt Disney films as a child is bullshit. Sorry. I know.

This takes A LOT of getting used to – and, unfortunately, is something you don't figure out until much later in life. The fairy godmother says, 'Soz.'

Finding a partner with whom to breed takes a lot more effort than running out of a nightclub high on pills, accidentally leaving a Louboutin on a staircase and hoping the bloke you danced with all night will track you down via Instagram. We're not suggesting there's no hope of finding 'The One', we're just saying he probably won't arrive on horseback/climb up your hair to rescue you.

As you exit your twenties, you'll find 'bad boys' tiresome and recovering from heartbreak a little harder. Please take note! Should you find yourself on an endless cycle of exhilarating dopamine 'love' hits when aged thirty-three-ish, seek help in the form of therapy. IMMEDIATELY. Recovering from childhood wounds and filling an emotional void is, in lots of cases, entirely possible. However, facing issues head-on can be frightening and create a ton of grief you'd rather spend a lifetime avoiding. Take it from us, you'll be much happier in the long run if you don't stick your head in the sand. Or a bottle of vodka.

As for gay men, we can confirm they are *not* interested in having sex with you. Best stay far away from Vauxhall if you ever want to meet a straight man. As for that time a gay man wearing a leather harness snogged you in a nightclub in New York, he was in a K-hole. As were you.

On a side note, WITH REGARDS TO MATES (as in, platonic friends): Find good people, find your tribe, hold them tight and never let them go. Put as much effort into friendships as you do romantic relationships; they're worth it. Communicate with your mates regularly, listen to them, and offer help when you have the bandwidth to do so. Make solo time for them – and believe us when we say that romantic relationships end, but friendships continue. Your friends are your REAL soulmates – a fact you'll figure out much later on in life. If you feel shocked by the notion of 'much later on in life', we can confirm that, despite existing on a diet of beige food for forty-nine years, you make it to at least, well, forty-nine.

WITH REGARDS TO MARRIAGE: The big day, a massive dress, five bridesmaids, masses of flowers, yadda, yadda, yadda. Like a lot of girls growing up in the West, marriage is something to aim for in life, right?

No. No, it's not.

By all means, go for it, but don't let so-called societal 'norms' – getting married, having kids, buying a house – distract you from finding your true happiness.

Before signing the marriage paperwork, do your research and ask yourself what happens if the ring comes off. Before we talk about break-ups, know this: marriage requires attention, and relationships are not easy. Take the rough with the smooth and always communicate. Plan date nights, take care of one another, have sex. Are you rolling your eyes? We know, we know, 'date nights' sometimes feel forced, especially after having kids, but you should plan alone time together. Keep talking. Oh, and it's essential to remain curious about one another.

As for the idea of a 'life' partner, word to the wise: it's not possible to find everything you're looking for in one person. That's why you need friends, a career, hobbies, etc. Leave space between you, try not to become 'one', work on retaining an air of mystery. Curiosity could help keep the sexy stuff alive – and anyway, you really don't need to know every single detail of their day and vice versa. This is not a green light for Hitchcock/Agatha Christie-themed rental costumes, BTW. Mystery can be low-key and drama-free. OK, perhaps not drama-free, but still – no costumes.

WITH REGARDS TO MOTHERHOOD: Apologies for the shocking news, but the stork may never fly past, and you may never find your 'mate'. Motherhood in a traditional sense may never happen; you might have fertility issues or struggle to conceive. The good news is, motherhood comes in many forms, such as caring for other people's children, having stepchildren, caring for your community, mentoring disadvantaged kids, and looking after beloved pets. If motherhood is your plan A, find a plan B.

If you do end up giving birth, be prepared for the following weeks to not be all cupcakes and people popping in for cups of tea. Ashamed to admit that motherhood is very far from what they'd expected, and certainly a million miles away from immaculate images of new motherhood on social media, many women keep quiet about what's really going on.

On that, never believe a word that comes out of a new mother's mouth. They're lying. Wolfy is NOT sleeping through the night, and Sophie, his mum, is as shit-scared as you are. These women may not be your 'type' per se, but do your best to make an effort at the mother and baby groups; you'll really regret not doing so. You need a circle of new friends now more than ever before, and these women will provide a vital support network. Time to leave your preconceived ideas at home. (And perhaps your GUCCI nappy bag. Just sayin'.)

WITH REGARDS TO MONEY: When you're young, someone you find extremely boring will mention the words 'savings', 'pensions' and 'investing'. Instead of faking a panic attack or looking at them blankly, as though they've just landed from Mars (the planet, not a new fashion brand), listen to what they have to say. Listen, learn, take action.

If you end up married or cohabiting one day, you'll need

to understand joint finances and know your legal rights. Joint ownership of a property is one thing, but what if you aren't married and then split up with someone with whom you have a child?

And what if the house you all live in is in their name? Your partner owns the house, so – what, you're homeless? On that note, always have your own pot of money. Save little and often every week. Save, invest and plan; I repeat, save, invest and plan. And avoid credit cards like the plague. One more time for luck: AVOID CREDIT CARDS LIKE THE PLAGUE.

As for the products social media influences you to buy, you don't need any of them. The algorithms fed to women via social media ads is money better saved. You don't need a whizzy new hair gadget; you need a pot of savings to fall back on. As for the miracle slimming powder as seen on Instagram, it's just another tax on women. Financial freedom is the ultimate freedom.

The End.

Best wishes – and here's to a very happy life,
The Life Department

PS WITH REGARD TO MAYHEM: Should you, for whatever reason, not receive this memo – or, indeed, the extended version covering holiday insurance, tornadoes in Thailand (aka how to survive a tsunami wearing an Alaïa swimsuit), buying a home alone in Spain on a whim, budget planning, preventing unplanned pregnancies and the perils of recreational drug use – please head to your nearest motorbike shop, buy a crash helmet, pop it on and don't leave the house or answer the phone.

Why? Because you're fucked. Especially . . . sorry for laughing . . . especially when you reach mid-life. You want details? Ha ha ha . . . OK. Sorry, OK. At around the age of forty-six, having ignored ALL my well-researched life advice, should you find yourself divorced, single, homeless, unemployed, and in a short but highly toxic relationship with a married narcissist – don't come crying to me. You may have a glorious collection of shoes, but, as I mentioned before, sadly, you're completely fucking fucked.

Apologies, I don't mean to laugh … it's just – ha ha ha ha – sorry, it's just SO hard to believe one woman could wreak this much carnage and chaos in her own life.

OK, I gotta go before I wet myself. Ha ha ha ha ha ha.

DISCLAIMER: I, HEAD OF THE LIFE DEPARTMENT, HAVE SENT MULTIPLE MEMOS TO WOMEN LIVING IN THE UK SINCE, WELL, FOR EVER. IT'S NOT MY FAULT IF YOU DO NOT RECEIVE – OR INDEED READ – THEM.

Erm, so, I didn't actually get the memo – did you?

That life memo – the one that was meant to explain everything – never reached me. It's clearly lingering in an out-of-use email inbox somewhere. Perhaps it was sent to the Paul Smith HQ, where I worked in 1997 (I say 'worked', but really, it was where I dragged my hungover body each morning and got paid for doing so). Could it be gathering dust in an old Hotmail account set up circa 1999? Or maybe it went to Giorgio Armani's head offices in Milan, from where I was fired in 2002.

Name of terminated employee: Stacey Duguid c/o Giorgio Armani, Milano
Date: Circa May 2002
Reason for firing: Dancing on a podium at the Tom Ford party while wearing a 'borrowed' new-season Armani gown.

Further detail: A) The dress was autumn/winter 2002, and not even out in the shops yet (and we ain't talking the Big Sainsbury's).

B) It cost £3,000, and she's skint.

C) There was only one sample in existence, meaning she definitely 'borrowed' it from the VIP celebrity wardrobe.

D) Cameron Diaz later asked to loan it, but it stank of Tom Ford fragrance and prosecco.

Apparently, Mr A hit the roof.

'Who is the blonde from the UK?' he fired at my Italian press office counterpart, who just went bright red and looked down at her Emporio Armani shoes. 'She was dancing on a *podium*,' he continued, at which point she knew he was talking about me. 'Last night. At the Tom Ford party. Wearing MY DRESS! My staff! My dress! *Vaffanculo!*'

Sheeeeeet.

But I digress ... So, a life memo, huh?

How unbelievably helpful it would've been to receive one. Exactly from whom I was supposed to glean this essential information, this precious intel that could've led to a far less bumpy life, I do not know. I imagine a glamorous Miss Moneypenny type, seated at a huge mahogany desk and firing off a heap of brilliant advice into a Dictaphone. She's wearing black patent shoes (extremely high and by Saint Laurent) and a bright red bouclé Chanel skirt suit. Her hair is held up by a single pencil, and her eyes are smothered in black eyeliner, messily smudged in that way only French women can pull off. Fiddling with a pair of vintage Chanel earrings, she delivers her insightful life lessons in one hit. She's not the PA at all. She's freakin' James Bond.

But I didn't get the memo. I didn't have a plan.

What I did have was more of a routine, one that had been passed down for several generations. I knew what life had in store for me.

Everyone in my family married young, bought a house young, had kids young. No renegades here; no one buggering off to research ancient tribes in the Amazon jungle. Born into a working-class family on the outskirts of Manchester, one didn't set off to far-off lands in search of adventure; one went to work and one 'holidayed' in a caravan in Blackpool once a year. And that, my friends, was that. Job done. Time to retire. Join the bowling club. Die.

At some point in my mid-teens, I knew I wanted more from life. Born in Ashton-under-Lyne, a town where generations of women in my family had worked in Lancashire factories, hard graft was definitely something I could do – but it was a *career* I wanted. Oh, and children, but not at the age my mother, grand-mother and great-grandmother had birthed their babies (when they were still children themselves). I wanted a version of their lives minus the outdoor toilets and a doctor who murdered his patients. (Serial killer Harold Shipman murdered hundreds of his elderly female patients – but not my grandmother.)

Coming of age during the nineties, the message was clear. I *could* have it all – career, kids, nice house – as long as I worked hard enough. It was all within my reach. I know many women who managed to walk the tightrope of having both a career and children while in their late twenties and early thirties.

As for me, I was still rolling around nightclubs.

I've spent most of my life broke, but hey, that's fashion for you. Sorry to burst the bubble of glamour, because God knows I hate to do that, but the way people dress on the set of *The Devil Wears Prada* and, more recently, *Emily in Paris* couldn't be further from reality. From fashion assistants (whose main job it is to pack suitcases) to writers to stylists, in films and on Netflix, the cast is dressed head to toe in new-season designer gear. In real life, the majority of us magazine gals earned shit money and had to clev-erly accessorise Zara to make it look like Prada/Loewe/Celine.

And so, single and earning shit money, the realisation I might never meet 'The One', never become a mother, never buy the happily-ever-after house, hit home hard about six months before my thirty-fifth birthday. Now what? Buy sperm off the internet? Where from? Sweden? Why would I do that when I could just book a flight to Stockholm and shag as many Swedish men as possible? Going to Stockholm for a shag sure beats ordering jizz off the internet.

If I was to be brushing organic crumbs off a wooden highchair by my mid-thirties, as opposed to dabbing MDMA crumbs off a loo seat at (insert name of party), it was time to take action. I'd have to go look for this mystical man, aka the prince I always knew was coming to rescue me. But hang on, why hadn't he showed up? Had he got lost en route? Was there a mix-up with the edits over at Disney studios? There must have been; there's no other explanation as to why no one – not a single person in any of the books or films – mentioned it was ME who had to go and hunt for HIM.

Well, I suppose I had sort of looked for him – at 4am in Soho. Turns out he lived in Shepherd's Bush, enjoyed cycling at the weekend and going to bed exceptionally early.

Thanks to Disney discourse soaked up as a child, then, I assumed life would unfold like a fairy tale, but it didn't. Six months before meeting the father of my children, having made the decision to embark upon motherhood alone, I fell pregnant. When I turned forty, I had a one-year-old daughter, a three-year-old son, a dog, a partner and a house. *TICK!* I thought. *I did it!*

Not for long, though.

Life isn't simple or perfect, nor does it always have a happy ending (not *that* kind of happy ending). It's supposed to be big and bonkers, miserable and messy, chaotic and funny, difficult and sad, bewildering and amazing. ALL that and then some.

This collection of short essays, divided into five parts, tells the story of a life that, until my marital breakdown, looked absolutely fucking fabulous. I'll talk about everything that is taboo in today's society, some of which you may have gone through, too:

miscarriage, abortion, debt, affairs, divorce, depression, sex in mid-life. The cracks in my life were glossed over with a big smile and an outfit I definitely couldn't afford. And then, in September 2021, fuelled by several glasses of wine, I took to Instagram and told my truth.

There's only so much I can squeeze into an Instagram caption, though, so I thought I'd write a book. Actually, I never dreamed I'd write a book and, having now written one, I can totally see why! To say it's been emotional is the understatement of the century. But I suppose that's the point. Life is an emotional roller coaster, one we are all too often ill-prepared for. Had someone told me not to worry about meeting a man, and to stop blowing money on credit cards just because the 'spirits' (as in dead people, not vodka) told me I needed 'a new wider-shoulder jacket', despite it being a week before payday and not having enough money in my account to pay rent, would I have listened? I'm not sure.

Had someone (or a spirit) mentioned that the so-called 'happily ever after' might not end up so happy, would my life be any different now? I doubt it, but in writing my story, I hope you'll feel less alone in yours. Over the past three years, I've connected with hundreds of women via Instagram: women who, in the middle of the night, when life felt unbelievably dark during the first months after my divorce, provided deep comfort. Some nights, I felt so afraid I thought I couldn't carry on. By sharing their vulnerability with me, these women made me feel less alone.

In many ways I wrote this book for them, and so, in the same way their messages helped me, I hope you'll find comfort in these tales. As for me, given this book is now officially 'out there', I should probably figure out what to wear to court.

Message me, get in touch! Assuming I'm allowed Instagram in jail.

Love,
Stacey x

PART 1

Mating

'We have been poisoned by fairy tales.'
  — ANAÏS NIN, *A Spy in the House of Love*

'We have been polluted by Hinge, Tinder,
Raya ...'

  — STACEY DUGUID

Perhaps it was lazy to allow Disney to be my guiding light, my North Star, the preordained trajectory showing exactly how life would play out. All that ingrained Disney shit is so unhelpful, especially when it comes to love.

In MATING, I tackle my life-long obsession with finding a partner, something I blame entirely on Snow White and her mates, the seven dwarfs. The message was clear: 'One day, my prince shall come.' But nobody mentioned when, where and how this prince would appear. Via toyboywarehouse.com? In a toilet in Ibiza? Will he arrive carrying a bag of chips on the last tube home?

Born in 1974, I'm part of Generation X, meaning I came of age in the you-can-have-it-all 1990s. Ladettes, pints, parties, strip clubs! I went from devouring fairy tales about princesses and finding true love, to approaching adulthood at a time when the wider culture was telling me to work and play as hard as the lads. Wait, so if I down as many pints as my prince, he's The One, right?

Erm, probably not, love. He's probably The One to Avoid, you muppet.

Shall we blame Disney? My parents' divorce? Not one but two absent fathers? Who knows? All I know is I've spent four years in therapy unpicking it all, and it's time to move forwards.

That said, low self-esteem resulted in many wasted years chasing men who weren't worthy of my love. When I found myself slipping back into old habits post-divorce, I decided to tackle what I now understand to be 'love addiction'.

Having never received the long-lost fertility memo – perhaps Mr Armani has it? – I reached age thirty-four and embarked on a mad rush to meet someone 'normal'. Oh my God, how I panicked. Actually, forget Disney; I blame the *Daily Mail*. They told me my ovaries were dying, and I believed the headlines. Cue screaming and arm-waving panic in the offices of my local GP. Waiting lists for fertility treatment were so long, I almost called an ambulance. Wary of the lack of NHS resources, I charged off to Harley Street brandishing a credit card instead.

I also joined Guardian Soulmates (an actual website, not an app; it was the closest thing we had to Tinder back then).

> **ME:** 'Hi, are you normal, or are you going to ask me to do a line of cocaine off your penis?'
> **HIM:** 'Oh, well, I wasn't going to ask, but now you mention it . . . '

I now understand the root of my attachment and codependency issues. I also know my 'triggers': a passing cat meowing too loudly, a pigeon flying too low, the dishwasher beeping – and romantic relationships. Thanks for that, Snow White.

In MATING (and throughout this book), you'll meet my

mates, as in the girlfriends who, as proven by the divorce tornado (plus that time I got into a fight with a drag queen after he accused me of stealing his 'lewk'), are my rock.

MATING also takes a look at the revelatory news that – hold the front page – it's actually OK to be single. Someone call a medic! Actually, scrap that – it'll take too long. Call Deliveroo. Nothing wrong with sipping a reviving glass of wine while laid out in the recovery position. I've done it before.

1

Fantasy Mating

Fairy tales, fables and Fendi

Forget Cinderella – hot like Snow White, now that's a beauty ideal to aim for. As opposed to her wicked stepmother, whose daily raging in the mirror proves that A) ALL women beyond a certain age lose their looks; B) older women are majorly cranky pants; and therefore C) is it any wonder Hollywood directors don't know what to do with us? Yes, I know, I too can name at least five older female actors still getting great roles. However, I cannot name twenty.

Thanks to exposure to Disney discourse and the patriarchal structures neatly laid out in every single one of Walt's nifty little fairy tales, by the grand ole age of five my internal narrative was set. By eight, I subconsciously knew that if I were to win at life, I had to be beautiful, passive, slim and, most importantly, quiet.

And young – for ever.

Thanks also in part to Disney, I internalised that being an older woman equalled looking like a witch. Already born with a slightly crooked nose, all I need now is a huge wart the size of an eyeball hanging off the end.

Oh, to be a man. Those cunning creatures don't age, they

'mature' into heavily shaggable silver foxes. Phwoar! Eighty and still hot.

I'll get my coat – sorry, I mean wimple.

In 2015, Phoebe Philo, the then creative director of Celine, cast writer Joan Didion to be the face of Celine sunglasses. The campaign featured a close-up shot of Didion's flash-lit face that had barely been retouched. Celine didn't attempt to eradicate fine lines and a sagging jawline. A celebration of grey pride, the campaign eschewed standardised, sexually objectifying imagery for something altogether cooler.

Under the creative directorship of Kim Jones, Fendi's catwalks and advertising campaigns have featured many a 1990s supermodel spinster. As have those of Versace.

Spinster: a word conjured up by some genius in the late Middle Ages to describe an older single woman whose job it was to spin wool. Can you believe such a word still exists? Throughout time, single, divorced and widowed women have had a rough deal. An elderly woman burned at the stake may not have been a real witch, but she was probably single.

It is about time we started to worship women of all ages, but it's not just age that's an issue. It's *singleness*. We've been told we can't 'do life' alone for centuries.

Way back in Ancient Egypt, circa 3100 BCE, women shared the same financial rights as men. They were legally allowed to strike business deals and sell, buy and inherit property without the permission of fathers, husbands, brothers – or any man, come to think of it. Well, they were until 700 BCE, when some bloke in Ancient Greece decided women were no longer allowed to run or trade a business, nor were they allowed to inherit property. By the late Middle Ages, unmarried women not only earned less on account of their marital status, they were only permitted to work in lower-status jobs.

In 1974 (which also happens to be the year I was born),

the UK Parliament passed the Equal Credit Opportunity Act, allowing single unmarried women to obtain mortgages without the permission or countersignature of a man. Prior to 1974, it was legal for a bank to refuse credit, loans and mortgages based on a woman's marital status. That included widowed women. If you were a widow, regardless of available funds, you had to find a man other than your dead husband (for obvious reasons) to add his signature to the paperwork.

In the case of a single woman making a mortgage application, her income-to-loan value was calculated based on only 50 per cent her salary. Even a woman with high earnings could only take out a much lower mortgage than her male counterpart earning the same salary.

Thank God for men, to be honest. Can you imagine how silly we'd get if we had full financial autonomy? (More on this in Part 4: MONEY.) Of course, basing a mortgage on only half a woman's earnings makes total sense. Taxi to Bond Street, darling!

As I've explained, I spent my childhood immersed in the fantasy of Disney, of princesses and handsome saviours, concepts spread around via some sort of magical fairy dust (societal diffusion). I came to understand meek women objectified for their infinite beauty always got the guy. They also got the castle, the baby, the happy ever after, the incredible couture gowns, the fabulous shoes, the great hair, the tiny waist (someone's obsessed), the amazing interiors and a fuck load of chandeliers. I fucking love chandeliers!

I filed this handy information under 'G' for girls.

My mind's library of unhelpful information: Girls – how to win your prince!

Must have a tiny waist (even when pregnant) and long hair – preferably either jet black or golden blonde (no gingers, especially fake ones). Must be of mild disposition; must collapse in a heap of dust at some point (from hunger, but also because you're so delicate and the slightest thing sets you off, like the smell of pigeon poop at Charing Cross station). Must have an array of small animals following you around singing. And you must NEVER argue. OH! And don't be too clever; it's embarrassing for you, for men, for everyone.

In addition to the list above, it's also worth mentioning that no one likes a show-off, especially in Manchester. Or, as my grandmother (whose doctor, as I've mentioned, was the mass murderer Harold Shipman), once said:

NANNY: 'I knew 'e were a wrong-un, that Shipman.'
ME: 'You knew he was a killer capable of murdering 250 of his female patients?'
NANNY: 'Well, 'e didn't murder me.'
(We both laugh for a good minute at this perceptive observation.)
ME: 'Well, clearly, otherwise we wouldn't be having this conversation, Nanny. But you only survived because you weren't rich enough to murder!'
NANNY: 'Cheeky devil! Bloody cheek of him! Any road, what an absolute wrong-un.'
ME: 'Killing all those old women. Yeah, truly awful.'
NANNY: 'Nooo, I meant when I used to go int' his office. Always bloody showing off. No one likes a bloody show-off.'

Proof, as if it were needed, that to be a show-off in Manchester is a crime worse than murder.

Court adjourned. Actually, no – case closed. Solitary confinement for the show-off.

So, how did I envisage this all playing out?

One day, my prince would appear and whisk me off to his kingdom. All frail and frazzled from being trapped up a tall tower my entire life, I'd ride side-saddle in a lady-like fashion, dress fluttering behind me in the wind. After a quick change into glass slippers by Jimmy Choo and a long, lavish white gown by Saint Laurent (that's my outfit, not his – this isn't *Strictly Come Dancing*) he'd bend down to kiss me, confirming the sex we were about to experience was guaranteed to be nothing short of electrifying. And we'd have a good old twirl and dance beneath a firework-lit sky.

The following year, a child would be born, sweet-faced, courageous and kind. And so, the story would end, and we'd all live happily ever after. Safe from harm, I'd have everything my heart desired. I'd be home; I'd be secure. I'd have the happiness I'd spent my whole life searching for. I'd be happy. I repeat, I'd be happy.

* insert sound of a needle screeching across a record player*

Sorry, sister – not *ugly* sister, obviously, I'm not that cruel – life ain't all Jimmy Choo slippers, hot marital sex and firework-lit skies. Newsflash: no one is coming to save you.

Oh, but until recently, I really believed they (he) would, in fact, turn up. But no longer. Not now – which I guess is thanks to a bucket-load of very good therapy.

Am I the only one to have believed such unhelpful-to-the-point-of-harmful things?

It makes me sound terribly old-fashioned. Sorry, can you hear me over the sound of my crinoline rustling as I pass through the hallway in search of my smelling salts?

No, of course I'm not old-fashioned; nor am I someone who believes the world owes me a living. Actively seeking out a man with whom to mate never crossed my mind, though, because ... OK, I admit it (cue trumpet sounds in the far-off distance, possibly coming from yonder turret): I just sort of assumed that sometime around thirty, a good-looking geezer on horseback would gallop through Soho and lasso me on to his horse.* In short, I assumed meeting someone was an absolute given.

Let's recap, because even I'm confused.

Despite the overwhelming evidence to the contrary gathered over the course of two decades spent dating douchebags, I assumed for reasons outlined above (I'm looking at you, Cinders) that one day this mythical 'he' would show up regardless. He would arrive in the nick of time, saving me from a lifetime of aforementioned douchebags, occasional drug binges, daily booze binges and a shopping addiction, and then he'd impregnate me. And (cue trumpets becoming louder as a Plantagenet-style band gathers ...) we'd live happily ever after.

Beat *that*, Cinderella.

Together, we'd canter into the sunset and get married (obviously). I'd wear a huge dress (clearly), and a year after the wedding, a perfectly chubby baby would be delivered by a stork as opposed to via my vagina. (Am OK with the last point, TBH.)

No fairy tale ever mentioned IVF, embryo freezing, egg donation, miscarriage, stillbirth or cocaine-addicted boyfriends whose sperm stopped swimming in their early twenties thanks to a rampant class A addiction. Or the fact Mr 'Prince' clearly got lost by the roundabout just off the motorway near the big Sainsbury's, because he never even turned up. If only horses had Waze.

*

---

* Please note – if ever a man cantering through Soho on horseback tries to pull you on to his horse, you're either at Gay Pride or he's a police officer and you're under arrest. Do not attempt to kiss him.

The fairy tales I absorbed, loved and returned to, time and time again, both onscreen and in books, damaged the way I viewed my gender's role in society. Fashion-wise, don't even go there. Aged five, I nagged Mum daily for a pair of plastic princess-heeled mules. Teetering on the brink of insanity, desperate to shut me up, she bought them. I'll never forget the sheer joy of the sound of a plastic heel clattering across stone. Up and down the garden path in bright red plastic-heeled mules I'd go. Clatter clatter clatter, swish swish swish. (Cut to twenty years later, when I have a shoe collection to rival the dressing room of *RuPaul's Drag Race*. Even today, the mere sight of a clattery heel is enough to send my nipples into an hour-long state of electrifying erectness.)

Despite her initial reluctance to buy me the shoes, my mum would greet me each morning by whispering softly in my ear: 'Wake up, it's time to marry a prince!' Eyes slowly opening, happiness radiating within my chest, I'd stare at her, knowing she was telling the truth. Of course I'd marry a prince! All girls do. Especially girls from a shit part of Manchester.

Post-divorce, I've only just begun to consider how much damage this inner narrative caused growing up. In order to be rescued and saved, I knew I needed to be slim at all times, beautiful at all times, obedient at all times. For God's sake, be quiet, woman.

These days, I'm trying to break with the 'prince rescues his princess and they live happily ever after' BS – inside my own home, at least. A brilliant bedtime read for little girls (and boys) is *Gender Swapped Fairy Tales* by Karrie Fransman and Jonathan Plackett, a book of traditional tales with a twist. The writing is wonderfully old-fashioned, but the female characters play the role of hero, and sometimes some of the men are even a bit objectified for their good looks. Just a teeny, tiny bit.

_____

Five Thoughts On ... Women and Beauty by Anita Bhagwandas

Anita is the author of *Ugly: Giving us back our beauty standards*

1. Beauty standards have meant that women are given this invisible job of 'beauty upkeep' that we didn't ask for, and aren't being paid for. Imagine if we were reimbursed for all the hours we've spent shaving our legs, for example – all to groom ourselves to a standard set by a patriarchal society and a capitalist agenda that, essentially, wants us to buy more and more.

2. We have to decide for ourselves *if* we want this extra job, and how much time and money we actually want to dedicate to it. So, I'd suggest doing a beauty audit: how much time and how much money do you spend on beauty and grooming? That's everything from putting on make-up each day, to having waxes or getting injectables. Tally this up for a month, a year, and then for five years. How does it make you feel? Is it more or less than expected?

3. During the audit, think about if you genuinely enjoy this routine. If doing your nails is something you love, or a place to catch up with friends, then that's fine, but if it's an hour that feels like wasted time, then those are the things we could gradually start to ease out of our lives, and replace with something we perhaps have always wanted to do or try but feel like we never have the time or money to do so.

4. Part of this audit could also include looking at what really influences you to feel like you have to look a

certain way. Perhaps it's social media, your peer group, or even your upbringing. It's confronting to be honest about these things, but if looking 'acceptable' to a certain standard is taking up too much of your time, money and headspace, then maybe, just maybe, there is another way. I always suggest that people remove or mute anyone who makes them feel lacking in any way on social media, but you can also hack your feed by following people who are growing out their hair colour and going grey, if that's something you've been thinking about, or if you loathe hours spent in the salon each month. Maybe it's relaying to friends that you're opting out of the weekly nail session this time. Even just trying a few of these things is a great way to work out what your personal non-negotiables are – and a way to take some beauty admin off your plate.

5. Finally, it's so easy to get caught in the treadmill of beauty admin that zooming out a little and thinking about the wider context can be helpful to shift our mindsets on beauty standards. Have you ever wondered where this pressure to look ageless, thin or like you 'woke up like this' has come from? Getting curious and informed about these things gives us the knowledge to set our own beauty rules, and to stop societal beauty standards from controlling our lives, time and finances. Because if we don't set our own standards, then others will absolutely do it for us.

I'll be honest: it's not all your fault, Walt. Even without Disney and fairy tales, the dominant role of men – both culturally and socially – was the background music played in my childhood home, and I can assume it probably was for you, too. In the

1970s, we lived in working-class Manchester (or should I say Hyde, close to Ashton-under-Lyne, the nearest town to the city – just so we're clear, never, ever pronounce the 'H' in Hyde).

On 29 May 1970, the Equal Pay Act 1970 – described as 'an act to prevent discrimination, as regards terms and conditions of employment, between men and women' – became the giant leap womankind had been waiting for. Despite this, in my home, the message was loud and clear: men went to work and earned 'proper' money, thereby earning the title of 'Boss'. Women, on the other hand, regardless of working full- or part-time, were in charge of the children, the cooking, the cleaning, the ironing, the everything. Even my style icon, Snow Freakin' White, had to cook and clean for seven men. All the women in my family worked hard, only to return home, where they worked even harder.

I watched them as they placed home-cooked meals on tables, put neatly folded clean clothes into skilfully stacked laundry cupboards, vacuumed beneath tables, washed up dishes and even turned off the lights and closed the curtains before bed, before checking doors and windows were securely locked. Tickety-boo.

Having witnessed an imbalance of power throughout my childhood and beyond has meant that whenever I've lived with a partner, I've naturally adopted the same role.

Despite not exactly being domestic goddess material, during the three relationships in which I cohabited with a boyfriend, I certainly knew how to make a home feel cosy and inviting. I just didn't quite know how to do the rest. 'Fancy some nachos and hummus for dinner? More beige food, anyone?'

'Are you waiting for a man to come along and save you, Stacey?'

Those were the memorable words delivered by The Therapist one Thursday in spring 2022, post-divorce.

'What I mean is, I feel helpless,' I told her. 'I just can't imagine my future. It's just . . . '

A minute of comfortable silence passed between us. Finally, after four years, I felt safe in this room.

I found the words.

'I'm older, and I'm single, and whenever I try to imagine myself even older than I am today, all I see is this lonely figure seated at a small kitchen table, her featureless face resting on the palms of her hands. It's scary. She looks lost. There's only one dining chair.' I could feel tears about to flood the room.

'I don't *need* a man. Well, a nice one – yeah, that would be, well, nice, I suppose, but that's really not the point. I can't fathom how I'm going to do it all alone. Any of it. All of it.' Tears shoot from my eyes like a fast-moving waterfall. 'Am I old-fashioned? Is it stupid to miss having a man around the house, even one who never took out the bins? Am I a terrible feminist . . . ? Don't answer that,' I added, balling up a sixth or seventh tissue, ready to grab another. 'Is it so bad to want – or rather, need – the support of a man? Like, really need it, as though your life depended upon it?' I asked.

'Perhaps it's not the support of a husband or boyfriend your life depends upon, Stacey. Perhaps it's the love of your father.'

Ah. Jackpot.

Man, I love my therapist. When I'm not consumed with hate for her.

Dear Therapist,

After four (often emotionally uncomfortable) years sitting in your front room, I'm writing to let you know, I've finally figured it all out. You won't believe this latest revelation, but it was Cinderella's fault all along.

Am now cured of anxiety, and my sense of self-worth has soared! Needless to say, you won't be seeing me again.

Best wishes – and thanks!
Stacey

PS Four years!? You really do deserve a medal. Strict 'boundaries' aside, I thought I'd buy one as a 'thank you' gift for all I've put you through on a weekly basis. The only medal I could find was one of those crappy (pun intended) flimsy things off Amazon, the kind you give to toddlers for doing a poop in the potty.

Fearing you may think the gift represented an enactment of some sort of 'Freudian' poop-related psychosexual developmental theory, signalling I'd officially entered the 'anal' phase, thereby relinquishing parental dependency on you, I deleted it from my shopping basket and bought a chocolate one instead. That's when, thanks to Google, I discovered 'chocolate trait theory'. Freaking out, I ate the medal myself, hence this written note instead.

And just to say, I know it's been four years, but as of this Thursday, I shall no longer be attending our regular 5pm slot. Wait, I already mentioned that.

Anyway, cheers!

2

Fantasy Mating B (or *Bis*, as They Say *en France*) – Or Should I Say D, D for Dad

Where did ya go, Dad?

Hello, my name is Stacey Duguid, and I'm a love addict.

Thanks for coming.

Goodbye,

Stacey x

If only it were that simple. If only I could close the book and breathe an almighty sigh of relief and say, 'Thank fuck that's over.'

The label 'love addict' is a headline drenched in shameful connotation.

I guess if I were to suddenly announce, 'I'm an alcoholic,' your rational brain would easily understand I have an issue with alcohol – and, if I were in recovery, I'd need to do everything within my power to avoid being around it. What you wouldn't know, however, is the underlying root cause of the alcoholism (unless I told you). Nevertheless, you'd easily understand alcohol is an addictive substance I can't live without. That's where this is different.

Love addiction is the constant need to feel loved – romantically or otherwise – to fill a void inside, and telling a human who, for whatever reason, did not have their needs met as a child to turn away from love permanently as a way of healing themselves is not only counterintuitive, it's simply impossible. With effort, time, therapy and rehabilitation, humans can recover from consuming addictive substances such as booze, cocaine, coffee and sugar. Humans cannot give up love. Nor should we.

For me, this issue developed in childhood as the result of an avoidant bond, and, like many love addicts, I've spent a lifetime craving, needing, wanting, desiring, yearning for love. Erm, that, and looking for a person to couple up with (roll up, roll up, anyone will do!). It's not my parents' fault – they were absolutely right to split up – but when a child goes through a parents' divorce when they are very young, their experience alters their view of attachment in relationships. I actually prefer the term 'attachment dysregulation' to the label 'love addict', but it's a bit of a mouthful. So, for argument's sake, let's call me a love addict. Way punchier.

This love addict has spent a lifetime not feeling good enough in relationships. When I'm in love (I use the word lightly, as I fall in love very easily), in the back of my mind there's always this creeping feeling of unease, as though I've done something wrong, as though I am not enough. It sets in after a few weeks, once all the hormones have settled down a bit. I manage to convince myself the person will see me for who I really am, and then I start acting up. Although it applies mostly to romantic relationships, I see this pattern in EVERY relationship, from those with work colleagues (especially bosses), to friends, social acquaintances, classmates and even family. I've blown up more work opportunities and friendships than I care to think about.

The idea of being single (alone) used to set my insides alight, rendering a part of me dead. Whereas a new love? Ooooh, swoon! Nothing short of electrifying. The first few weeks feel euphoric. In the arms of a new lover, I can fly. Alone, I can barely make it out of bed.

But what *is* love addiction? Well, quite.

Five Thoughts On ... Love Addiction, by Lucinda Gordon Lennox

Lucinda Gordon Lennox is a mentor, coach and trauma therapist, and author of *Nobody is Broken*

1. Love addiction is not a technical term nor a clinical diagnosis, but it is a phrase that is used when an aspect of our trauma is playing out in our romantic relationships, to the degree that the connection with our partner is not healthy or balanced and there is a high prevalence of codependence in the relationship. In love addiction, usually the addict will be terrified of being abandoned by their partner, will people-please, will change their life to work around their partner's needs at the expense of their own, will be susceptible to abuse such as narcissism from their partner (or other emotional, physical, or sexual abuse), will have feelings of not being good enough in their core, and might put their partner on a pedestal. They will not have a strong sense of self from which they can allow their partner to come to them; they will step out of themselves in order to meet their partner where the partner is.

2. To avoid love addiction, we need to have a very solid sense of self before we enter into a relationship with another person. There is an element of 'losing oneself'

in a relationship, especially at the beginning when the chemicals are running high, and in many ways, there is nothing wrong with this at all – it can be fun and really lovely. But this has to be examined and kept in check. If we do not check ourselves during this process and we have a propensity towards addictions and codependency, then we will probably become lost in, and codependent with the relationship. We need to continually give ourselves time to step out of the dynamic and back to ourselves, to check in with ourselves. 'Is this absolutely working for me? Am I in the truth of who I really am in this relationship? Am I able to speak my truth in this relationship? Am I continuing with my own inner growth and my own life while I'm in this relationship? Am I absolutely not neglecting myself, my family and friends while I am in this relationship? Am I proud of myself in this relationship?' These are all really good questions to ask ourselves to ensure that we do not step into codependency within a relationship.

3.   True love addiction comes from a deep, unresolved childhood attachment trauma. And when we have a lot of unresolved trauma, we will probably be in denial when answering these questions. The best way to protect young girls – and boys – who might be vulnerable in this way is to provide a safe, nurturing, nourishing, empowering and boundaried childhood at home. The feminine energy is soft, and holding, but it does not require 'saving' – and neither does the masculine! Support? Yes. Saving? No. The fairy tales imply that a girl will be 'saved' by a boy (or a young woman by a young man). This implies that the girl is not powerful enough to save herself and will thus need a man in order to be able to conquer life. If we provide the 4 Ss of attachment to our

children – Seen, Soothed, Safe, Secure – then our children will grow up with a deep inner knowing that they are enough exactly as they are, and that they do not need to be saved. Nor do they need to save anyone else. [They will understand] that loving romantic partnerships can be just that – loving partnerships.

4. It all starts at home, and it all starts in childhood. For many in our generation, as children, we were, on the whole, very much and very subtly left to our own devices, seen and not heard, ignored, belittled, shamed, put down, expected to be raised by our schools, invalidated, disrespected and not honoured in the truth of who we were. This is, of course, no fault of our parents; they were simply doing what they thought was best for us, and it was probably an improvement on how they were parented. But over the past few decades, science has caught up and we now know that this rather abstract and apathetic type of parenting is not in the best interests of the child with regards to developing a strong sense of self. We want to be educating young girls and boys about the feminine and masculine energies and how incredibly beautiful and important they are in their own right, and how they make both sexes different, and how they can support each other to create a wonderful partnership.

5. We need to be educating young girls (and boys) on the importance of developing a strong sense of self, a good relationship with oneself, feelings of enough-ness without the need for validation from another, feelings of worthiness without having to prove anything, abilities to trust themselves in their core, and belief in themselves as powerful beings with ultimate control over their

lives; we need to be educating people on the beauty of remaining whole. We need to educate young people on how extraordinary and incredibly beautiful a romantic partnership can be when each person comes together to complement the other as a whole being, rather than to 'save' the other as a fragmented and wounded being. Once this is mastered, a young person will not even entertain a relationship that could be potentially unhealthy or love addictive.

————————

A strong sense of self? Until embarking on 'The Work', I had no idea who I was. Nor did I know my father at all well.

Dad was always very bright – not that I knew it, given I didn't grow up with him. At the age of eleven, he was awarded a place at the local grammar school. He lived in council housing, and his parents worked at ICI, the local paint factory. Like many working-class parents of children bequeathed grammar-school places, they found it a struggle to pay for his uniform.

After grammar school, Dad took an apprenticeship and slowly made his way up to 'draughtsman'. As I was to discover many years later, had the family been able to imagine such a thing as university, Dad might have trained to be an architect.

Mum has always been canny and hardworking. Her unwavering and relentless work ethic flows through me like a fast-moving river. She inherited her work-yourself-to-your-bone modus operandi from her mother, who inherited from hers. Working hard wasn't optional in our family. It's called survival. If you didn't work, you didn't eat. Simple as.

My earliest memory is of being three years old. Mum was still married to Dad, and the three of us lived together in Hyde (Eyed). Mum and Dad both worked and needed to share childcare, so Mum took a job at the local supermarket, where she worked as a checkout operator in the evening. Years later, when

I was a teenager, I discovered Mum had really wanted to be a hairdresser, but no one took her seriously. To be a hairdresser, you needed to train, but in northern working-class towns in the 1970s, girls didn't train; instead they went to work in cigarette factories.

Dad was famously tight with money, but, to his credit, he was also a keen saver. One winter, despite her working hard and earning her own money, Dad apparently told Mum she wasn't allowed to buy a camel coat she'd fallen in love with. Dad should've known what he'd signed up for, considering they were both well-dressed mods.

Heavily into music and fashion, the mods formed one of the most important subcultures in England at the time, involving scooters, parkas, immaculate clothes and an obsessional eye for detail. Dad's hair was cut into long sideburns, and he had a fringe to rival Noel Gallagher in the nineties. With his big blue eyes and skinny zoot suits, he was 'dead' handsome. Mum, meanwhile, was all long bleached-blond hair, fake eyelashes circled in black kohl, and long legs in micro miniskirts sitting on the back of Dad's scooter. I mean, wow. They looked amazing.

Aged three, I'd lie in bed, listening to Mum and Dad shouting downstairs. Then, one morning, Mum and I took the bus to my grandparents' house. Although I didn't realise it at the time, the two plastic carrier bags Mum was carrying contained the sum total of our worldly belongings. As we sat on the bus, she said, 'We don't live with Dad any more; it's just us now.'

Apparently, I replied, 'OK.'

Dad was just twenty-four, and a lot of women found him attractive. I remember Mum saying he was good-looking, but she hated him, with a disdain she couldn't possibly hide. Dad allegedly refused to pay her enough – or any – money towards my upkeep, according to the conversations between Mum and Nanny I overheard as I lingered in doorways, trying not to be seen.

'It's because he works freelance; the CMS can't force him

to pay,' Mum would say, thinking I couldn't understand. Of course, I could.

I remember being very happy at my grandparents' house, sharing a bed with Mum. At the weekend, I'd stay at our old house with Dad. Always late by at least an hour, he'd come each Saturday morning to my grandparents' bungalow to pick me up. As I waited, my stomach twisted like trapped moths. Dragging a shiny black leather stool with dark wooden legs towards the window, I'd stand on it, looking out for his car. A lifetime perched precariously on polished leather. By the time he arrived, I'd be in a state of heightened anxiety. Anxiety I managed to internalise, so nobody noticed.

This happened every week. Perhaps he was late in order to coincide with pub opening hours? Climbing into the front seat of his car, my usual spot, we'd head to The Rising Moon, The King Bill, The Cheshire Cheese. They all looked the same to me, as did the chain-smoking locals with whom we hung out all day. Not that Dad actually spoke to the chain-smoking locals – or to me. Occasionally stretching out his hand to stroke a passing dog, the only regular sound coming from Dad's direction was the rustle of a newspaper.

Crossword completed, Pepsi drained, last ale for him, my lunchtime packets of empty crisps littering the table, it was time to go. On our way out, I'd stop to marvel at the gloom of cigarette smoke hovering above. Over the course of the afternoon, smoke formed a horizontal line above our heads, dividing the pub in two.

After a short while, staying at Dad's house became less boring, because now there were new girlfriends to meet every Saturday. I got to know some of the women, but a few I met only once. One, a blonde woman called Cathy, stayed a bit longer. Someone, I don't remember who, mentioned she was only nineteen. That wasn't something I could really contextualise at the time, but I knew deep within that she was different, somehow, to my mother.

One Saturday afternoon at the pub, Cathy took hold of my hand. 'Come to the toilet with me. We're going ice-skating; let's get changed,' she said, apparently oblivious to the fact I had nothing to change into.

In the cubicle, Cathy undressed revealing a type of underwear I'd never seen before: garters and a suspender belt. I found the strappy sexiness of it all unsettling and strange. I stared at her in confusion, an odd feeling rising in my tummy.

I remember imagining this feeling as a bouncy ball, the brightly coloured one I'd lost ages ago and still couldn't find. When I felt stressed, the image of the ball would appear, its kaleidoscopic colours soon overtaken by the sensation of loss, shame and guilt. I was the one responsible for losing the ball; therefore, whatever terrible thing was happening in that moment, whatever uncomfortable situation I faced, it was all my fault.

Forty or so years later, thanks to therapy, I now realise that, as a young girl, I blamed myself for a lot of things – including my parents' divorce, the fact my father's house was messy and cold, and many more out-of-my-control scenarios – as a form of self-protection. If it was my fault, I could control it. By blaming myself, knowing the divorce was all my fault, I could do something about it. Not that I could ever do anything about the young women I met each weekend.

After ice-skating, the three of us drove back to Dad's house to watch a film and have our tea. ('Tea' is northern for dinner – and, even more confusingly, up north we serve dinner with a cup of tea. I grew up being asked, 'Do you want tea with yer tea, love?')

Back at the house, I sat on the big chair in the corner, while Dad and Cathy snuggled up on the sofa. They began kissing. I tried to focus on the film, but all I could see was the colourful lost ball. Cathy was giggling, whispering in Dad's ear. I'd never heard anyone giggle like that before. Out of the corner of my eye, I could see she'd sat on top of him, both legs straddled across his hips. The room began to spin, and as I looked over, I saw she'd changed out of her ice-skating jeans and into the dress she'd been wearing earlier that day at the pub.

Cathy's dress was hoicked up, and I could see her thighs and the strange strappy black suspender belt I didn't know had a name. The ball bounced in my tummy, and I ran out of the room towards the front door. I rattled the door handle to get out. It was a 1970s double-glazed special, and I had no clue how to open it.

Dad and Cathy came running in from the lounge.

'What's the matter, love?' asked Cathy, running after me.

'I want Grandad.'

'Why?' she said.

'I want to go home to Nanny and Grandad.'

Picking up the receiver of the wall-mounted phone, Dad didn't argue or protest. He jabbed his left forefinger into the holes of the circular dial, and one by one, he slowly swished to the right. The silence in the small hallway was claustrophobic.

'Hiya, Ralph. Stacey wants you to come and get her,' said Dad, in a monotone Manc accent.

Grandad arrived faster than Superman, and I hopped into the front seat of his Ford Capri. That car was his pride and joy. As was I – and as was my mum. Nanny would often say, ' I wish Grandad would look at me the same way he looks at you two.'

Cathy was still there the following weekend, smoking as many fags as Dad. She seemed to have lost interest in ice-skating or fun adventures, so we just sat in the smoky pub all Saturday afternoon, with nothing to do but watch northern men play darts and pool.

Bored of the lovebirds, I waited for my favourite TV show to come on the telly above the bar. Transfixed by the audacious outfits and dramatic posturing, I was obsessed with wrestling. For a good hour every Saturday afternoon, Big Daddy and Giant Haystacks would chuck one another across the ring.

Cathy wasn't there the following weekend. In celebration, I took my dolls' pram out for a walk around the estate. Instead of dolls, it held the two large pottery dogs Dad kept by the gas fire-place, wrapped in tea towels.

During this time, Mum, still working nights at the supermarket, met a man named Ron, who happened to be the manager of the store. Imagine the gossip as the night-shift checkout girl shags the BIG CHEESE!

One day, she introduced me to Ron, her 'new friend'. Then, on another day, he popped over to meet my grandparents, bringing with him an autograph book for me containing not one but two autographs. On the first page was Rod Hull. I couldn't believe it! Emu was my third favourite puppet after Kermit and Miss Piggy.

The second autograph was none other than the legend that is Noel Edmonds! I knew Ron worked at Fine Fayre as store manager, but this was proof he was also a celebrity.

In 1979, Mum and Ron announced they were finally 'together' together. When I was six, they bought a house that felt like a palace, located on a corner on a nicer housing estate than the one we'd lived on with Dad. The day they were married, Mum was hugely – and I mean *massively* – pregnant with my little brother.

We weren't destined to live there long, and I only have a few memories of that house. One was her morning whisper of, 'Wake up, it's time to marry a prince,' which eventually changed to, 'Wake up, it's time to marry Prince Charles.'

At around this time, I told Mum I didn't want to go to Dad's house any more.

'I don't like it there, it's cold and dusty,' I said, using my asthma as an excuse.

'We're moving to Scotland soon, anyway,' replied Mum.

This life-changing news was delivered in the upstairs bathroom, as Mum folded bath towels and I brushed my teeth, watching pink toothpaste gunk mixed with clean water swirl down the plughole.

In the year I was due to turn seven, my baby brother was

born in Ashton-under-Lyne hospital, the same birthplace as me, and where our Great-Aunty Doreen, Nanny's sister, worked as a 'teasmaid'.

'What shall we call the baby?' Mum asked me, delighted she had a boy.

'Kermit,' I replied. 'No, Ken. No, wait, Lee.'

Lee was a boy I fancied who lived opposite Dad's house.

At around this time, Dad met a new girlfriend called Cheryl. I really liked her, and I remember my excitement as Dad told me we'd be going away with her that summer: a caravan holiday to Blackpool, my family's favourite choice of accommodation and destination. Dad picked me up, an hour late as per usual, and then we drove to pick up Cheryl from her mum's house. Her mum opened the door.

Cheryl was nowhere to be seen. Her mum asked if I'd seen *E.T.* As it had only just come out at the cinema, I replied, no, I hadn't. Cheryl's mum bent down to slip a VHS tape into the machine. As she left the room, she gave me a funny little wave, then closed the door shut behind her.

Straining to decipher the story of a lost alien through white strobes of pirate-video fuzz, I could barely make out a thing. When the film ended, Dad and Cheryl's mum finally reappeared. There was still no sign of Cheryl, and we set off on holiday without her. Cheryl's mum came instead.

At the caravan, Dad shared his bedroom with Cheryl's mum. One day, looking out of the window, I watched Cheryl's mum put her hands down the front of Dad's shorts. Her hand stayed there for a long time. Seeing them both laugh in the sunshine made me feel even lonelier. I couldn't name the indigestion feeling inside, so I tried to visualise the ball again. I couldn't trust adults any more. Especially not Dad.

We made the move to Scotland, and after a short period of being bullied for my 'Deirdre Barlow' from *Coronation Street* accent, within a few months of living there, I developed a Scottish twang overnight for self-defence reasons.

Dad called our new house every Sunday, and when the phone rang, my stomach lurched to the other side of the room. Stretching the telephone's curly wire across the hallway, I'd sit on exactly the same carpet swirl each week, on the second step, close to the side table displaying Lladró figures and bowls of potpourri. I would count everything three times – the Lladró figures, the swirls of the carpet, the pictures hanging in the hall – and by the time I'd finished counting everything, I knew it was time to end our conversation.

I say 'conversation' . . .

With the landline phone hugging the side of my seven-year-old face, I'd say, 'Dad?'

'Yer, I'm 'ere,' he'd reply.

'Dad?' I'd ask again, a few silent minutes later.

'I told ye, I'm ere,' he'd reply once more.

'OK.'

For ten excruciating minutes, we'd sit in silence. It was like torture. I'd hang up knowing he didn't love me. After we moved, I only saw Dad when my stepdad Ron drove us all to Manchester to stay at Nanny and Grandad's bungalow during the school holidays. After the age of six, when I moved to Edinburgh, I'd see Dad, or, as I began calling him, 'real Dad', four times a year.

It was only when I had my son that I began to understand my 'real Dad'. We'd tried many times over the years to have some semblance of a relationship, but it never lasted. Not until 2011, that is.

When I reached out with news of his grandson, I made a promise to myself I wouldn't be a daughter by her father's deathbed, a million 'what ifs' plaguing my mind for ever. We now speak regularly (regularly for me – I'm not good on the phone or even planning a phone call). Thanks to therapy, I've moved on from the past; I forgive him because I know life is not easy and we all have our limits. I also know he loved and loves me, and that's worth a lot. When he first said, 'love you' as he hung up the phone three years ago, for several moments afterwards, I stared at the receiver. Had I accidentally picked up a banana instead of my iPhone? With that quiet, 'love you', something inside healed. At the end of the call the next time we spoke, aged forty-five, for the first time in my life I told my dad I loved him.

By the time I was a teenager, my early childhood spent in Manchester felt very far away. Scotland was total bliss, my home. At around the age of twelve, I no longer felt 'English'; on the contrary, I felt proud to identify as Scottish. Ach aye. Perhaps it was to do with my stepfather, who, from the moment he moved in with my mum, was the best dad I ever could've hoped for.

I loved school, and had a great group of close girlfriends. Mrs Dyer, my English teacher, provided constant inspiration, as did a shared fascination with George Orwell. One day, another muse, Ms Cameron, head of the art department, slid a book across my desk and said, 'I have a feeling you'll like this.' Georgia O'Keefe. My fourteen-year-old mind was blown. Long before I realised it was my passion, Ms Cameron noticed how much I enjoyed painting and drawing.

Creativity, fed daily, fuelled a fire that didn't burn out when school closed. I wanted to paint all evening and weekend. Even though it meant his company car had to sit on the driveway, my stepdad set up an art studio in the garage, complete with a Calor gas heater so I could paint throughout winter. I felt alive. I felt so unbelievably alive.

I was seven when I began calling Ron 'Dad'.

I was eleven when the kids at school voted me to be their 'Gala Queen', and Ron decorated the outside of our house with turrets made from MDF covered in fake brick wallpaper bought from B&Q. It took him weeks, and our house looked incredible. People from all over the village came to take photographs all week long.

I was eighteen when Ron hosted a party in our garden to celebrate my prom.

I was twenty-three when my mum left Ron. Desperate and lost, he jumped on a plane to London to meet me for lunch. Coming from a different world (the Highlands), he hated London. After our lunch, I remember standing in the middle of Piccadilly Circus, both of us lost for very different reasons. Incongruous, the Highlander's rugged face lit by the bright lights of Soho, the world whipped around us. We walked to the entrance of the tube station.

'Bye, Dad. I love you.'

He crumpled into my arms and cried.

I was twenty-three and a half when, despite having never cooked more than a baked potato, I organised Ron's first Christmas at his new home. Cooking for five people, an elaborate red cabbage dish from Jamie Oliver's cookbook almost finished me off. I remained upbeat for his sake, making sure everyone was happy: Nanny, Grandad, Lee, Ron. But I wasn't. I missed Mum, who was on a cruise with her new boyfriend, Mike.

I was twenty-four when my beloved grandfather died, suddenly and out of the blue, aged just seventy-two.

I was twenty-seven when Ron met a woman at the local bowling club where he was the club manager.

'I've always wanted a daughter,' said Sandy late one night, after she and Ron came to visit me in London.

I was thirty when Ron invited me to his and Sandy's wedding, back home in Edinburgh. 'Stacey plus one,' read the invitation. Single, I asked every unattached man in my phonebook. Then, two weeks before the wedding, I met an art director on Guardian Soulmates. Working in the same industry, we had lots of people in common, so the blind date didn't feel as awkward as it should have. On our second date, I mentioned Dad's wedding and, without hesitation, he volunteered to join me.

'Are you sure?' I asked, feeling quietly relieved. I chose to ignore the sharp twitch of a right eyebrow raised too quickly as he replied, 'Sure! It'll be fun.'

Three days before the wedding, his brief text read: 'Sorry, this is all too much. Terrible idea, me coming to your dad's wedding.'

Staring at my phone in disbelief, I thought back to the flicker of uncertainty. A red flag, an immediate sense of regret running across his brow, mouth having spoken before brain had had the chance to engage. We didn't bother to meet for a third date. Where's Prince Charming when you need him, eh?

Dateless and thirty, I called Sandy to cancel my plus-one, and felt embarrassed for the following two days.

Right from the get-go, the wedding felt off. I couldn't quite tell what it was, but it appeared to me I wasn't being invited to join the photographs alongside my brothers – Lee, plus Mike and Brian, Ron's two sons from his previous marriage.

Sunshine bouncing off red kilts, the men all wearing Ron's family tartan, the Stewart clan. More photos, more family members switched in and out. Brian's wife, Mary. Then Sandy's son. Time moved fast and slow, then it stood still. Had the photographer been briefed to leave me out of every picture?

'No, no way; it must be a mistake,' I told myself, ordering another cheap white wine in an attempt to quell the nausea ruminating inside.

Unable to look at the happy photo formations outside, a creeping pain strangling at my throat, I numbed it by standing at the bar.

The ceilidh started, and soon enough I found myself in my stepfather's arms, swinging across a slippery fake wooden floor.

Trying to dance in too-high heels, I said, 'Great wedding, Dad.'

'Well, I'm technically not your dad any more.'

'TECHNICALLY? Yes, you are!'

'Not really. Not now I'm remarried.'

'Dad, you brought me up! I'm Scottish because of you! I have your surname!'

'But I'm technically not your dad any more.'

The room began to spin . . .

It's 1980. I'm around six years old and we still live in Manchester. Ron-dad is turning an unused outdoor coal store into a guinea pig hotel. Set into the side of our house, it'll make a cosy den for the guineas I've decided to name after my favourite comedians, Little and Large. I watch as he finishes the whole thing off with a handmade sign. In swirling red paint, it reads, 'Stacey's Pet Shop'.

It's 1981. I'm seven. We now live in Edinburgh and I'm hiding in the gang-hut Ron-dad built behind the shed, even though Mum said he shouldn't build it there. It's where I go for quiet time alone, when everything feels overwhelming.

It's 1986. I'm twelve and just got my first period. I'm stirring a pot of mincemeat on the gas stove at our house on Turner Avenue. Dad's arms wrap around my shoulders from nowhere as he kisses me on the cheek and says, 'Mum tells me you have your first period. Congratulations, darling.' We both laugh at the absurdity of 'congratulations'.

It's 1990. I'm sixteen years old and I'm in Ron-dad's car, speeding towards Edinburgh. I'm meeting my best friend Natalie at an under-eighteens disco in town. I'm wearing a flamboyant homemade outfit, and he took one look at me in the hallway at home before quickly informing Mum he was driving me the mile to the nearest bus stop 'to save scaring the neighbours'. We have such a good chat on the way, he drives me the whole eight miles into the city. As he always does.

It's 2006. I'm thirty-two years old and I've just fallen over drunk on a slippery fake wooden floor at Dad and Sandy's wedding. The familiar twang of the Gay Gordons begins in a far-off corner. A man's hand reaches down to grab mine. A stranger in a room full of strangers. I stagger to my feet, blaming high heels and cheap white wine, and use it as an excuse to go to bed.

I walked wonkily back to my room to collect my things, but all trains from Edinburgh to London had stopped three hours before. Four hundred and sixteen miles between me and London; I paced the floor like an injured animal as tears turned to a howl.

I cried myself to sleep. No man can break a woman's heart like a father can.

Although to this day I remain close to his son, my little brother Lee, I never saw Ron-dad again.

With my self-esteem at rock bottom, I spent years in the pursuit of men clearly wrong for me. Rather than be by myself, I preferred to be with a mediocre boyfriend. Even though regretting the past is a total waste of time, I can't help thinking the younger me was so lost she didn't even know herself, never mind what she wanted from a relationship. None of us really know ourselves when we're young, but I felt like six different people all at the same time, constantly switching personas – posh, not posh, creative, serious, wacky, dorky, sensible, intelligent, gossipy – depending on who I was with.

Before meeting my ex-husband, I never allowed myself to be with the 'nice' guy, preferring instead the distant guy, the game-playing guy, the drug-addicted guy, the narcissist guy, the guy who made me feel fat, the guy who only called at 1am for a hook-up, and – worst of all, and just because it made me feel good for One Week Only! – the needy guy.

Puts fingers down throat. I'M THE NEEDY ONE!

But most often of all, I wanted the 'unavailable guy'. At least I now know why.

April, 1980

Dear God,

Me again. I need you to please, please listen this time. It's urgent.

I am praying HARD for a Miss Piggy bendy, rubbery doll. It's the one wearing a tight purple satin dress that's split high up the side of her leg. She's wearing matching purple high heels, which I think are painted on. I'm not sure if they're plastic or painted on, come to think of it. I love plastic heels, and so have one more request (but Miss Piggy first – I've seen her down Ashton Market).

I also saw a pair of red plastic high heels I really, really need. Princess shoes, like, erm, have you ever watched *Cinderella*? They're like that, but red and plastic, not glass.

Mum says they look tarty. Not sure what that means, but it sounds great. If you can't find the red plastic high heels or the purple Miss Piggy doll down Ashton Market, then if you've got time, you can pop to Hyde Market?

I'd send Uncle Tony, but he's on a mobility scooter at the minute. He needed one to get to the Man City game.

Amen

3

Wot, You Woz a Virgin, Mate?

*I lose my virginity to a gangster on the
Balearic island of Majorca*

'Now pierced is her virgin zone;
She feels the foe within it.
She hears a broken amorous groan,
The panting lover's fainting moan,
Just in the happy minute.'
— JOHN WILMOT, *The Complete Poems*

Yes, that's right, I'm quoting a male rogue from the 1600s, who died a slow, miserable death on account of his penis killing him. It didn't strangle him; it — the penis — acquired several sexually transmitted diseases. Regardless of his rotting penis, in five spare lines, Wilmot succinctly sums up the biggest anticlimax of our lives: virginity loss . . .

This is not a feminist essay on virginity loss in contemporary culture – many wonderful writers have already tackled the subject in great intellectual detail – but we all know society fetishizes 'virgins' and demonises 'sluts', yet only in the context of girls and women, never boys and men. I grew up believing that to 'sleep around', (or in other words, to shag everyone you liked the look of), was a terrible thing for a woman. In some cases, if you're vulnerable, it can be.

I've been that vulnerable young woman, flinging myself into the icy depths of one-night stands, totally off my box on drink and drugs. Experimenting is very much part of sexual evolution, of discovery, of youth, and as such I don't want either of my children to come of age thinking sex, having a lot of sex or enjoying sex is a 'bad' thing. I want them to know that sex is to be enjoyed and explored. I hope my daughter loses her virginity with some semblance of knowing who she is, and also who he, she or they are, too. I hope the person with whom she chooses to have her first sexual experience is someone she knows and likes. I hope she feels confident. I hope she can look back at her virginity-loss sex experience and feel happy. I also hope she's sober. Actually, forget sober.

As for my son, I worry about how he'll navigate the choppy waters of sexual consent. Something I discuss regularly with friends – and also random strangers – consent is nuanced beyond a simple 'no means no'. Many of us have found ourselves in situations where, in a heartbeat, a 'no' easily slides to a half-meant 'yes'. And yet, only five minutes ago, the person you're now shagging said, actually uttered the word, 'no'. So, now what? Forget they said it? What if they didn't mean 'yes', and they stand by their original 'no'? Was the sexual act consensual? Or was it rape?

As a wise mother of four children once told me by the water cooler in the kitchen of the Net-A-Porter office (where all the best conversations take place): 'Tell your son, "THE WOMAN TAKES THE MAN'S PENIS AND PUTS IT INSIDE HER VAGINA."'

I stood there, frozen, mouth agape, for what could only have been ten seconds but felt like five minutes. Standing in the kitchen of Net-A-Porter with your mouth wide open is not acceptable behaviour in offices of high-octane global fashion empires. Ditto, smiling, laughing, eating crisps, or eating anything with a calorific value above 500.

Eureka. I'd found my answer. I knew immediately this was how I'd address the issue of consent with my son. As soon as he is old enough to understand, I plan to tell him. The placing of the penis inside a body also applies to non-heterosexual relationships. A penis entering *any* body – male, female, non-binary – is, by definition, an act of *doing*. Meanwhile, those of us without a cock (or those with a cock who prefer to be entered rather than enter), lie there and take it. But the purposeful act of *placing* a penis inside you, making it clear consent has been given, is the opposite of passive. It's another act of doing. To me, it feels like progress for both parties. Or am I just clutching at straws in an attempt to find a crystal-clear standard for explaining consent to my children?

From when I was thirteen, on a fairly regular basis, and always totally out of the blue, Mum would say, 'Keep your legs crossed; no one wants to marry a bike.' She'd impart this wondrous wisdom whenever and wherever she could: at teatime, walking down the road, shouting loudly over the dulcet tones of Gary Davies playing on the car radio – 'Oooh Gary Davies, oooh Gary Davies, ooh Gary Davies on your raaaaadio.' (Dearest Millennials, that's how catchy radio jingles were back in the 1980s. Bet you're sad you missed it.)

Aged thirteen and with a fertile (pun intended) imagination, I pictured my imminent death. I visualised myself as a seventeenth-century prostitute living above an ale house, riddled with every sexually transmitted disease imaginable and rotting away to translucent skin and bone. That's what happened to our friend John Wilmot (otherwise known as the 2nd Earl of Rochester), after all. Having poked his penis into everything he possibly could, the filthy rascal died of gonorrhoea and syphilis at the grand old age of thirty-three. Technically, though, he died in grandeur, wrapped in silk robes on account of being landed gentry and best mates with King Charles, as opposed to above an ale house covered in flies.

At around the time my mother began scaring me to death with words meant to protect me, a girl at my school 'put out' and lost her virginity, aged thirteen, to one of the boys in the upper year. Cherry well and truly popped, she threw caution to the wind and started shagging various upper-year boys for the rest of the school year. The boys our age remained so unevolved; they were practically playing with Lego at breaktime.

Being sexually active, this girl – let's call her 'L' – was viciously gossiped about. From year one to year six (in England, that's year seven to year twelve), the entire school knew every detail of her sexual adventures. Cast as a slut, she became a social pariah and only hung out with the other so-called 'bikes'. Awful label. Witnessing what happened to L and her 'bike crew' not only ensured my legs stayed clamped shut; as I grew older, I vowed that if my vagina *were* ever to open, no penis living within a sixty-mile radius would gain permission to enter. As sad as it is to admit, Mum was right, people treated L differently after that.

There's no denying that thirteen is very young to start having sex, but it wasn't L's age that freaked me out so much that I still remember the girl's name thirty-five years later.

Instead, it was because, at the tender age of thirteen, I'd subconsciously figured out that the act of sex had not been for L herself, but for adoration and male attention. The thought of L giving herself away so freely haunted me for months – and I hated the boys who took her.

It's fair to say that my 'knowing' she'd had sex not for herself but for the validation of boys can't ever be confirmed, and of course I never dared ask her, but I sensed an air of heaviness around her.

Rather than discuss how I felt about L with my parents at

home, I internalised a swirl of feelings until my insides were like a food processor set to 'high'. L losing her virginity and then becoming the school slut collided in my mind with Disney princesses and a quietness I'd developed around Dad.

When I think back to 'sex talks' in our house, 'No one wants to marry a bike' is the only advice I can ever recall. I'd found out how babies are made at around the age of ten. Watching telly while off school sick, I'd accidentally watched an hour of life-changing daytime TV.

'Mum,' I had screeched down the short, dark hallway of our bungalow, 'I know how babies are made!'

Given the unthinkable act of turning off the vac without actually finishing the 'vackin' (vacuuming to the rest of you non-Mancunians), Mum poked out her head from behind my brother's bedroom door.

'Go on,' she said, even though there's no way she wanted to know what was about to spurt forth from my gob (a loving term for 'mouth' in Manchester).

'I always thought babies are made when a man wees in the toilet and a woman wees on top of it. Then her wee splashes on to his wee and the wee ends up inside her . . . '

'Yessssss?' Mum replied, vac still in hand.

'Well, it's nothing to do with wee! It's when a man puts his willy inside a woman's wee place!' I said, both revolted and completely obsessed at the same time.

Such a macabre titbit picked up from daytime TV – who'd a thunk it! I can't remember Mum's reaction, but the information I'd gleaned from whatever TV programme I watched that day made sense in the context of books I read the following year by Judy Blume. Delicious: I devoured them with voracity, inspiring a different kind of bloom.

When I turned sixteen, I applied for a weekend job working at Habitat in the West End of Edinburgh. It was there I met Sarah, a beautiful brown-eyed goth who introduced me to the city's metal music scene. I was already buying clothes from charity shops and wearing Doc Marten boots every single day even throughout summer, even when they were falling apart and my stepdad had to glue them back together, but under Sarah's influence, my style went up a notch. Or, if you're one of the unfortunate family members subjected to living with me during this tumultuous teenage stage, down a notch.

After work, we'd change out of our Habitat staff uniforms and circle our eyes with black eyeliner like pandas. Draping multiple beaded necklaces over psychedelic-print minidresses, we'd pull on our mid-calf-length Docs – hers in burgundy, mine in black – and head to Leith Walk to drink pints in grubby pubs. Pre-gentrification, Leith Walk was very, very rough. Like, Begby in *Trainspotting* rough. I was jealous of Sarah's battered black leather biker jacket – I thought she was dead cool.

When I was seventeen, my mum and stepdad booked a package holiday to Majorca and asked if I'd like to bring a friend. My best friend couldn't afford it, so I asked Sarah and her parents agreed she could come. Each of us packed a suitcase filled with gothic hippy clothes that were about as 'summery' as the Addams Family at a funeral. My hair was long and dark, and I'd moved away from the awkward, gawky stage: my thicker legs had grown longer, my blue eyes were framed by thick, dark eyebrows, and I'd developed a handsome kind of beauty.

Sarah, on the other hand, was tiny and pretty, like a nymph, with long, dark lashes that she batted at boys, knocking them over with a glance. She got all the attention. It didn't bother me.

After a day on the beach wearing as little sun cream as possible, we'd head back to our apartment to have dinner with Mum, my stepdad and Lee. Lee was ten, too young to join us. After shuffling a few chips around a plate, we'd tell them we'd be back by midnight. Quick loo check, more eyeliner, a top-up of Body Shop perfume, and we'd charge into the night.

And we'd get raging, rolling, rambunctiously drunk. Pissed like a scene from *The Inbetweeners*. We'd stumble into apartments with boys from Manchester, Newcastle, Leeds. We'd dive into swimming pools fully clothed. We'd drink until we could barely stand. Within five days, we'd managed to snog one boy each! Result! Except I couldn't remember *my* boy's name. Thankfully, he returned to the UK after two days.

For an entire week, we knocked about with funny, daft northerners, lads wearing garish T-shirts with mismatching shorts, always paired with white socks and Adidas trainers. The northern lads existed within the realms of our tribe: the same suburban state schools, the same faceless housing estates built between 1965 and 1980. With different music but shared cultural references, we understood them and they understood us.

It wasn't until the second week of our holiday that I found him: Marlon Brando good looks; black, slim-fit round-neck T-shirts; slim-cut black jeans. He wore perfect boots, of a kind I'd never seen before, which I later discovered had a name: 'Chelsea boots'.

It was early evening. The sun was a whole hour away from disappearing to the other side of the ocean. Witching hour: my favourite time of day. Sarah and I headed to our favourite cocktail bar, safe in the knowledge that the northerners we'd snogged had already gone home.

There was an alien among us. A man we'd never seen before was sitting at the bar with a friend. I was aware I was staring, but I couldn't pull my eyes away. Every minute or so, he lifted a tanned hand and combed it through his shoulder-length hair. It was the most erotic thing I'd ever seen. I'd had no idea watching a man smoking could induce a full-body flush – that had always been omitted from Judy Blume novels. As he pulled a cigarette towards his full lips in a pout, the beautiful alien was so handsome I froze, heart pounding beneath a layer of beaded necklaces. For the first time ever, I was turned on.

Suddenly self-conscious, I felt like a peacock trying to hide behind a tree, flashing a fanned tail. My bright blue paisley-print minidress was impossible to hide. Compared with the alien in shiny black boots and slim-cut black jeans, the dress suddenly felt all wrong. Although I didn't realise it at the time, this out-of-sorts feeling was something I'd learn to get used to when I became a fashion editor attending Fashion Week.

Under all that long, chocolatey hair, his doleful brown eyes caught me staring, and within five minutes, I somehow knew his name. He was from London. Of course he was from London.

Within thirty minutes, we were holding hands.

'I'm leaving tomorrow,' he told me, as we folded into one another, mouths, bodies, hair, our smells entangled together. We left the bar as one; I'd lost Sarah. We were in his apartment, on his bed. My clothes were on the floor. He rolled a condom along his dick. I looked down, enthralled.

'I'm a virgin,' I told him.

A pouty side-smile suggested he didn't believe me.

A new dawn lit up the apartment complex outside. He was inside me now. A sharp pain, deep, reminding me of the snap of a Christmas cracker. I closed my eyes; my mother's face floated into view, like the ghost in the Dickens classic *A Christmas Carol*. Too scared to close them again, I fixed my gaze on the side of his face. *Handsome*, I think to myself. *So, so handsome.*

Maybe ten minutes later – definitely more than five – a deep groan indicated his cock was releasing cum inside the condom. It was over and I was ecstatic. *I did it!*

Cherry popped, hymen broken, blood the colour of a cardinal's cloak seeping into white, virginal sheets. Blood running down my legs. Handsome went to the bathroom to fetch a towel.

'So, you *woz* a virgin,' he said, in a thick cockney accent I'd been struggling to understand all night.

Yes, Handsome. I was.

As for what happened next, I hot-footed it back to our apartment, praying Mum wouldn't catch me coming home at 6am. Without waking Sarah, I took a long shower, scrubbing my body, terrified Mum and my stepdad's Spidey senses would detect evidence of my new, non-virginal state. Later that day, Handsome left Majorca, but not without coming to find me. We snogged for ages. I already knew I was in love.

Four days later, I returned home. In Scotland, schools return from the summer holidays earlier, so even though it was only July, I was due to return to school for my final year in a couple of weeks' time. Lovesick, in total agony, I spent hours on the phone to Handsome. Pining for him, wanting him, needing him, loving him; I was a woman possessed. Intoxicated. I told Mum I had to go to London, pleading that my life depended upon seeing the boy in black. No such luck. My parents said I should stay in Edinburgh. No running off to London with Highers on the horizon.

My heart no longer belonged in this small town; it belonged to Handsome – and every man who would come after him. My body was on fire, and it's how I would feel in every future relationship until I eventually sought therapy. Lovestruck, I was blind. Down in the depths of the abysmal sea, the love addict was awakened.

A week after returning from Majorca, I caught a bus into central Edinburgh from Balerno, the small town eight miles outside the city, where we've lived since leaving Manchester. I alighted the bus on Princes Street, feeling like a crook as I navigated the cobbled streets. I'd never pawned jewellery before.

By combining the pawn shop cash with some unexpected wages, on account of Habitat paying me double time to work on a Sunday, I managed to scrape together enough for the bus fare to London. Pockets laden with Scottish pound notes, and ten- and two-pence pieces, I headed to the main bus station in Edinburgh to buy a return coach ticket to London. Later that afternoon, I broke the news of my imminent departure to my parents, informing them I'd be 'back in a week'. We all shouted. We all cried. Beneath the tears and anger, Mum and I both knew we needed a break from each other.

Lying on the floral bedspreads of suburbia, I'd already soaked up London via the pages of *The Face*, *i-D* and *Vogue*, and the city had been embedded in my soul since the age of fourteen. Not that I'd ever actually been. Ten hours after leaving Edinburgh, the coach hit London traffic. Famously slow and annoying, it hasn't bothered me for decades now. These days, when I wake up in the dead of night, knowing London traffic is thrumming around Piccadilly Circus just a few miles away, it comforts me back to sleep. Life. I need to be around it.

Handsome was waiting for me at Victoria bus station. I felt awkward, out of my depth, this small-town girl in the big smoke. Handsome ushered me towards his car, a sporty thing, brand new, given the smell. At least, that's what I assumed the smell was, given I didn't care about cars.

He drove too fast, and the glove box flung open. Two spare number plates dropped heavily to the floor, narrowly missing my kitten heels. He leaned across and shoved them back into the glove box, slamming it closed.

With lovely views of Blackheath Park, the immaculate 1930s private apartment block smelled of Brasso. Golden handrails and not one fingerprint in sight. A glamorous Bond Girl greeted us at the door in head-to-toe pink: blonde bob, thin, huge boobs bouncing braless in flimsy T-shirt, dark brown eyes lined with kohl.

'This is Mum,' Handsome said, beckoning me towards the creature.

'Oh,' I said, shocked, having assumed her to be a model or on her way out to perform a West End play. Leading lady, of course.

''Allo darlin'!' she said, gripping me to her boobs. Her south London accent was so Barbara Windsor, I thought for a moment she might actually *be* her. She was doused in Poison by Dior, and her smell remained on my clothes six hours later: horrible, like fly spray. I felt suffocated by it. I sat on her huge bed. The walls were lined with tinted mirrors. In their reflection, we all looked a bit weird. I asked whether she could see herself properly, in the dulled tint of her already dark bedroom. She said she reckoned she looked better in the dark.

'No, you're beautiful,' I said.

The following day, I was told we were going 'out-out'. I had no clue what 'out-out' meant, but it sounded serious. The restaurant was 'posh', down by the River Thames. I was instructed to 'Go see Mum.' Back in Handsome's mum's bedroom, I was handed a deep pink Valentino shift dress and told to put it on.

'And 'ere are the 'eeels,' said Handsome's mum, throwing the most beautiful shoes I'd ever seen on to the bed.

From the front room, a man shouted, 'Fank fuck, she can't go owwwwt dressed like faaacking Janice Joplin.'

I pulled on the dress and heels, oblivious to the fact I was wearing head-to-toe stolen goods.

After a few days, I began to feel at home enough to help myself to food from the kitchen. Handsome's mum only ate Ryvita with sliced tomatoes on top, a diet she suggested I try, given I was two stones heavier than any woman I was introduced to during my time in London. After another late night, I meandered towards the kitchen in search of cereal. No more Ryvita – endless red packets of crackers wouldn't placate the familiar blizzard of a hangover.

Grabbing a nearby chair, I raked along every shelf. Reaching to the highest one, finally, a prize! A box of cornflakes nestled behind a stack of pots.

The box felt heavy and the cereal poured out too quickly. A thud in the bowl suggested congealed cornflakes, but upon closer inspection, it turned out to be a ginormous bag of white powder inside a freezer bag. I carried it to the window to take a closer look, holding it up towards the light. *Why would anyone keep icing sugar in a cereal box?* I wondered, just as Handsome walked in wearing only his Calvins. Seeing me inspecting the bag in the sunlight, my smile was unreturned.

'I've gotta tell you somefink,' he said, gently placing the icing sugar back inside the cereal box, hiding it on an even higher shelf, way out of everyone's reach. 'That bag, it ain't old cereal, it's uncut cocaine. And the tins of Coke in the fridge? There's more in there.'

For a long while, Handsome refused to allow me to sample the drugs his family sold for a living. I was a drug virgin. Eventually, he caved and racked up a line in the loo. 'You sniff it,' he instructed, rolling a twenty-pound note (otherwise known as a 'score', fair reader). Two virginities lost in one month.

High on the purest cocaine, twice a week we ran around London nightclubs – Love Ranch, Gaslight Club, Gardening Club – and danced all night wearing stolen designer clothes.

I avoided suburbia for as long as I could, and stayed in that fourth-floor apartment for two weeks, not one week as initially planned, blithely ignoring my parent's phone calls to the landline. Eventually, Handsome's mum forced me to speak to Mum, who begged me to come home to finish the final year of school.

'You won't get a job,' she said.

Don't need one, I thought, looking around at the mob I'd moved in with.

I did agree to come back, but I spent every half-term, Christmas, bank holiday, Easter break – every second I could – back in London, spending the money I'd made from my new job working in an old people's home as a carer. In May the following year, I turned eighteen, and the following month, I left school. The feeling of freedom tore through my body. On the final day, I walked out at noon, went home, grabbed my case and boarded a 2pm train to London.

And it's goodnight from me.

My little brother was so upset at my quick departure that he ran along the platform, chasing the train. I knew Mum was both worried and relieved to see the back of me. Living together had become a strain.

Make-up-free for school, I sat on the train swooshing a thick layer of eyeliner across my top lid, on top of which I applied several swipes of mascara. Two posh boys sitting opposite openly discussed how much better I'd looked without make-up. It made me think of L and the judgement I'd cast. I felt guilty and ashamed. Arriving at King's Cross at around seven, no longer a fish out of water, I gulped in the familiar stench of a hot London evening, revived by the manic hustle and bustle.

Summer bobbed along. Handsome assumed that, come September, I'd take up my place at Camberwell College of Arts a few miles away. But I was withholding information; hedging my bets, as it were. I'd been offered a second art school place, at Manchester Poly. Attending Camberwell would mean living in London with Handsome and his mum, whereas accepting the place in Manchester would be a different experience altogether. I reserved a room in the Manchester halls of residence, just in case.

His family were beginning to frighten me.

My university conundrum was decided late one night in a restaurant by the River Thames. Handsome's mum's boyfriend – let's call him 'P' – booked a table for ten at his favourite restaurant. Sitting next to P, I wore a black dress by Chloé – stolen, naturally. The staff approached the table cautiously. They were visibly on edge, as though walking on tightropes, seeming afraid to make an approach.

'You alright, darlin'?' P asked, leaning his head towards mine. 'I used to come 'ere back in the day wiv the Krays. Naughty boys, they woz.'

I nodded politely, praying no one would bring a live lobster anywhere near my face.

Then came the incident that changed the course of my education. It was Handsome's grandad's birthday, and I felt drunk. I saw a flash of metal before I realised it was a gun. A gun held to a waiter's head. Everyone began to flap.

'For fucks sake, put the shooters away!' shouted the women.

I couldn't move. Handsome grabbed my hand and stood up to leave.

P's face turned dark and violent. 'Sit your faaaackin' arse down, boy.'

Apparently, P had begun smoking joints at breakfast and continued to smoke weed all day, as well as drinking hash tea in the afternoon, before getting started on loads of cocaine (sniff) at six o'clock. By the time he'd had a drink at dinner, he also decided to drop a tab of acid. As did Handsome's elderly grandad, along with his brother and uncle.

'Faaaaackin' great night out, last night, wannit, eh, gal?' he asked me the next morning.

I nodded and continued to walk down the hallway towards the kitchen. The kitchen where toast was way safer than cereal.

Things turned darker from that day. Even when I was just out with Handsome and his mates, I noticed a change in his behaviour. He was always encouraging me to dress up when we went out, and when men glanced my way, he turned, becoming verbally violent. 'Want me to faaackin' shoot him?' he'd whisper in my ear.

So as not to upset him, whenever we were out, I stopped meeting people's gazes, and spent weeks staring at the floor.

I felt derailed. The only person I could call was the person I'd run away from.

'Mum. I need to get out of here'.

I'd been living in Manchester at university for a month after my disappearing act. Handsome had assumed that after a 'quick trip' back to Edinburgh, I'd return to live with him to attend Camberwell College of Arts. I'd told him I'd be back 'before mid-September'.

I'd lied, of course.

I had to lie. What with the guns, his violent family, and his out-of-control, cocaine-fuelled paranoid jealousy, I was scared to death.

One night, using a payphone in the halls of residence, I called Donna, a girlfriend I'd met through Handsome.

'Where you living?' she asked me.

I should never have answered.

When Donna told her boyfriend I was living in Manchester, he, of course, told Handsome where to find me. After driving two hundred miles in a rage, Handsome stalked the streets like a panther all day. In a city of two million, it was late and dark when he found me. There was no point apologising for my secretive departure now, I remember thinking, noticing his face growing angrier with each fast step.

Heartbreak and rage flickered across his face, and I didn't notice his fist as he raised it. 'You faaaackin' slag,' I heard him say, followed shortly by the loud thump of his right fist as it met my face. As blood poured from my nose on to my suede ankle boots, I silently clutched my face.

He got back into his white sports car. 'Faaaaaaack you, you faaaackin' slaaag,' were his final words to me, shouted from the car window by the man with whom I'd lost my virginity.

4

Love Mating

*The love of my life arrived wearing
a skirt, eyeliner. No horse*

The one thing I miss about being much younger – as in, below the age of twenty-something – is the 'not knowing'. A script unwritten, a life ahead without a plan, the sexy sizzle of excitement felt imagining what's yet to come.

Rooms decorated with embossed shiny wallpaper and those floral borders as seen at the edges of countless ceilings in suburbia? No. I wanted to live in a flat with pale wooden floorboards and whitewashed walls. I wanted to sleep in a bed with white bedding, in a room with no ornaments.

I was nineteen on the sunny afternoon I met Rob outside the City Café, a bar located halfway up a cobbled hilly street in Edinburgh's Grassmarket. The legendary City Café is nothing like a café, it's a bar. Having recently flunked out of art school in Manchester, I'd returned to Edinburgh with my tail between my legs.

Not that I let Rob see I was deeply ashamed of my recent academic failings. I was showing off; I remember telling him I'd dropped out of art school because I'd lived on the same street as seminal nightclub the Hacienda. I vaguely remember saying Bez from the Happy Mondays was a 'friend' (he wasn't), and that I'd been on tour with the Stone Roses (I hadn't).

Studying English lit and about to begin his second year at Edinburgh, I assumed Rob might be gay (I think, at one point, he may have thought the same). His gentle energy made me feel safe, and we soon sank into an easy friendship. His outrageously camp mannerisms made me laugh. His daily 'look' was a tight-fitting, ankle-length black tube skirt, black eyeliner, a white shirt with extra-long sleeves dangling way past his hands, topped off with a shrunken black jumper. Within two months, we were dressing in matching outfits. Then, from out of nowhere, we looked at one another, both realising at exactly the same time that we'd fallen madly, deeply, passionately in love.

Best friends and now lovers, we quickly moved in together. At a loose end work-wise (had just been fired by The Body Shop), with nothing else on the horizon, I convinced Rob to do the obvious thing and start a club night, a night at a pre-existing nightclub, one that had, until we turned up, been pretty empty of punters.) Rolling around the backseat of a friend's car on our way back from the Tunnel Club in Glasgow early one morning, our bedazzled E brains came up with the name 'Burger Queen'. Because that's exactly the type of name you come up with when you're totally off your tits.

With no clue how to run our lives, never mind a club night, neither of us took it particularly seriously at first. We weren't in it for the money or local status; we were in it for the laughs, the dressing up, the outrage, the rebellion, the drugs, the music, the dancing. How could we have possibly predicted that within a few months, the club would be famous up and down the country? It was rammed to the rafters every Saturday night. DJs, journalists and photographers made their way up from London to witness the Scottish spectacle, and clubbers travelled from all over the UK to attend. In all our dressed-up madcap innocence, we'd accidentally put Edinburgh on the nightclubbing map.

Complete with tall, powdered white wig, I hired a full Marie Antoinette outfit (no comment) from a local fancy-dress shop and wore it to do the door. Dancing all night in floor-length blue silk, the hemline soon became tattered and torn, and the fancy-dress shop refused to take it back. I vaguely remember them threatening court action. I also vaguely remember the cat crapping on the dress one night, and me soaking it for hours in the bath (the dress, not the cat). (If you're the owner of a fancy-dress shop in Edinburgh and you happen to be missing a Marie Antoinette costume, please DM me on Insta, and I'll happily cough up.)

Everyone made money from the club except us. Our promoter and the DJ had the business smarts to make a living out of it (for a time at least) but we were out. I was unable to pay my share of the rent, so we were both living off Rob's student loans. It was impossible to live on such a small amount of money, and I'd constantly doorstep the local council offices begging for housing benefit. After the fourth or fifth trip, I resorted to wedging my face into the small cut-out in the thick plastic screen designed to stop lunatics like me from throwing themselves on to council employees. Sobbing, I threatened not to leave until someone helped.

As I left the council offices and walked back to our cottage wearing a 1970s skinny black leather coat, my white-blond hair shaved to one centimetre long and my high heels clattering on the cobbles, I realised there was nothing left for me in Edinburgh. The Body Shop had fired me, and bar jobs interfered with my only hobby, nightclubs. As for a career, I had no real concept of what that even meant.

At this point, I was no longer on speaking terms with any family member, so I convinced Rob we should move to London. He was half up for it, half terrified. I imagined a speech bubble floating above his head: 'This is a fine mess you've got us into,

Duguid.' As for delivering the 'we're moving to London' speech to his academic parents, I'm not sure they ever forgave me.

Regardless, the decision had been made; we were moving. I took a train to London to look for flats, while Rob stayed in Edinburgh to carry on with university. We were so skint that although I'd scraped together enough to buy a cheap train ticket, I had no budget for a hotel or even a B&B, so I looked for lodgings advertised in the *Edinburgh Evening News*.

'Lovely room for rent. Available short-term. South Woodford, London. £40 per week.'

I quickly moved in and decided to use this as a base while I searched; I found imagining parts of London overwhelming and difficult. I looked at the tube map, a confusion of colour and possibilities. I studied the opening credits of *EastEnders*, hoping an aerial view might provide a clue. I walked around W1, popping into random estate agents', only to be quoted rents so high, so casually suggested, that I assumed they were for a whole month, not just a week.

Having discovered on day two that I was unable to afford a Kensington postcode, I had to make a decision. I knew two areas in London: the shops and tube surrounding the council estate in South Woodford, and the streets edging Blackheath where Handsome and the Mob lived. The streets leading uphill from Greenwich to Blackheath felt endless and green, and were pretty and familiar. But after what had happened the night Handsome had finally found me, moving anywhere south wasn't an option.

South Woodford it was, then.

I went back up to Edinburgh to fetch Rob. He was penniless, as per; his parents had to put money into his account so we could hire a middle-management-style car and buy petrol.

Because Daddy was a well-connected scholar, Rob managed to transfer his degree from Edinburgh to UCL. Surprisingly, The Body Shop didn't want to hire me in London – or, in fact, ever see my face in one of their stores again. Instead, we found part-time work on the shop floor of Harvey Nichols (we couldn't bear to be apart, even at our Saturday jobs). Once we were earning, we broke out of the grim, dirty, old South Woodford flat and moved closer to central London. Shoreditch back then was gritty and alive with young artists destined for future fame. Thanks to housing benefits and free education, those artists became world renowned. To this day, I remain grateful for the three months' worth of housing benefit I was able to claim.

I took a job in the pub opposite our flat, and poured pints and G&Ts three nights a week. Serving booze to all of humanity, the Golden Heart buzzed with taxi drivers and prostitutes coming off their night shifts. Bored of shop work and pub shifts, I applied to attend fashion school, a thing unheard of at my state-school secondary in Edinburgh. Halfway through the September term, I applied to the London College of Fashion. Even though they said no, I got Rob to call them. Still no. I remember the phone calls made from our white BT landline phone as though it were yesterday. But then I got a yes from the University of East London, where I applied to study Fashion Design. I managed two terms, after which I applied for a marketing degree. I left that degree, too, but only after spunking a loan on a catsuit from Vivienne Westwood. Three universities, two student loans, and not one qualification. I did, however, become a huge success at going OUT.

Rob became friendly with Julie Burchill and Mariella Frostrup via a magazine he wrote for called *The Modern Review*. ('It's *postmodern*,' he'd say, lying back, practically wearing a smoking jacket and feather boa.) Burchill had made Rob and his mate walk down a catwalk wearing 'ironic' underwear (as in, a pair of small underpants with two inverted commas made out of felt stuck to his bollocks).

'Geddit?' he'd ask.

'YES!' I'd reply, even though I really didn't.

Julie invited us to her coming-out party. She'd left her husband,

Cosmo, and had fallen in love with a woman named Charlotte. All I remember is a dark blue kitchen filled with a lot of lesbians.

If the much younger me believed life was mine for the taking, by the time I reached my early twenties, hope and a sense of discovery were soon replaced by an overwhelming sense of doom and dread. Joy evicted by fear, my unwritten future felt as destabilising as a bad hangover. Moving in with the mob aged seventeen, a year at art school in Manchester at eighteen, back in Edinburgh at nineteen, before moving to London once more with not a penny to my name, at the age of twenty-one, finding myself distanced from my family and isolated. Fear, it turns out, had moved in for the long haul.

As fear made itself comfortable in my life, I even began to dress differently. Trying hard to fit in in a city where literally no one knew my name, gone was the experimental version of me, a young woman who'd think nothing of pairing an old-lady skirt suit found in a charity shop with black fishnets and sexy heels. I'd transformed into a somewhat vanilla version of myself I hardly recognised, losing my innate eclectic style.

I knew it was happening, knew I was morphing into someone I didn't want to become, but I couldn't do anything about it. I didn't need a *plan*, I needed a witchy type, all haggard and tiny, clutching an old porcelain cup with some musty old leaves stuck to the bottom of it.

'Cross my palm with gold and I'll tell you what your future holds.'

Actually, forget tea leaves; a future as dazzling as mine deserves to be delivered by a well-dressed ghost wearing head-to-toe Issey Miyake.

Fashionable Ghost: 'Would you like to know what your future has in store?'

Me: 'Oh, yes please!'

Fashionable Ghost: 'What would you like to know?'

Me: 'Love. Tell me all about my love life. My handsome husband . . . my beautiful babies . . . my career, my home . . . '

* Cue swirl of dramatic smoke, plus a couple of bright lights that could also be a sparkler – or my glaucoma, hard to tell.*

Fashionable Ghost: 'The person you're currently dating is the man you'll love for ever.'

Me: 'Rob! Yeah! Course, I will! But not *for ever* for ever.'

Fashionable Ghost: 'For a very long time.'

Me: 'Tell me all about my fabulous life ahead. My husband and all that.'

Fashionable Ghost: 'Rob is married with children. You are not the wife or mother.'

Me: 'OK. That's cool. What about me?'

Fashionable Ghost: 'You're lonely with a massive mortgage, many, many doomed relationships under your belt. Far too many to mention, actually.'

Me: 'What?'

Fashionable Ghost: 'Anything else you'd like to know before I disappear into a puff of Japanese designer, fashion-forward smoke?'

Me: 'Erm, hold on. Don't go anywhere just yet. So, if the love of my life is Rob and he marries someone else, who the hell do I end up with?'

Fashionable Ghost: 'Two years after ending the relationship with Rob, you remain heartbroken. And so, regretting the day you ever left, one day you pick up the landline phone at work.'

Me: 'OK, thank God. So, it's only a two-year break-up? What about his kids? Actually, I'd be a great stepmum, I've never fancied actually pushing a baby out of my fanny.'

Fashionable Ghost: 'But it's too late. He's moved on. You are just a distant memory, fading into his past. And what's worse, you spend the following fifteen years with a Rob-sized hole in your heart.'

Me: 'I don't fall in love for another fifteen years?!'

Fashionable Ghost: 'No, you do.'

Me: 'Oh, thank God. Go on, then. What's *he* like?'

Fashionable Ghost: 'Irish.'

Me: 'A Fellow Celt! Excellent. Looks? Occupation?'

Fashionable Ghost: 'He's difficult, homeless and food obsessed.'

Me: 'Homeless?'

Fashionable Ghost: 'Until you adopt him from the Mayhew Animal Rescue Home.'

Me: 'OK, you can go now.'

With a whole life ahead of me – great friends still to meet, places still to see, a career yet to imagine – ending up with the first person I fell in love with was never part of the plan. Ever. I had bigger ideas, as backed up by my Mancunian aunt, who chose two minutes before the coffin arrived at my grandfather's funeral to tell me my ideas were 'above my station'. My crime? Turning up looking 'too showy', and, an even worse crime, as if I was 'from London', wearing a bright red coat to such a sad occasion. Little did she know I'd purchased said 'showy London coat' for eight quid after an hour-long rummage in the sale bin at the Cats Protection League, Willesden Green.

Big ideas, no actual plans. There was only one thing I knew for sure, which was life did not involve getting married young. I had hope coursing through my veins, I had huge dreams of – well, nothing I could quite put a finger on, but *big stuff*.

Rob and I threw ourselves into London headfirst. On a dancefloor late one night, I met the woman who changed the course of my life. Lighting up the dancefloor in a shimmering silver Red or Dead blazer that flashed like a glitter ball, I was mesmerised – both by her and the jacket. She had short cropped red hair and a ballsy Essex twang, and over the heavy bassline of pumping house music, we managed to exchange numbers.

'Alright, babez? What? Yeah, alright. Yeah. Call me at the

office,' she said, flicking a large silver stud pierced through the centre of her tongue that clattered against her teeth as she spoke.

Within a month, I was her fashion intern and a runner at London Fashion Week. A fire, a flicker; so this is why I'd moved to London with not a single penny. I was finally dipping a toe into the inner workings of a world I'd read about in my teens in magazines bought with money earned at the pound shop.

Seeking excitement (and without a fortune-teller to guide me), I ended the relationship with Rob almost out of nowhere. The day he moved out of our Shoreditch flat (taking all the furniture, because I still owned nothing) an infestation of silverfish moved in, transforming our stained, grotty beige carpet into a bright crystal sea. With zero clue who to call, I put on a pair of platforms instead.

I was twenty-two, with no furniture, and a flat I could no longer afford. Rob's parents were unavailable to bail me out, I had a pest infestation, and all I owned was a second-hand bed meant for two.

Had I known that fifteen years later I'd spend nights poring over a new thing called Facebook, staring for hours at photos of Rob and the babies I wished were mine, would I have stayed? Each click of the keyboard was a sharp scratch to my heart. After the birth of his third child, thank God, Rob blocked me.

Should I have stayed? Probably. Yes.

Hindsight can be most unhelpful.

5

Mating Call

I fall in love with a small thing decorated in
florals and it's NOT a Prada handbag

Around my thirty-third birthday, I began to feel very strange. Not 'tired strange', or 'hungover strange', or 'comedown strange'. Not '1992-consuming-too-much-ecstasy strange', when even attempting to get out of bed would send my tiny ping-pong-ball brain ricocheting around my skull. This was way stranger than the usual 'strange', and that's saying something. The pilot light of the broken-down boiler, otherwise known as my womb, had suddenly – inexplicably, alarmingly – flickered into action.

The first time I noticed traces of this new feeling inside was on my way to a shoe appointment in Milan. I couldn't put my finger on why I felt so odd. It seemed like more than fashion-show fatigue. I'd been on the road for four weeks straight, and after a week of New York nightlife, four nights of parties in London, fourteen days of back-to-back fashion shows, as per usual, I'd arrived in Milan running on empty.

It's normal to feel somewhat worse for wear in Milan – not that you're allowed to show it. Home to the world's biggest-selling designers, it's where serious business happens. It's also the best city for food (unlike Paris, the *finalement pièce de résistance* on the show schedule, where, for several days, because the French think chicken is vegetarian, I'd live off buttered bread, green beans and wine).

A month of living in hotels while travelling around the four fashion capitals in chauffeur-driven blacked-out vans may sound amazing, and a lot of the time it was, but as with anything that you have to do all day and night without a break, it soon becomes deadly boring. And teary. And emosh. And messy. I sound like a dick.

Within days, our swish transport inevitably morphed into a chaotic moving walk-in wardrobe on wheels, with compartments overflowing with sweet wrappers and discarded show invitations littering the floor. I'll never forget pulling up outside the Armani show. As the electric doors slid open, with our driver looking ever so fine in his immaculately pressed suit (Armani, obviously), several empty bottles (water not wine, thank God), notepads, packets of nuts and a couple of pairs of shoes tumbled out of the van, decorating the Armani-greige carpet below. We sashayed off, huge sunglasses hiding our faces, pretending it had never happened (a lot like eating carbs). I'd heard the *Vogue* van was always serene and calm, with fruits, healthy snacks and sparkling water served at regular intervals. Friends told me the previous Net-A-Porter team played gospel music to calm their frazzled nerves. Even in the van, there was a strict seating arrangement (allegedly).

With no time to eat in restaurants, but being massive fans of food, Team *ELLE* scoffed paninis in the back of our van, washing them down with a full-fat Coke. JUST Team *ELLE*, to be clear; never *Vogue*, and certainly never Net-A-Porter, where bread is considered an illegal substance. I'll never forget joining the extra-fabulous queue at Versace with my face covered in ciabatta flour.

'Erm, you have white powder all over your nose,' said a well-known buyer, before carrying on his conversation about the death of the bejewelled headband and whether green or pink was the colour of the season.

I'm grateful to this day that he didn't realise the white powder smeared across my face was in fact ciabatta flour. *Bread!?* Talk about blowing up your career.

Crap diet, no sleep, too much booze – there's only so much a woman can handle, so it's no wonder there was always a tiny drama, a fall-out, a devastating loss. During the season of the ultra-shiny black patent Prada pencil skirt (as in, THE iconic skirt of the week), it was decided unanimously (we took a vote) that the fashion director HAD to wear one to the Prada show the following evening. After making around six hundred phone calls, we tracked down the only size ten left in the whole of Italy.

Our fashion director was famous for her wardrobe prep, so, before jumping in the shower, knowing the Burberry dinner would end late, she tried on the Prada skirt in preparation for the next day. Satisfied, she wrapped it back up in the now scrunched-up tissue, and popped it back inside the lightweight paper Prada shopping bag before flinging it somewhere across her room in her hurry to get ready.

During their evening turn-down service, the hotel cleaners assumed said bag was rubbish, so popped it down the hotel garbage chute, along with several hundred other bedrooms' worth of trash.

Trying to explain this level of emergency to the night watchman on the front desk was impossible, and, as it was midnight, I gave up and decided to give it another go in the morning. For round two, with the only Italian at my disposal being '*vino rosso*', and with 8am being the busiest time of day at reception, I decided the only option was to mime the emergency instead. Picture a sort of cross between Manuel from *Fawlty Towers* attempting to take a dinner order, and Patsy from *Ab Fab* ordering a drink in Harvey Nichols.

We looked everywhere for that bastard skirt. Everyone helped, including the entire concierge team, waiters and a random person carrying a stepladder, who came along just in case the Prada carrier bag had been mysteriously flung in the air and was hanging invisibly from the chandelier or lodged in the curtain rod. But the last black patent Prada pencil skirt available to buy in the whole of Italy was gone, never to be found again.

A terrible tragedy.

Early nights during Fashion Week? Pffft, forget it. Which would you choose: parties at Donatella Versace's apartment with Kevin Bacon and the Backstreet Boys, or a quiet night in with a bowl of vegetable soup ordered on room service? DUH. My point is, it's totally normal to feel strange during Fashion Week. It is not normal to feel strange while looking at a *baby* at Fashion Week.

While I am well versed in the 'I simply must have that right now or I shall die' desire that courses through one's veins after seeing a handbag (especially for impulsive types like me, especially when Jil Sander hires a new creative director who designs a bag that looks like it's landed from the future), I did not expect to feel the same way about an Italian *bambina* wearing a floral dress and matching bonnet. I saw her being carried by her handsome father through the streets of Milan, and I didn't know what to do. Even when broke, I can buy the goddamn bag. It's called whacking it on a credit card (actually, it's probably called stealing, given the lack of intention to ever pay off the card). But the adorable *bella* baby girl? There's only so much Prada can deliver.

Wherever I went, I noticed babies. I could hear them, smell them, feel them. I remember standing in Gail's one morning buying my daily expensive coffee. Upon hearing a nearby newborn scream its head off, my body turned to jelly. I stared at it (for a bit too long), and then, as though dredged up from a long-lost sea of feelings, the strangest, most discombobulating mix of emotions floated over me, slicing through me like a knife. I couldn't tell whether I wanted to run away from the newborn's screams or pick it up and dash out with it smuggled inside my Saint Laurent tote. Can you imagine? Me, huge tears rolling down my cheeks, crying, wheezing, making noises a bit like an asthmatic accordion played by a five-year-old jacked up on Coco Pops, running through Queen's Park (dead posh part of London now, but it was awful when I first moved), with a stolen baby (also crying) stuffed into a YSL tote?

'Hello, it's Jeremy Kyle on the line; what time can you be in the studio?'

Up until this point, I had not usually been a fan of children (with the exception of my close mate Sara's child Donovan, who, I have to say, was perfect from the day she birthed him). But now, the deep gnaw inside me could only mean one thing: Christ alive, I was broody!

A tug and a pop, every twenty-eight days like clockwork; I could feel every ovulation. I'd lie in bed at night, cosy and relaxed beneath my duvet, palms gently pressed on my tummy somewhere above my aching ovaries. I'd lie there, imagining what this month's egg might look like if it collided with a sperm cocktail that evening. Ovulation became borderline painful, eggs pop-pop-popping like cannonballs. I wanted to be a mother. I needed to be a mother.

Of course I was going to be a mother: white, cisgender, living in the West. I'd worked hard, I told myself, and now my prince was on his way. We'd have babies, and we'd live happily ever after in our Pinterest-worthy home. Obviously, I'd go back to my career after birthing a few sprogs. Got to save up to retire so we can enjoy our grandchildren . . .

Check out me and my white Western privilege.

Like the turn-down service at the hotel, though, there's always going to be the odd spanner in the works of life. To this day, I'm convinced my fertility spanner came in the form of 'the Ladettes'.

From newspaper headlines and TV programmes, to billboards advertising Wonderbras, and images of Sara Cox wearing low-cut tops and being gobby in nightclubs, if you're around my age or above, perhaps you too received a message from the wider culture sometime around 1995 informing you that 'she' (religion notwithstanding) is finally equal to 'him'. Young women had been liberated; it was official. Leading the shouty broadcast like an impassioned speaker standing on an upside-down crate stolen from Tesco was *Cosmopolitan* magazine:

'ATTENTION PLEASE, ATTENTION PLEASE. WOMEN, YES, YOU OVER THERE IN THE PINK CARDIGAN AND KITTEN HEELS – YOU. ALL OF YOU! FORGET EVERYTHING! IT'S ALL CHANGE! YOU CAN OFFICIALLY HAVE IT ALL! I REPEAT, YOU CAN NOW HAVE IT ALL! YOU CAN WORK AS HARD AS THE LADS, PLAY AS HARD AS THE LADS, *BE* ONE OF THE LADS AND STILL FUCK THE LADS. GO, GO, GO, GIRLS, GO!!!!'

The megaphone had spoken, and I'd heard it loud and clear. In all their messy, outspoken, raucous, uninhibited, wild, hedonistic glory, Zoe Ball, Sara Cox, Gail Porter *et al* were our new poster girls. Wearing low-slung bootcut jeans, silky lingerie tops, big-buckled belts and a lot of lipstick, we attacked the night like Boudica. We drank pints of lager – at least, according to *FHM*, the magazine that coined the phrase 'Ladettes' in the first place, we did. In truth, we drank pints of prosecco or vodka and tonic, and whisky chasers, coz we iz ladies, innit.

When the Met Bar opened in 1997, the only chaser that followed my sea breeze was a big fat line of coke. Not naming names because, you know, being taken to court is such a bore, but every week I'd end up in a toilet cubicle with a ragtag assortment of celebs, huddled together in a snowstorm, snorting white powder off urinals. The after parties were always, um, let's just say *interesting* and leave it at that. Ending up naked in a jacuzzi with a model being a particularly memorable moment.

It's interesting to note that not once during the you-can-have-it-all mid-nineties megaphone moment did anyone stop to question the gender pay gap. 'Work as hard as the lads, but don't get paid as much as the lads.' I'd never even heard of the gender pay gap until a few years ago.

Earning crap money, living in a boxroom near Marble Arch with three flatmates I despised, one thing's for sure: I was miles away from suburbia.

Pint of vodka, please.

Throughout the nineties, I tried very hard to behave myself in corporate jobs, but somehow every single one ended in an explosive drama. As I'm not a doctor working in A&E (thank the dear lord for small mercies), nor have I ever had to undertake the kind of shift work requiring early nights and even earlier starts, personally speaking, the seismic cultural shift of this era was, for me, nothing short of freeing. Chaotic, creative, funny, madcap, ridiculous, emotional, strong, loud but sometimes shy – thanks to the legacy of the Ladettes and a new career at *ELLE* magazine, aged thirty, I finally gave myself permission to give up the charade and be my true self.

Hog wild. Carefree. No responsibilities. I travelled with work, attending lavish parties in palaces in Paris and private dinners in the homes of household-name designers. I ate in the best restaurants in New York on *ELLE*'s expense account (we're talking pre-2008!). It was all unimaginable to my working-class Mancunian family. I was happy dating the kind of men willing to provide the kind of catastrophes a woman addicted to DRAMA enjoyed. I had a continuum of awful boyfriends, and despite my rather pathetic love life, I also owned a property – well, at least in name, and regardless of a truckload of debt and being mortgaged to the max. When I wasn't depressed or on a comedown, I rushed around, loving my job, my mates, my house, my clothes, my rescue dog – and life felt good. I did whatever the hell I fancied.

After I'd been at *ELLE* for a year, my then-editor pointed out that my 'emails were very funny' and asked, 'Do you really get up to all this stuff at the weekend?' Before she pointed it out, I had no clue I could even write. Then she gave me a column, and we named it 'Mademoiselle: Confessions of an *ELLE* Girl'. It featured on the back page for several years.

Writing. At last. Finally, I enjoyed doing something that didn't involve a strobe light and being surrounded by twenty homosexual men wearing leather harnesses.

And so, in many ways, I was happy. At least, until one day when, tottering off to a shoe appointment in Milan, the sight of a baby wearing a floral dress and matching bonnet made my insides scream.

6

Mates

Finding intimacy in close friendships

There are people in my life I wish I'd stayed closer to, but unlike my friend Jill, who can somehow manage her very full-on career, being a single parent (with both of *her* parents living in the States) *and* keeping in touch with thirty-seven people per day, I can't. I've tried writing a list at the front of my diary, the names of people I really care about and would love to see more. Before I know it, a year has passed and I still haven't seen them. That said, there are a handful of women I have come to rely on in ways in which I've never relied on a romantic partner. Women who are my family, whose presence in my life is critical to my well-being.

I met Natalie at school. Even aged twelve, I sensed her energy was electric, and knew she was exactly on my wavelength the moment I saw her. Sounds very 'chakra tat' and 'woo woo', but Natalie started working as a full-time energy healer before ayahuasca was even a thing, and way before the biggest cocaine-takers I know retrained to become yoga teachers – so, you know, I reckon it's more than OK to say we spiritually connected the moment we met. When I tell my kids this story, and explain that she and I sometimes communicate telepathically, they take the piss out of me. 'Sure, Mum,' they say, before putting their fingers to their temples and shouting, 'Natalie, are you there? Come in, Natalie.'

I met Sara aged nineteen, working behind a bar in Edinburgh. Harry's Bar! A sort of city-boy bar meets gangster hangout. Mum got me the job, obviously. I'd heard about Sara before we'd even met; several people warned me she was a horrible bitch, a mean person to be avoided at all costs. It's extraordinary to think that, having only just returned from Manchester, and a couple of weeks into establishing myself in the Edinburgh 'scene', I'd have heard all about this evil Sara, and then, on my first night working at Harry's, we ended up on the same shift together. Strikingly beautiful and very, very funny, I loved her the minute we met. Women are jealous of beautiful women, especially when they are bright, confident and knowing. Warned off her? Pffft. OK. We're still friends thirty years later.

The minute we met, Kim and I were inseparable. We met outside a pub the day I'd been dumped by Tom Stoppard's son. Just off the back of a heavy week in Ibiza, I went to meet him for lunch, and he dumped me. Can you imagine being dumped *two hours* after returning home from Ibiza? Me neither, which is why I went to MatchesFashion (now online only) and spunked money I didn't have on a pair of YSL shoes. I was sitting alone with the box on my lap, drink in hand, when Kim asked if I was OK. We were joined at the hip for many years before I met my ex; a few years ago, she moved to LA. Prior to all the big grown-up stuff – proper jobs, kids, husbands – we'd spend entire weekends together, going everywhere and anywhere. The following day, ecstasy comedowns incoming, her flatmate Luc would cook Sunday lunch and serve it to us in bed. As we approach the next phase of our lives, knowing we'll spend it together, growing older no longer holds the same sense of fear.

As is also true of sexual relationships, one person can't possibly provide everything you need and want from a friendship. So, it's

Sara who makes me laugh more than anyone I know. Like sisters, we quarrel and squabble, falling out dramatically, with harsh texts exchanged back and forth until someone messages after a few days of silence and simply says, 'Pub?'

She's bright, and she challenges me, and when it comes to a difference of opinion, the friendship can sometimes feel volatile and difficult. The rough is balanced by the smooth, though, otherwise it wouldn't work. Sara is generous of soul, spirit and humour, and she's also financially bailed me out of a rough patch or two. It's her I want to be on a dancefloor with at 4am. It's her I message with a sexual exploit overshare. I love her like family.

We all met Jill during the Oasis backstage years, when she was dating Phil, an old friend of Noel and Liam's. Phil was the Oasis warm-up DJ, and also had the responsibility of hanging up the Man City flag backstage. Phil's also from Hyyyyyyde. EYYYYED. Soft, sensual and devoted to justice, Jill's the kind of friend I spoon on the sofa or in bed, and when we met in 2006, we'd spend our weekends hanging out in north London pubs during that Chris Evans, Billie Piper, Sadie Frost, Kate Moss north London 'phase', after which we'd go home to her flat and crawl into bed with our two dogs, Chaplin and Bo. When Jill and Phil split up in 2009, she moved into the spare room of my house, joining me, my dog and my lodger Suzy, plus her oversized Labrador. Three women in their thirties, plus three dogs. Quite a scene.

I met Claire through Sara, but it wasn't until many years later we became really close. She is steadfast, sensible and strong, but what I love most about her is she isn't afraid to express her vulnerability. Claire held me through my divorce like no other. One morning, after a particularly unfortunate incident involving a hotel room, I took a cab to her house at around 9am (you'll read about that in the Mayhem section). Knowing I was distraught, she'd already prepared the bedroom: the blinds were closed, a big bottle of water was by the bed. And as she tucked me in for the morning, she squished a pipette of Rescue Remedy directly into my mouth, which I drank like a lost baby bird. Which, of course, I was. By handling most of the admin for my divorce, she gave me the strength to carry on fighting.

I met Kate Spicer on a night out, and found her an intimidating presence. Back then, when I was totally hung up on the idea of not fitting in, of not being posh enough or privately educated, she always seemed so self-assured. She scared me to death. She was also extremely bright; I couldn't keep up with her. I still can't, but I've laid my insecurities to one side. It's weird how we do that, making assumptions about someone we don't really know. So, no, Kate and I don't sit long into the night discussing GDP (she does that with her mate Potty), but I am at least relaxed in her company. She can be a complex woman, but more importantly, she's thoughtful and kind, well-meaning and well-mannered (except for the fact she loves turning up an hour or so late), and she writes the best thank-you cards.

No spoilers, but you'll meet Nicole in Mayhem. I only met her a few years ago, but my God, that woman has been there for me. She's great, and, like the rest of the women in my life, I could never have coped over these past couple of years without her. I've leaned hard on my friendships of late, but thankfully they were solid enough to be able to take the weight. Built on proper foundations over many, many years, I know they're always there. Well, always there until a point.

There's only so much being 'leaned on hard' a person can handle. Having experienced what I've gone through over the past few years, one of the most important things I've come to realise is that friendships only thrive when there's an equal amount of give and take.

Gabriele Hackworthy, Kate Monro, Tara Germain . . . so many women I love. When you're done 'leaning in hard', it's your time to do some giving. I'm now in full 'giving back' mode. Until the next drama . . .

Five Thoughts On . . . Friendship, by Dolly Alderton

Dolly Alderton is the bestselling author of Everything I Know About Love

1. When you commit to someone, commit to the whole experience of them. This may sound over-simplified, but friendship is so much easier when you make a decision to accept someone. If someone is really irritating you or upsetting you, it's worth having an honest conversation about it, but otherwise, I am a big believer in letting things slide. If someone talks too much, drinks too much, is too late or too early, or sometimes a bit moody, I wouldn't call them out on it unless you know that you yourself are perfect. Best-friendship is a great place to try to exercise radical acceptance.

2. Vulnerability with each other is the hardest thing to maintain as you get older, and I believe it is the only thing that sustains proper friendships. When we get to our thirties, something new and weird occurs: we all become worried about people feeling sorry for us. Even the people closest to us (especially the people closest to us). We don't want to be the subject of anyone's pity, so we stop being honest when we feel lonely or sad or restless or unsatisfied. The minute a group of friends starts doing this, the group is doomed. When things go wrong, the hardest thing to do is text a friend and tell them how unhappy you are or how unsure you are of the choices you've made. If you can swallow your pride and push through this embarrassment, your friends will feel safe to do the same. And I genuinely believe this secures a friendship for life.

3. You don't need to spend loads of time with each other's

partners. I don't think this is the big deal we've been led to believe it is. You need to spend a long weekend or a long lunch with your best friend's partner once or twice a year, and I think that's about it. Time with your friends is increasingly precious as we get older. I don't think we should feel bad if you want to spend it without partners and children.

4. You need to do stuff together. If you're not making memories or experiencing new things together, you're going to lose sight of why you fell in love. It's sort of just like romance. If your relationship is reduced to WhatsApps listing grievances, complaints, illnesses and admin, and occasional meet-ups where you just list what's going on in your lives, the friendship will fade. You need to do things, see things, eat new things, go to new places, meet new people together, and then you'll be able to keep falling in love with each other.

5. The biggest test of female friendship is when women start having babies. The worst of this is between the ages of thirty and forty. Schedules and priorities suddenly change, child-free women feel left out, the women with kids feel left out, conversation is dominated by babies. It's an absolute shitshow for everyone, on all sides. But I've seen friendships that have come out the other side – it does calm down. Ride out the storm. Because life throws a whole bunch of new shit at you in middle age, and you'll need your best girlfriends more than ever, so hold them close, even in those years when it's difficult.

7

Mating Memo

Life's a mess (miscarriage, men and me)

Did anyone receive the fucking memo yet?

Checks old Hotmail account AGAIN. Calls Hotmail head office.

'Hello? Answer the fucking phone, my ovaries are on the turn!'

Boom! And just like that, I wanted a baby. What fresh hell is this on yonder horizon? What do you mean I have to hurry because I'm running out of time? Running out of time? I'm only just getting started! I have my whole life ahead of me! There's so much more I want to do! So many more dancefloors to trot across. So many more drinks to drink, a thousand late nights to spend skittering through Soho with my mates. Many more cat-walk shows to attend wearing clothes I can't afford, so I have to 'borrow' them. There are many more art classes to attend – and so what if I always quit after three weeks because I'm always hung-over on Saturday mornings?

What do you mean my chances of conceiving drop rapidly after the age of thirty-five? Did someone just say 'medical inter-vention'? Is that why I got my period at the age of twelve? Am I supposed to have got all this procreating drama out of the way

Dear Cosmopolitan Magazine,
    I trust this note finds you well.
    At least that means one of us is.
    With regards to the **far too many to list** articles published from the mid-nineties until approx. 2002, you appear to have omitted one major detail. Usually entitled 'YOU CAN HAVE IT ALL', we all lapped them up like a cold beer on a hot summer's day, probs while some of us were giving our boss a hand job. However, the major point omitted from your au courant feminist missives was an inarguable fact of biology.
    I'd like to point out that yes, I have in fact been pregnant and decided to terminate; however, it's the career stuff. It takes a lot of time to get off the ground, and by the time one has found a decent mate with whom to mate (sorry to go all David Attenborough on you), well, you know, one is in one's mid-thirties and above!
    It doesn't take an A in O Level biology,*† to figure out female mammals cannot continue to reproduce for ever. ALL female mammals, that is. What would have been SUPER helpful to hear, while we were busy rampaging through Soho in our Wonderbras and bumster jeans, is that, should we someday wish to birth a child, it's probably best to aim to meet a mate with whom to procreate said child no later than, I dunno, shall we say . . . thirty-one-ish?

Best wishes,

Stacey Duguid
Aged thirty-three and three-quarters
Currently single
Currently childless
Possibly a candidate for a liver transplant

---

* No one was more surprised than me to receive an A in O Level biology. To this day, I remain convinced it was more to do with my mum's love of wearing very short red skirts on parents' evening than me possessing a deep understanding of science.
† An O Level is basically the penny farthing equivalent of a GCSE, should you be a millennial or Gen Z.

in my teens and twenties? How archaic. How absurd. How, how, how?

HOW DID THIS HAPPEN!?

How did this happen to me, a woman that's hardly supermodel material, but not exactly gopping, either? No, it can't be. It's all made up. It's bollocks. I don't believe it.

Shit. Shit. Shit. Shit. Shit.

I fell down a rabbit hole of panic, had dreams of whizzing down water slides that turned into fallopian tubes. Newspaper headlines screamed at me: 'Geriatric mothers are at higher risk of death during childbirth'. I googled 'geriatric mothers', imagining it to mean celebrities over the age of fifty – you know, rich Notting-Hill types – only to discover the NHS considers any pregnancy over the age of *thirty-five* to be geriatric. OMG. Pass the Ovaltine. Where's my Stannah stairlift?

'Sod this, I'm out,' I shouted in the direction of the dog, who couldn't even be bothered to open an eye. How had I, a genius with an A in O Level Biology, only just figured out this 'fertility' nonsense?

'Women over the age of thirty-five who assumed pregnancy was a given are "deluded"'. So read one newspaper headline that kept me awake all night.

I thought my fertility would last for ever. Now I was one of the *deluded* millions.

My thirty-three-year-old ovaries were almost past their sell-by date, and the countdown to expiration was on. I mean, who the hell knew? And if they did, why the hell hadn't they mentioned it? Working, boozing, shagging – I'd spent a lifetime avoiding pregnancy, and now that I wanted it my ovaries were shrivelling. I imagined my insides looking like tiny raisins lingering in the crack of a highchair, or E.T.'s long, wrinkly finger, only without the lighting-up bit at the end. No lighting-up bit over here, not in my dark, empty womb.

I am doomed.

I am deluded and doomed.

I am deluded, doomed and empty wombed.

Fuck.

Never the type to sit around waiting for life to pass me by, I knew if I wanted to be a mother, I had only one choice: get on with the important job of mating. But with whom? A gay guy? A friend? I didn't have any straight male friends, and the last time I'd checked, none of my girlfriends had a penis.

I imagined myself walking along Oxford Street, wearing a sandwich board. Instead of a neon arrow pointing to the words 'GOLF SALE', mine would read: 'Urgent Insemination Required, Enquire Within (Literally)'. I'd invest in a Hollywood-style set of light bulbs that would flash around the arrow, thereby proving the urgency of the situation. I'd string the leftover lights around my M&S big-girl pants and wear them to an actual straight club where actual straight men might go. Going to a straight club – Jesus, why would anyone do that? Everyone knows the music's better in gay clubs.

Perhaps I'd pick up some delicious ingredients and cook a nice meal for one. Light a candle, pour a large red in one of those posh glasses I usually kept for Christmas Day, then log on to Guardian Soulmates to sift through thousands of dating profiles in an attempt to find someone sane. I might even check out images of sperm and egg donors while I was at it. Perhaps I'd masturbate, too, just to make the whole thing feel more authentically romantic.

None of it felt romantic. It all felt totally and utterly surreal. While I was too busy having fun, had I ignored warnings that my fertility was on the wane? Had Mum mentioned anything about not 'leaving it too late'? Had anyone? I asked a few friends my age, all of whom appeared as shell-shocked as me. Surely, I'd remember receiving something as major as a fertility memo. Of course I would.

Naked on the top deck of a ship about to hit choppy waters, I clung to the mast developed in early childhood that kept me from going overboard. I was bound to meet 'him'. A life without a 'mate' was unthinkable; it would force the ship to take another route, a journey I couldn't fathom without a compass. A life without children wasn't part of the plan. I clung to the mast, knowing the long-lost someone was out there somewhere. I'd taken it for granted I'd fall in love, find my mate, settle down, have kids, get married – or perhaps not get married. To be honest, I've always struggled with the notion of marriage. Two people reduced to a single entity; one half expected to change her surname to his. No thanks.

The bleat of babydom followed me around daily, reaching an almighty crescendo at 5pm on weekdays. Minding my own bloody business – just, you know, sitting at my desk – I'd have to endure ten minutes of excruciating pain as women (often my juniors) picked up landline phones to boyfriends, fiancés and husbands.

'Hi daaaarling, good day? Yeeeeeah, me too. Did you speak to your mum? She OK? Yeeeeeah. Awwww. Yeeeah, I'm leaving soon. Shall I pass by M&S? I walked past this morning, there's a special offer on meals for two. Yeeeeeah. I knoooowww. Buy one "meal for two" and get another "meal for two" free. Thought we could get the chicken curry meal deal tonight and save the Thai for tomorrow? Yeeeeeah, OK. Yeeeeeah. OK, brill, you get the wine. Love you, see you soon . . . ha ha . . . no, you put the phone down first . . . love you more. No! *I* love *you* more!'

Shoot me now. No gun? Pass something, anything. I'll sniff all the goddamn hairspray from the *ELLE* cocking beauty cupboard.

The university-educated head-girl types I worked with could go home and eat Thai food with their boyfriends who worked in marketing, but I had a wild reputation to uphold. So, you know, fuck it. Off I'd trot, to drink cocktails on an empty stomach.

Curry for two, my arse.

The autumn that followed the 'Come to Me Baby' moment in Milan, I entered my local pub wearing a thick plaid coat by Preen slung over a navy-blue jumper minidress and ankle boots. Legs-out Friday, and all that. Each time I left the house back then, a small part of my heart wondered whether I'd meet someone, so I was always dressed to impress. Because, you know, meeting some-one decent, clever, funny and sane, ideally at some point before my sixtieth birthday, would be ace.

Recent relationships had all been an absolute fiasco. Even the guy I'd lived with for just over a year. He'd seemed normal enough when I met him on the dancefloor of a hardcore gay leather club (insert shrugging shoulder emoji). Handsome – nay, hot as hell – the minute I discovered he had zero friends, I should have skedaddled. Ditto when I noticed that whenever we were out, he'd go completely mute. A gaggle of friends, all talking over one another, and he wouldn't say a single damn word. Even worse, when we went out with his parents (who were lovely, by the way), I'd do all the hard work making polite chit-chat the entire night, practically balancing a ball at the end of my nose while cycling around the table on a unicycle. Exhausted within an hour, by pudding, I'd resort to setting my nipple tassels alight.

One night, though, I didn't. I don't mean I didn't set the nipple tassels alight (obviously, I never leave the house without them). I mean I didn't speak. I kept totally quiet, and the four of us sat in silence. His parents asked whether I was OK, wondering if I was tired, or had had a bad week. I just shrugged and looked over at my boyfriend, willing him with all my heart to say something interesting. He never did, and it wasn't because he was incapable; he just preferred to sit back and let me do the entertaining. So I hung up my unicycle, put down my ball and my nipple tassels and I vowed to never again enter a relationship where ALL the red flags are flapping in the breeze like a funfair.

The hardcore gay club should have been a clue, *non*? *Oui*.

The golden Friday-night glow of my local pub was a beacon of hope. Ahhh, The Chamberlayne, where all the good guys go. Pulling open its heavy doors, I remember holding back for a moment, surveying the busy scene I was about to step into. It was packed full of creatives and everyone was out and bang-up for it. Men were lining the bar, pints in hand, all adopting the same stance: elbow on bar, right hip out, the occasional glance around to survey the women in the crowd. They wore the latest Nike trainers, jeans rolled up high to reveal jaunty-hued socks, Japanese selvedge-denim, beanies, Barbour jackets, fishermen's jumpers. Super stylish, the same motley crew of men propped up the bar four or five nights per week. Sometime around 8pm, they'd all begin their nightly dash downstairs, packets of white powder passed from one to the next like a drug-fuelled relay race. Newly animated, they'd settle in for a night of barstool banter before going back to someone's house to continue sniffing Columbia's finest until the sun came up.

'This can't be it,' I said to my close friend Jill, as I swung my coat across the back of the chair, Mulberry cross-body bag whacking the table, making her dog Chaplin jump.

'What?' She'd been gazing at her phone.

'This!' I gesticulated with my right hand. 'This utter fucking bollocks!'

'What, the guys? Oh, yeah, they're hopeless. A total waste of time.'

American Jill, or Alabama Jill, as she is sometimes known, is beautiful in a way that's unusual. Full, soft lips; long, brown hair; thick, dark eyebrows – and her southern drawl has men eating out the palm of her hand. Not that she'd notice. Or rather, if she did, much like me, she'd only pay attention to the kind of men we should have been avoiding like herpes.

As we were edging into our mid-thirties, having fun, working hard, staying out all night, the glow of what had once felt important was beginning to lose its shine.

It would be Christmas soon, and I still didn't have a boyfriend. I'd had dates with men I'd met on Guardian Soulmates.

There was a musician named Rick, who was so nervous when he got up to go to the loo, he somehow caught the edge of the tablecloth in his belt buckle. Drinks, dinner and the contents of my handbag all spilled across the floor. My borrowed Louboutins were tragically splattered with red wine. But it was the lone Tampax rolling beneath a nearby table that finished things off. A man bent down to pick it up and handed it to Rick in a panic. That's when I thought about calling an ambulance, because, despite being only thirty-two, it looked as though he'd had a stroke. He couldn't really speak after that, so we left.

Then there was Nick, the owner of a chain of restaurants. Within ten minutes, he'd burst into tears, blubbering about how much he missed his ex-girlfriend. I held his hand across the table, and, after two hours of him describing her 'great beauty', I was one wine away from booking a facelift. Or punching him.

Oh, and there was Dominic, who, on our first date, gave me a long lecture about being online (on Guardian Soulmates) too often.

'How do you know?' I asked, puzzled.

'Because when I'm online, I can see you are too,' he said. 'Makes you look desperate.'

I'm not sure which was worse: having to sit through dinner with such a twat, or failing to argue the point that, given he was online at the same time as me, we were clearly online as much as each other.

At around this time, I met a much younger man on Guardian Soulmates. I barely fancied him. He lived in east London and hung out in a very different scene to me. He was a hipster, and took me to bars and markets and coffee shops in Clapton I'd never heard of. Still, I knew I had no future with him, mainly because he annoyed me to death. Despite my disdain, I continued to see him, and one night threw caution to the wind by suggesting we have unprotected sex.

Blame the deep ovarian ache within, the yearning for a baby, the vodka and tonic – whatever it was, one night I just thought, *Fuck it, I'm old, this won't work, but let's see.* Four weeks later, I took a pregnancy test, and bejeezus – pregnant! Pregnant after one (intentional) slip-up (slip-*in*)!

By week six, I was throwing up. Mum rang and said she was really worried about me having a baby with someone I barely knew, asking how I would cope. I remember the phone call well. I sat on the edge of my bed, telling her I'd be fine.

Close to the twelve-week scan, I did the maths on nursery places. Childcare vs mortgage repayments vs my salary. I was already in the red; there was no way I could do this alone without leaving London. Then the hipster father asked if he could move into my house so we could look after the baby together. The enormity of the situation hit me. I turned off my phone and stayed in bed all weekend.

The hipster father told his family and friends 'we' were pregnant. I shouted at him for saying 'we'; unless he fancied putting on a stone in six weeks, he was not allowed to say 'we'. Hormones raged and I spent my entire day puking.

'How exciting!' chirped a message from his mother on his phone. A High Priestess witch, she was delighted. Her little wizard (aka the father of my foetus) was *extremely* delighted. I just felt suffocated and out of control, like my body no longer belonged to me. I guess because it no longer did.

'Twelve weeks pregnant, do we think?' asked the doctor, her calm bedside manner as soothing as a mug of hot chocolate on a winter's day.

'Yes, I think so.'

She helped me on to the bed and guided my feet into stirrups, after which she unwrapped a condom and pulled it down the shaft of the ultrasound wand that would soon enter my vagina. She squeezed KY Jelly around the tip, and, still able to look me straight in the eye all the while and using only one hand, she managed to get the condom on it on the first go. Skillz.

'Nice and gentle,' she said. 'Make two fists and pop them under your bottom, that's it. In it goes, there we are. OK, let's see . . . '

As the wand wiggled around inside my vagina, I settled down to watch the screen over her shoulder. Peering through round spectacles at what looked to be a scene from *Star Wars*, the doctor edged her stool closer to get a better look. Her hand gripped the top of the wand as she directed it inside my vagina like a joystick. I was half expecting to see a Storm Trooper appear. Right, left, right, middle. Stop. Right. Left. Middle. No. Back again. Stop. Right. Left. Middle. Stop. Back . . . Middle. Stop.

Eventually, the video game came to an end.

I felt the wand pull from my vagina.

'I'm sorry, there's no heartbeat,' she said, her smooth, hot-chocolatey voice no longer a comfort.

Expecting to see a fully-formed baby wearing Petit Bateau, I glanced at the screen. What was it? An alien-blob, an unidentifiable splat?

The doctor clicked off the monitor with a loud snap. White lines turned to darkness. A blazing silence engulfed the room. Closing my eyes to gather myself, I saw my baby in the darkness. I followed her floating outline until she eventually disappeared. As I swung my legs off the table, the doctor looked up from her paperwork.

'Have you ever wondered where they go?' I asked, struggling to pull on a pair of skinny jeans.

'Where they go?' she said.

'Yes. These beings,' I said, gesturing towards the blank-screened monitor.

'You take care,' she replied, preparing to leave the room.

'They go to outer space,' I said, when she had left. 'They're all out there,' I said, out loud to an empty room.

Mating material: Items of clothing in the context of red flags

From now on, do not date anyone wearing:

1. Round tortoiseshell glasses – unless they have a prescription. In other words, men who wear opticals purely as a fashion statement as opposed to for a medically proven issue should, from now on, be avoided like that guy Peter who refused to see a dental hygienist.
2. Rugby socks worn with slip-on checkerboard Vans. Need I say more? I rest my case.
3. Barbour jackets with cuffs rolled up to show off a tattoo.
4. Very big beards. Awful to snog (well, apart from that guy in Paris, but I'd taken quite a lot of MDMA).
5. Hats. All of them. Unless it's snowing, in which case a beanie is OK. A beanie worn high on the head during summer is a red-button-alert, ejector-seat-vibe red flag.
6. Boots made in UK that cost more than my Pradas. It's not right.
7. Fishermen's jumpers in cream, worn with a pork-pie hat on holiday in Cornwall.
8. Commes des Garçons Converse. Twat.

8

Internet Mating

Love doesn't live at my local pub. Who knew . . . ?

As the morning sickness subsided, the sweet relief was short lasting. A week after the scan, with the non-viable foetus and placenta freshly scraped from my womb, I looked down at my puffy belly, now filled only with a sense of loss. I'd been so sick all day and night, all I was able to do was lie down and eat carbs, and now my stomach stuck out like a double-decker bus. Not one vegetable had passed my lips in six weeks, and the smell of cooked broccoli made me heave.

I was happy to be able to stand up without feeling I might fall over, glad the all-day nausea was no more, pleased the deafening ringing in my ears was gone. And as for the end of that 9am tiredness? Oof, sweet relief. But still, I knew I'd wanted that baby, who, in my heart, I knew had been a girl. Just a hunch, no actual evidence; a feeling more than anything.

The brief encounter with Hipster Dad was over the minute the nurse clicked off the ultrasound. I called to tell him that A) he wasn't about to be a father, and B) I needed space and time alone to process. His initial enthusiasm for fatherhood quickly gave way to audible relief. Deep down, he hadn't wanted a baby with me.

We said our goodbyes and agreed to remain friends. We needed a break; both of us needed to settle back into life as it had been before.

So, now what? Back to searching online for dates and sperm donors while enjoying a romantic meal for one with a vibrator? For over a year, an inner physical craving had consumed me, but having had time to reflect, the biggest lesson learned during those intense few weeks of pregnancy was knowing I wanted *more*. Having a baby with a random I didn't even like wouldn't be enough. Forget not being able to make the baby-maths work as a solo parent, thereby welding he and I together for eighteen years of joint custody, shared childcare and all the ensuing inevitable disagreements therein. During those dark hours alone in bed, I realised it wasn't just a baby I wanted more than new shoes. It was the love of a significant other.

A month later, and it was already December. Ahh, the infamous Christmas of 2009: me, aged thirty-four, driving to Newcastle with my rescue dog Bo (otherwise known as my Irish husband). I'd splurged on a Miu Miu jumper featuring a cat motif. I planned to wear it while drinking neat vodka locked in Mum's downstairs loo.

When Nanny and Grandad were alive, Christmas smelled of Yorkshire puddings and hairspray, gin and tonic, and Grandad's horrendous homemade red wine. Seven adults squeezed around the orange-tinged kitchen table, while my brother and I, plus our cousin, squished at a tiny folding table in the corner by the boiler. What a laugh. Drinks flowed, delicious home-cooked food appeared, then dishes were cleared to make way for a night of telly. Grandad lit a cigar, comedy shows blared – *Morecambe and Wise*, *Little and Large*, *The Muppets* – followed by pudding back at the kitchen table, and a fist fight over *Uno*. Magic.

Christmas was never the same after my grandparents passed. Nanny cooked with confident ease, endless pans and pots simmering despite the small cooker; she made everything look effortless. In a stroke of interior design genius, shiny purple Christmas decorations that twinkled and clattered whenever a door opened matched the swirls of her garish purple carpet. Gaudy 1970s decorations stuck to the ceiling, a purple tinsel Christmas tree, and four generations of women stuffed on the sofa together, laughing until one of us weed our pants.

We laughed at everything and nothing. We were famous for it. Grandad would walk into the room to find my little gran (aka Great-grandmother Eva), my nanny (Joan), my mum (Gaynor), my younger cousin Keeley and me, all laughing.

'What's so bloody funny?' he'd ask in a broad Lancashire accent, rendering us even more hysterical.

'Bleedin' 'ell,' my uncle would say, as we staggered outside, knowing the only cure to be a blast of cold air.

But times had changed. So: ho, ho, ho, off to Newcastle to stay with Mum and her husband I go.

Arriving around 11pm, no sooner had I dropped my case in the hallway and kissed Mum and Mike hello, than I heard my Irish husband rustling beneath Mum's immaculate fake Christmas tree.

When I say immaculate, I mean it. Each branch aligned perfectly with the one below, above, left and right. Decorations were symmetrically placed, arranged in order of size and colour. I walked into the sitting room to find the dog stuck under the tree, torn-up wrapping paper in his mouth, dog slobber all over a once-neatly wrapped silk dressing gown.

'And to think *this* is my only grandchild,' said Mum, before walking out in despair.

Barking mad and on the edge, I couldn't figure out who Mum despaired of most – me or the dog. It was hard to tell. The miscarriage, plus the sudden realisation that in six months' time I'd be in the second half of my thirties, rendered me paranoid and edgy. I was halfway through my thirties and nowhere near where I'd thought I'd be. Panic began to nip at my toes.

By the way, when it comes to age and achievements, the idea of knowing where we 'should' be in life is ludicrous. Plans are there to be broken, and life isn't linear – it's messy and chaotic. Having carved out a fairly decent career from genuinely nothing – an achievement I allow myself to recognise these days – I was very mean in the way I spoke to myself in my early thirties.

I'd begun to feel lonely in a roomful of people: lonely at work, at the weekend, in my thoughts and imagination. I spent days and nights looking for something to plug the emptiness, from cocktails to clothes to cock (now there's a book title if ever I've heard one). Buying expensive things I didn't need didn't make me feel better, nor did dates with men I'd turn into an insecure wreck around. But still, I didn't call off the search. Instead, I looked higher, lower, harder for what I thought I needed.

So: Christmas 2009. Hands down the loneliest few days of my life so far. The three of us rattling around the Edwardian house Mum and Mike used to live in, located conveniently off Gosforth High Street. (I loved that red-brick three-storey house. Mum convinced Mike to move in the end because she couldn't keep it clean. Only children of Celtic northern mammies can possibly understand the levels of cleanliness to which I refer.)

The too-big rooms echoed like a party nobody had bothered to turn up to. At around 3pm on Christmas Eve, bored, I suggested the three of us head to a nearby pub. It was busy with men only, their dear wives and women at home peeling spuds. In true Christmas style, an argument kicked off. I can't really remember what it was about, but it culminated in Mum storming home.

By the time I'd caught up with her, the kitchen was kind of on fire. Black smoke poured out of the oven and the sink, and I think something was on fire in the backyard, too. Christmas things in tin foil smoked in the bin.

'Oh God,' I said. 'Everything OK?'

Mum didn't know it at the time, but the drunken argument that followed the fire in the kitchen changed my life for ever.

'I'm too old for this,' she said, throwing a tin containing an unidentifiable burned something across the kitchen table.

'Too old for what?' I asked, nervous for the answer.

'Too old for this shit,' she said, holding back tears, gesturing up and down the kitchen as if seated before a burning banquet. 'I should be at *your* house with *your* family. You should be cooking for me. I should have grandchildren, and—'

I didn't hear the rest. Using all my strength to not say a word, I left the room and walked upstairs to lie down.*

Unable to decide whether I was sad, upset, or just plain fucking furious, after ten minutes of lying in bed, I turned to the dog – I mean, my Irish husband – and said, 'Fuck this, fuck fuckety fuck this'.

Like robbers, we crept into the spare room, where Mum kept her ancient computer, which potentially needed to be attached to an eighteenth-century watermill to get going. A Christmas miracle: the thing cranked into action, and after managing to log on without the help of a steam engine or an extra battery pack, the homepage of Guardian Soulmates flickered across a blurry screen. After the miscarriage, with a round, soft belly and larger thighs the only thing I had to remember the pregnancy by, I had left the

---

* Mum, if you or any of your book-club members or Women's Institute friends are reading this, we all say things in the heat of the moment, especially when we've had a drink, especially at Christmas. Even if your words stung at the time, hearing them jolted me into action. No more playing the role of the forgotten woman sitting on the sidelines of life, expecting to meet someone while off her tits on drugs in a gay club (apologies to all at the Newcastle arm of the Women's Institute).

Also, Mum, Christmas is really stressful, and you and I will never live up to the kind of day your mum hosted. We're just not like her. We don't rustle up a delicious chocolate cake while making a roast dinner for ten. We don't even *like* cake. We like crisps and gin, short skirts and heels. We're good at linking arms, making sure neither of us trip over after too much wine. So how about we stop pretending? How about we go down the pub for a bottle of wine and a packet of crisps? I'd like that.

site. But now I was back. If there was a soulmate out there for me, by God I was gonna find him. No stone would be left unturned.

I knew a 'soulmate' connection wasn't waiting for me at the local pub. Nor was it to be found in an establishment for homosexuals, nor hiding in an office filled with women. There was only one thing for it – a strategy.

I needed a username. I pondered this, leaning down to scratch the dog behind his ear. A lone safety pin shone on Mum's desk in the moonlight. It was odd of Mum to leave a mess. I decided it must be a sign. So, at 2am on Christmas morning, hangover already kicking in, I typed 'Punky Pins'. LOL. *WTF am I thinking!?* I hit delete, but too late: the name was irreversible.

Shit, really? Punky Pins? I sounded mad. Perfect.

I googled my actual name and grabbed a screenshot from *ELLE*'s website. It had been taken after two weeks in Greece, when I was white-blonde and my face was too tanned. The photo was snapped on my last night by a much younger French manboy I'd ended up having sex with. I worried the tan combined with the stolen sailor's cap might make me look 'fun' in the wrong way, but decided to go with it.

I checked the site a few times per day, ensuring I only replied to men I didn't initially fancy, thereby avoiding my usual 'type'. If I wanted to date the kind of guy that littered the bar at my local pub in Kensal Rise, it would have been easy, but I didn't. I wanted more than a boyfriend with a penchant for trainers and taking cocaine at the pub. So, in a bid to change my old ways, I avoided men wearing high-top Nikes and anyone on a skateboard. I checked for good grammar and kept an eye out for messy-looking flats in the backgrounds of photographs. I deleted anyone with the job title 'musician' or 'art director'.

It was mid-January when I saw his profile. Thick-rimmed dark spectacles, dark hair, white shirt, photo taken at the most awkward angle, making his Adam's apple look as big as a tennis ball.

I stopped. Clicked on his profile. Impeccable grammar. Funny, too. I sent a message, probably just, 'Hi.' He replied that evening and we messaged back and forth for around ten days before he suggested we meet up. As I was about to leave for New York Fashion Week, I suggested we meet the following week during the London shows, perhaps after Burberry.

Overwhelmed, when the time came, I cancelled our date and went home to pack for Milan. Milan Fashion Week passed, and by then it was on to Paris.

We'd rearranged our date for when I got back in March, but after a month on the road, all I wanted to do was sit on a sofa with a close friend and have a cuddle.

Alabama Jill suggested we meet the day after I arrived back in London – on the same evening I was due to meet him. After the relentless churn of air kissing and fakery, I decided I needed my mates more than a date. When I sat down to compose the text to cancel our date once again, I was, unusually for me, at the gym – only to take a shower, obviously.

'Hey, sorry to do this again, but I'm absolutely knackered and feeling deranged. Really want to meet you, so hope we can make it work another time?'

And then the oddest, weirdest, scariest thing happened. Something so weird and spooky, I will forgive you if you don't believe me. As I pushed 'send' on the text that would cancel our date, before he'd even had a chance to reply, I heard a voice. Not quite human, but 'other'; not he, not she or even they. It said, with a boom, 'GO!'

The words appeared to echo around the changing room. I looked up to find no one there. I walked around the corner, past the shower cubicles, flinging back curtains to check for someone hiding. The place was empty. I looked at my phone and mouthed, 'Shit.'

I sent another text: 'Hi, me again. Ignore that last message, I'm fine. See you at the Hospital Club (Covent Garden, yes?) at 7.30pm.'

Within a minute, he replied: 'Hi. You sure? It's OK if you're too tired.'

Within a second: 'I'm sure, 100 per cent. See you there.'

So, on 12 March 2010, wearing a pale blue silky wrap dress by Vanessa Bruno and over-the-knee black suede boots by Miu Miu, I plonked myself down in front of him. Bare-legged, I accidentally flashed my pants, but he was too polite to acknowledge my M&S three-for-the-price-of-two black knickers. He ordered a decent bottle of red instead.

I liked his hands.

A couple of moments in, I excused myself from the table. The heavy bathroom door slammed behind me. A line of three sinks edged a large mirror along one wall. I didn't need a pee; I needed space to think.

Palms sticky, I leaned against the cool ceramic walls. Deep breath, release, exhale. I looked at myself in the mirror and mouthed, 'Fuck. Now what, Duguid?'

An internal voice, very different to the one I'd heard earlier, suggested I look for a window to jump out of. I was in fight-or-flight mode, scared and wanting to escape. Not because the date was an unmitigated disaster – quite the opposite. Because it wasn't.

I went back to the table and, somehow, out of my mouth poured the words, 'Have you googled me?'

'Errm. No.'

'OK, well, if you do, you'll see I'm in the top twenty most eligible single Scottish females list.'

'Oh. OK. So who's number one?'

'Susan Boyle.'

Atoms bounced, my scalp felt electric. If it wasn't love at first sight, I don't know what else you'd call it.

Two hours later, we walked outside. No attempts made to kiss, no weird innuendos, no awkward lunge. He pulled on his black overcoat, which I noticed was GUCCI and slightly too short for him, the hem hanging at an odd angle, rendered cockeyed by *Madame Bovary*, the thick tome stuffed in his right-hand pocket. I waved goodbye and watched as he disappeared inside a corner shop in search of a packet of Twiglets.

My Irish husband only walked into establishments that served food on his hind legs, having at some point during his street-dog days figured out that making himself taller made it easier to steal food off passing tables. Once a rescue, always a rescue. But on our second date a few days later, the dog behaved so badly, I swear he was vibing off my high anxiety.

After lunch, we went for a walk – and the dog decided to continue walking on hind legs only. I said goodbye, half expecting a kiss that never came. Getting off the tube, I called Alabama Jill.

'Hey, so the second date went well. He didn't kiss me, but said he'd been dating a few people off the site, but nothing serious. Jill, I think I might be in love.'

The phone went silent.

Then: 'Stacey! What, OMG! AMAZING! You've been so quiet about him! I couldn't tell what was going on!'

I put the phone down with a deep sense of unease, so I quickly bashed out a text that immediately made me feel better.

'Hi, loved our two dates! Thanks for lunch today! Sounds as though you've got a lot going on, though, so let's leave it. Nice to meet you and good luck on the site! Stacey.'

9

Love Mating

I'm home

I can't believe I sent that text. Nor can I believe I attempted to detonate all future relations with the most 'normal' man I'd ever met. 'Normal' as in, he didn't even ask me to do a line of coke off his penis. Can you believe it?

During the moments that followed pressing 'send', I felt a shitload better. A wave of relief washed over me as I congratulated myself on the 'wise' decision to never again see the handsome, sane, bright, solvent, kind, funny man. *God, I'm so smart! What a relief. I wonder if that guy who asked me to do a line of coke off his penis is still single . . . ?*

One banal Monday evening in March, sitting on one of two matching cheap white cotton IKEA sofas intended as a temporary purchase and yet somehow never replaced, I stared at my phone, waiting for a reaction. *Come on, son, let's see what you've got.*

I used to do that kind of thing: sending a message that was cathartic to write but suicide to send. Regularly wheeling out my fucked-up damsel-in-distress act, I'd test the boundaries of someone's love for me, knowing I'd be right whatever the outcome. I didn't care. Either way, I'd have won.

If they walked away, that meant, 'See, I knew he didn't really care.'

If, undeterred by whatever brush-off I'd doled out, they came back, that would mean, 'OK great, he cares,' followed quickly by, 'But! I wonder how *much*?'

No amount of reassurance was enough for me and there are only so many detonations a person can handle. Depending on how far I pushed them – family, boyfriends, friends – after one too many blows, they'd inevitably jump ship, abandoning me and my inner child as they left. My inner child, however, would remain victorious. *Thanks for the confirmation. See?! I am unlovable.*

He came back.

He wasn't having any of it.

His reply was long. Back in 2010, when phones were a bit rubbish, messages longer than five sentences were chopped up and sent separately. After the sixth chopped-up text, I leaned against the grubby white cotton of my IKEA sofa, relieved he'd sent enough texts to prove he actually liked me.

A date was arranged for the following evening. As in, the third date within seven days of meeting. And we all know what happens on date three. We kissed, we had sex, and afterwards, I said the most frightening five words I'd ever uttered to a stranger.

'I'm in love with you.'

After my declaration of love, we spent every weekend together. My Irish (now newly ex-) husband harassed my boyfriend's asshole cat every time we arrived at his flat, eating everything in her bowl. My dog soon gained weight – as did I, although my weight gain was not due to cat food, but carbs, wine, chocolate and love. The cat continued to mock me by remaining sleek and slender.

Now in love, I stopped going out, preferring instead to cosy up together on his giant sofa, crunching Twiglets, drinking red wine and eating Sunday roasts. I even ate the potatoes.

We went to Greece that first summer together. I ate a shedload of feta and watched him hand-feed a dying cat. As he scooped cat food out of a can with his fingers and held it out to the skinny creature, I fell even more in love.

By the time autumn rolled around, Nanny was sick, so we took the train to Manchester. Nanny stopped greeting houseguests at the end of her short driveway when Grandad died. She always used to be there, clutching two gin and tonics, ice clinking, huge smiles turning to laughter the moment the car door swung open.

The image of Mum putting on lipstick in the car mirror in time to greet her parents also stays in my mind: dressing up for her hosts and spraying a spritz of fragrance, regardless of the fact they were her parents and lived in a bungalow in a housing estate in Hyde (Eyed). It's just good manners.

My grandparents – immaculate, holding the gin – would greet my family as we rolled out of the car, dishevelled – bar Mum, who now looked like a supermodel.

Until Grandad died, and dementia danced across Nanny's neurons, reckless and drunk.

Nanny's bungalow no longer smelled of freshly baked chocolate cake. No more tinkling Christmas decorations clattering whenever you opened a door; no more purple tinsel Christmas tree glistening beneath several strings of colourful lights; no more cramped kitchen Christmas lunches, kids so jacked up on Vimto, eventually one of us puked.

No more fresh strawberries, radishes and rhubarb grown in the back garden. No more Grandad arriving at the back door, handing over a new crop of something-or-other for Nanny to bake into a delicious feast. No more tinkering in the greenhouse, marvelling at the season's bloom of tomatoes.

Nanny's incredible cooking disappeared along with her memory. Her making dinner was now a thing of the past. The oven had been unplugged and taped up for fear she'd set the house alight, so we took her out for lunch instead. Confused, she ordered the same dish four times, not to mention a couple of gins – 'That'll put some lead in yer pencil,' she said, laughing. Back home, she fed my Irish ex-husband fifty-five dog treats, because apparently 'he looked 'ungry.'

As she told the same story on repeat, my boyfriend leaned forward to listen, nodding intently, as though the tale told only moments before was the most fascinating thing he'd ever heard. Watching him interact with my precious nanny so carefully, her hair still immaculate, still dressed to impress but her eyes beginning to dim, I knew I'd love him for ever. It was the first and last time he'd meet my beloved grandmother, Joan.

Two weeks later, on a Tuesday in mid-October, sitting in a meeting that clearly bored me, I made my excuses and left, citing some bullshit emergency that could never possibly happen – unless, of course, you believe a fashion-obsessed person could possibly leave a Chloé cape on the Bakerloo line? Erm. No. Who would do such a thing?

It was never my intention to 'head to Oxford Circus to check lost property'. I popped to Boots to buy a pregnancy test instead.

All the way from Oxford Circus to Kensal Rise, I contemplated jabbing the white stick into a hot stream of pee. Whatever the result, I'd need a drink, so I poured myself a large glass of red the minute I got home. The pregnancy kit was so firmly wrapped in plastic that I ended up stabbing it with the corkscrew to prise it open.

Recollections of previous pregnancies floated towards the surface, autumn leaves scooped off the surface of a swimming pool.

'Are you sitting down?' I said into the phone, bum sore from the plastic loo seat, pants and fifty-denier M&S tights still wrapped around my ankles, despite having peed on the pregnancy-test stick a whole twenty minutes earlier. It was dark outside; rain lashed against the bathroom window.

'I'm pregnant,' I said in a matter-of-fact tone, before taking an extremely large swig of wine.

'Move in with me,' he said, after a pause to rival Pinter.

I put my house on the market. In hindsight, I should've kept the house, had the ghosts not followed me around, tugging at my dressing gown like memories I couldn't quite shake off. And the debt, of course. And all the shags.

To help me pack up my piles of crap, Mum came down from the north, which sounds very *Game of Thrones*. I should buy her a bearskin. Surrounded by stuff I couldn't remember buying, I had zero appetite to continue to carry it around. A heavy load of too many things, it felt arduous and difficult. Turns out, I'm a shocker of a hoarder, as confirmed by the piles of unopened mail stuffed into Miu Miu shoeboxes. That, and clothing bought but never worn. That, and letters from the credit card company reading, 'Dear Ms Duguid, we're writing to inform you that, given you are nearing your £15,000 credit limit, we'll raise your existing limit to £20,000 for the next twelve months.'

Cue taxi to Selfridges.

Gripped by pregnancy nausea, I had to lie down every five minutes or so, so I fashioned a fake-fur leopard-print coat into a sort of dog bed and lay down on the kitchen floor.

'God, you own a lot of crap. Do you really need five teapots?' he said, before relenting, sinking to his knees, preparing to lie down on the floor beside me.

We both lay there, laughing at an absurd teapot decorated with a clown's face. I'd carted it back from New York.

'I need it.'

'No, really you don't.'

The night before the house sale went through, he helped me gather the last of my single woman debris. A lot had happened at 14 Victor Road: good times, bad times, lots of sex with a confusion of men, mostly while high. Relieved to leave, I dropped the keys I'd carried with me every day for the past four years on top of the note I'd left for the new owners on the kitchen counter. Glancing over my shoulder, I bid farewell to the house, to the fun times, to the laughs, to the benders, to the loneliness.

At 8pm on a dark October evening, we piled the last of my crap high in the boot of his car. I turned around to look out the back window. Victor Road was already a green screen, a memory, a film that's not really there. In a 1930s black-and-white movie where I was the leading lady, I'd found my guy. And look at me now, driving off into the sunset with my prince.

I sat in the front of his trashed green Golf, my Irish ex-husband on my lap, the dog's bad breath made even worse by a heightened sense of smell. A flicker of a baby boy growing inside me. Even the streetlamps shone brighter that night.

The warmth within was a sign telling me I'd finally made it home.*

---

* Home? Despite the fact I'd only known him for eight months, had met him online and therefore had no friends in common, despite the fact that he was posh and I was – and still am – not, and despite the fact that he'd gone to boarding school and I'd gone to state school, over the years I grew to love him deeply, in ways that went far beyond that initial hit of oxytocin. Having placed my fantasies of safety into the hands of another, little did I know finding my way back home would be far more complicated than I could ever have imagined.

In Pursuit of Happiness

Spellcheck mating

To cum or not to come, that is the question.

Me: Hiya. Is it cum or come?

Sara: Come again?

Me: lol. No, seriously. How do you spell cum?

Sara: I hate the word cum.

Me: So, it's 'come', then. Gotcha.

Sara: Why?

Me: Just a thing I'm writing.

Sara: OK, sure.

Me: OK, bye.

Sara: Cum on – what are you writing?

Me: This thing about cumming/ coming and how difficult I find it, and how I haven't really enjoyed sex, even after having loads of it.

Sara: Bullshit.

Me: What? Why bullshit?

Sara: You LOVE sex!!!

Me: Well, kinda, but only
recently. As in, the past year
recently. Before that, I was just,
I dunno, playing along. Or high.

Sara: Errrr. OK.

10

Motherhood Mating –
The Second Coming

Cum again?

I never cum. Have I mentioned that? Well, I *can* cum very quickly, but only when alone, never with a partner during sex. In other words, someone blithely banging their willy in and out of my vagina does not do it for me. A penis inside my pussy is not enough to make me cum. A vibrator set to FULL BLAST on my clit as he whispers filth in my ear, and maybe I'll think about it.

On my own, the whole thing is done and dusted within ten minutes – and that includes two orgasms, because I'm greedy. I go through phases of masturbating daily, cumming/coming anytime between school drop-off and the first deadline of the day. I call it my 'stress wank'.

In the years before baby-making sex, I never felt fully in the room. Like an actor watching from the sidelines and willing the sex to be over so I could stop kissing the stranger and get on with my day, I never felt connected. Even if the stranger was replaced by a boyfriend or long-term partner, no matter how hard I tried,

I never really enjoyed it – not really. Not enjoying sex or feeling fully in the room didn't stop me from putting on a bloody good show, though. Like, Only Fans style. Porn vibes. *Look at me, I can do tricks and I have a ridiculously long tongue.* All show-off moves to hide my embarrassment.

As a younger woman, I had a lot of sex, none of it particularly satisfying. I don't remember properly enjoying it, not least because I was often off my head, too high or too drunk to remember, but mostly because I didn't engage. This is not the norm for all young women, of course, and I have several friends who've enjoyed explorative, sensual sex right from the get-go. The way we mentally engage with sex is, I think, to do with ideas formed in childhood.

No one wants to marry a bike, remember? And yet there I was, pulling all the porn moves but never able to connect. Connecting to him, I now realise, was not the point. Connecting to *myself* was the crucial part missing, the reason I was so reluctant to cum/ come. Even more ironically, the first time I ever watched porn was when I was forty-seven; my so-called 'porn moves' were borrowed from Madonna videos as opposed to Pornhub.

Sorry to come over all Cher, but if I could turn back time, I would spend more time getting to know and understand my own desires. In my twenties and thirties, masturbating felt like an urgent need each month, usually around the time of ovulation. Coming/cumming was explosive, but I never took the time to enjoy my body, to feel my own skin, to gently stroke massage oil along my limbs, to caress and feel inside my vagina, to run a finger slowly along my clit.

Kids. I told you not to read this book.

The wall I built around myself protected me from exposing my true, vulnerable self – but good sex requires conversation and connection. When I eventually had babies, I turned away from myself and him, and focused on being a mother instead. You could argue that's exactly what a mother should do, but looking back, I disagree. Why did I lean so far into motherhood when I could have sought out balance?

In her book *Mating in Captivity*, Esther Perel writes:

'The psychology of our desire often lays buried in the details of our childhood, and digging through the early history of our lives uncovers its archaeology. We can trace back to where we learned to love and how. Did we learn to experience pleasure or not, to trust others or not, to receive or to be denied? Were our parents monitoring our needs, or were we expected to monitor theirs? Did we turn to them for protection or did we flee them to protect ourselves? Were we rejected? Humiliated? Abandoned? Were we held? Rocked? Soothed? Did we learn not to expect too much, to hide when we are upset, to make eye contact? In our family, we sense when it's OK to thrive and when others might be hurt by our zest. We learn how to feel about our body, our gender, and our sexuality. And we learn a multitude of other lessons about who and how to be; to open up or to shut down, to sing or to whisper, to cry or to hide our tears, to dare or to be afraid.'

Later, as the babies grew and my body went back to looking more like the one I was used to seeing in the mirror, I attempted to walk back towards my old self – but I couldn't. I couldn't find her. She had gone. Had she even been there in the first place? *Who was I? Who am I?*

My younger self was built on such flimsy foundations: wild nights and a glamorous job. It was as if I didn't know who I was to begin with, so how could I possibly rediscover the old me?

The old me was a shadow, and shadows can't be seen in the rain. The old me once destroyed a 'borrowed' Roberto Cavalli sequinned minidress by rolling along the pavement outside Soho House. That was an expensive mistake. The old me danced on podiums when nightclubs in Ibiza were open-air and ecstasy was cheaper to buy than a bottle of water.

A pram replaced my Prada work bag, and this new me didn't forward-roll around Soho wearing stolen dresses. This version of me went to meet strangers for coffee mornings, trying hard to bond over feeding times and sore nipples. We all looked the same. Shapeless slogan sweatshirts, hair that hadn't been coloured or cut for a while.

Why am I telling you all this? Oh, yes: to cum or come, that is the question. As we saw on page 100, Sara doesn't like the word 'cum', and ever since she mentioned it, I've gone off it, too. Whichever way you happen to spell it, I'll stick my neck out and say that, in my experience, 'baby-making sex' tends to be not exactly satisfying. Rather than screaming in ecstasy, there've been many times I've wanted to yell, 'Just cum already, let's get this shit over with. Impregnate me, bad boy.'

Whenever I initiated 'baby-making-sex' (which, by the way, is the only time I ever initiated sex, or indeed *wanted* to have so much sex with a partner I've known for more than three months), I wanted the whole thing to be over as quickly as possible. Sex with an end game felt forced and weird, diarised with an agenda. Obviously, he knew nothing about Operation Ovulation; he just assumed I was momentarily horny. You know, now I have a toddler and a full-time job . . . sure.

When trying for baby number two and beyond, there's an unspoken awareness between couples that if this month's 'try' turns out to be mission complete, at least one of you won't fancy having sex for a very long time to cum – I mean, come. Unless it's a reluctant blow job administered under duress (code for: aggressive, with teeth). Or a quick hand job in the shower before baby number one wakes up – as long as the overpriced shower gel from Planet Organic (aka 'expensive lube') hasn't run out. He may need a hand job, but a woman still has standards.

Forget the frizzle-sizzle-dizzle of days gone by, if I'm too tired to flick breakfast crumbs off my cardigan come bedtime, why the fuck would I want to get 'sexy' after the herculean effort of removing mascara AND applying moisturiser? Forgetaboutit. Oh, wait, sorry – actually, I do. Impregnate me, and make it quick.

Still wearing Mamas and Papas maternity jeans that ended beneath my newly low-slung tits, having never enjoyed sex before, why would I choose now – three stone heavier, a too-tight wardrobe, several hundred pairs of shoes I could no longer walk in – to go all 'sexy temptress'. No way, babes.

My new life was all polite coffee mornings with women wearing Breton, confusion sketched across our faces, none of us admitting how we really felt. Were they as out of their depth as I was? We had surface-level conversations about feeding routines, sleep patterns. I missed my actual friends.

Friendships change when you have a baby. Relationships change, too. And when you don't feel like *you* any more, no wonder the last thing on your mind is sex. I wish someone had told me that sex (in its many forms, not just penetrative) is the glue of a relationship. Without the glue, relationships become unstuck.

Unstuck and broken, pieces falling apart. Catch the pieces before they shatter to ashes on the floor.

Too late.

11

Un-Hinged Mating

*Dating apps: safer than cruising for
men in bars, right? WRONG!*

Dear Hinge,

*I'm forty-eight years old and currently spend roughly – let's
round it up – £200 per month on dating apps.* Two hundred
pounds. That's right. *That's a third of the way to a half-decent
pair of shoes. I dread to think what I've spent on this bullshit so
far. Let's hazard a guess – erm, ooh, WAY TOO FUCKING
MUCH!*

*I'm writing to tell you that the men that use it, make Hinge
the worst dating app on the market. It's the absolute bleedin' pits.
Men on Hinge are psychos. On travel mode recently, a man asked
to 'purchase' me. He said he'd give my mother a donkey. Not a
stallion, a* donkey. *I asked him why a donkey and not a stallion,
to which he replied, 'You fuckable but no fertile, no children, so
donkey no horse.' I told him Mum has no need for a donkey. She
lives in a bungalow on a housing estate in Newcastle.*

*Donkeys aside, let me tell you what happened last week. I
connected with two wonderful-looking men, both very different,
both clearly interesting and bright. Toby lives in a part of north*

London where only clever people live (it's a proven fact), and Amir lives in the States, and travels a lot.

Last Sunday, both men asked whether I'd like to 'head to WhatsApp', which, in case you didn't know, is the online equivalent of a marriage proposal. So, I gave both guys my number. Amir, I have to say, is ever so impressive on LinkedIn, with a big job in government connected to climate change. Toby? Well, he's a little trickier to figure out, some kind of career in tech, which, these days, frankly means anything from billionaire to broke. I remained positive throughout both exchanges, reminding myself money doesn't necessarily bring happiness. (I just choked on an olive writing that.)

Within ten minutes of sending my number, my WhatsApp exploded like bonfire night. In quick-fire succession, I receive a ton of images (don't panic, no dick pics). Cherubic angels, trees, seaside scenes, the sun rising behind mountains. I assumed Amir must be drunk.

It got worse. Each aesthetically offensive saccharine image contained a nifty motivational mantra. Then came Rumi. Rumi quotes! For God's sake, by this point I was one mantra away from 'Keep Calm and Throw a Plate at the Fucking Wall'.

The messages continued to roll in. Poetry, questions about what I wanted from love. What do I want from love? I'd never even met him!

Rather than block him outright, which is cruel, I wrote to say I found his communication overwhelming and that it wasn't what I was looking for. Then I blocked him. To be honest, his profile had provided enough red flags. Never trust a man in a bow tie.

Toby didn't text me immediately, which I liked. Play it cool, baby! But he did send a message within the same day, which I also liked. Don't play it too cool – that's boring!

(As an aside, Hinge ought to provide an information 'box out', as we say in publishing, providing a set of communication guidelines that are easy for men to understand. It could be a timesaving tool for all involved. I'd be happy to help write? See page 110 for my thoughts.)

For ease, I've copied Toby's WhatsApp message below.

Toby: *Hiya, it's Toby from Hinge.*
Me: *Hi Toby, what are you up to?*
Toby: *Am at dinner, nothing Michelin-starred, but the company's good.*
Me: *Oh, lovely. Are you with your family?*
Toby: *No, I'm on a Hinge blind date. You might know her, she's called Katie. She works at Apple Music.*
Me: *Um, wait, have you spoken to her about me?*
Toby: *No! Why on earth would I mention you to a woman I'm on a date with?*
Me: *It's just I'm confused. You asked whether I knew her, so I assumed she knew me?*

I can't properly remember the minutes that followed, on account of my head spinning 360 degrees like Beetlejuice.

'Anyway!' I continued. 'Regardless of who you're on a date with, that's so not the point. It's the fact you're messaging me FROM A DATE. That's so disrespectful – to both of us. How incredibly rude!'

I walked away from my phone at this point, dear Hinge Boss, and went upstairs to bed where I face-planted the pillow so aggressively, my neck hurt for three days. Considering radioing the starship Enterprise *to beam me up, I then downed three glasses of wine in quick succession. That's when I had the idea to cancel my subscription, but you bastards had already taken the money from my account.*

Anyway, I'm off to Tinder – so 'naaah'. In case you were wondering what 'naaah' means, I have my right thumb placed at the end of my nose, with four fingers flapping manically in your direction (the screen). Think 'Prince Louis at the Jubilee', but more pissed off.

Best wishes (which I obviously don't mean, because you're a wanker),

Stacey Duguid

How to communicate with women on dating sites

1. When making the first approach, be curious. Kick off with something about your day, but ask questions. Not too many, mind. Maybe just one, max two. Sample text: *Hello, nice to connect with you. I've been in meetings all day, just finished. On my way out to watch a film. How about you, what've you been up to today? Any plans for this evening?*

2. When she replies via the dating app, do not immediately ask for her number. It's tiresome and presumptuous.

3. Should she offer up her surname, do not snoop on her LinkedIn. She can see you've viewed her profile, you doughnut.

4. Assuming you haven't video dialled her via the dating app at 3am 'by mistake', after a couple of days, ask if she'd like to move to WhatsApp.

5. If she suggests moving to WhatsApp first, ask for her number and tell her you'll be in touch later on. If she has children, avoid messaging during kids' bedtime, home-work time, bath time, teatime, school pick-up time. Try between 2pm and 2.20pm. Even if she works full-time and is out of the home all day, she'll be micromanaging every single move her children make. It's what we do. We cannot help it. It gives us shit to complain about.

6. After a couple of WhatsApps, suggest a phone call. Not via Zoom, Microsoft Teams or Skype. Just a plain old phone call – and one that's not set up by your PA.

7. If the call's going well, don't hang up without asking whether she'd like to meet. Do not expect a firm plan on the first call; give her time to figure out her diary. And

whatever you do, don't WhatsApp several times a day to check if she's 'found a spot in her schedule'. If she hasn't committed, despite saying she'd like to meet you, it's a firm no. Got that? No.

8. After date one, don't ask to share Google Calendars.
9. After date one, if you split the bill and made a fuss about the food, you can delete her number immediately. She offered to pay half because she's a feminist. Doesn't mean to say she *wants* to go Dutch on a date. What do you mean, the rules are complicated?
10. Don't try to kiss her on date one. But do try to kiss her on date two. If you leave it to date three, she'll assume something is wrong with her – insert long list of physical attributes, but for argument's sake, let's go with: teeth.

12

Mating in Midlife

*The time a man I met on an app tried to
throttle me outside a five-star hotel*

We met in a fancy cocktail bar on the ground floor of a hotel.
It was panelled in dark rosewood, and candles twinkled to the
rhythm of a piano.

Not my kind of place, filled with not my kind of people.
Tonight's blind date was seated in a far-off corner. It was his hair
I noticed first. Brutally shaved high up the back and sides, he'd
intentionally left a section of long, floppy hair on top. *Odd*. That
was my first thought, imagining him instructing the hairdresser,
directing him this way and that, two middle-aged men deliberat-
ing in earnest concern over a small yet highly prized patch of hair.
I imagined his hipster hairdresser had tattoos across his fingers
and knuckles, and the word 'Mum' inked on the side of his neck.
Ironically, of course.

Walking past the pianist towards my blind date, I instinctively
knew this prized section of well-groomed hair had been swept
back using overpriced wax bought from an exclusive brand mar-
keted at exactly this kind of man.

Not my bar, not my people, not my music, not my man.

His puffy face seemed vain; his jacket looked expensive. I'd sensed a mean streak the second I'd opened the heavy, polished wooden door, but he'd already clocked me. Too late. Had he not, perhaps I would've scarpered.

Only perhaps.

'Stacey from the *Telegraph*, the famous dating columnist!' he said, shoving his face towards mine with a force that sent the prized patch of hair bobbing forward like an Afghan hound wearing a topknot at Crufts. The dreaded double kiss. I never get it right. I've kissed ears and grazed many mouths with mine – always awkward at the start of a meeting in a small boardroom.

He noticed my leather miniskirt move up my thighs as I sat down. No matter how subtle, women are highly attuned to body parts being looked at, registering the dart of an eye, even if it lingers only for a nanosecond. We see it.

'Oh,' I said, forcing a smile, inwardly vowing to use a fake first name and remove any mention of the *Telegraph* across all dating app profiles immediately. He ordered two negronis, then quickly ordered two more. He talked about himself without pause. I am used to this: men and women of all ages talking at me about themselves, me sitting there like a nodding dog. Must be my face.

Perhaps he felt he already knew everything about me, given he'd googled and checked out my social media. I hadn't given him my surname, but he'd found me, nevertheless. Of course he had. It was my fault. Who uses their real first name on a dating app? Who tells the truth about where they work? Take my advice: don't do it.

Five minutes before we were due to meet, he'd messaged to say how much he'd enjoyed discovering my 'Midlife Dating Diaries', the column I wrote each Saturday for the *Telegraph*.

'I'd better not be "research"!!!!,' he continued in a separate WhatsApp, adding a laughing emoji at the end, as if to let me know in advance that he was a fun, cool guy.

How boring, I thought, glancing at my phone, wishing I had a tenner for every man who'd said the same thing.

'Research? Doubt it! Bet you're far too fucking boring to end up in one of my columns!' That's what I wanted to say, but didn't. 'Course not,' I replied instead. 'See you soon.'

And now here we were. As the second negroni hit, I excused myself and went to the bathroom. In the dark interior of the cubicle, I fired off an SOS to a close friend I knew was at Soho House nearby.

'FUCK!!!! HELP!!!! Save me, this guy's a total dick!!!!'

'Hold on, girlfriend. I'll be right there!'

As if we'd planned it, Jill opened the hotel door to the pianist playing Elton John's 'I'm Still Standing'.

Two negronis can give a woman such confidence. I jumped up with a squeal. 'My friend's here!' Running across the heavily patterned carpet to hug her, we danced an impromptu comedy waltz around the piano. Everyone stared in bemusement. My Hinge date's face turned from vain to mean to livid to puce.

'OK, how do you wanna play this?' Jill whispered in my ear.

'Erm, I dunno.'

'Shall we just leave?' she asked, leaning in.

'What, do a runner?' I said, imagining us making a dash for the door but somehow accidentally ending on top of the piano. Tripping over while trying to do a runner. That would be so us.

'Yeah, kinda. Oh God, Stacey, he has terrible hair. It's giving me Nazi Third Reich vibes.'

'Ha ha ha, I know, the hair is AWFUL. I'm OK, you go home. Sorry for being dramatic; he's actually quite nice.'

'What? Are you joking? Come on, look at him! Bad hair, jeans way too tight – which I wouldn't usually give a shit about, but he looks really fucking angry. Are you sure you want to stay?'

'I'm fine, you go! He's looking at me as though I'm crazy.'

'You ARE crazy,' she said, in her delicious Alabama drawl. 'You're fucking batshit crazy, and that's why I love you.'

She disappeared as quickly as she'd arrived, and I skittered back to the table and sat down. 'Well, that was odd! Had no idea Jill planned to pop in for a dance!' I said.

He knew I was lying, but smiled nevertheless. Pulling his seat closer to mine, he ordered two more negronis. Two made me dance, the fourth made me cry. I cried about my marital breakdown and how much I missed my kids. I cried about my soon-to-be-ex-husband. By way of comfort, he reached out his hand and began stroking my leg, slowly making his way up my leather miniskirt.

His right index finger ran to the top of my inner thigh and continued upwards until it could go no further. Staring at this stranger with his hand up my skirt, I wondered what he'd do next. His finger lingered for a while, and then, I guess because I didn't ask him to stop, he began stroking my clit, willing me to cum in public. Such a display of dominance.

I'd spotted him on Hinge two days prior. Forty-eight hours later, his right forefinger was on my clit, and we were eight negronis down between us (plus whatever he'd had beforehand). Dating in midlife is treacherous. And also clichéd. The overpriced cocktail bar in a boring part of town could've been straight out of a Netflix series. Extramarital-affair tacky – an excellent look at the age of forty-seven.

Middle-aged and drunk, with a stranger's finger jabbing my clit as though I were a fucking jukebox, by the time the bill came, I'd already decided I didn't want to sing for my supper. Already knowing how the next scene would unfold I got out my card to pay half.

'I'll get it,' he said, because that's what men like this do; invite you to swanky bars where they 'impress' with expensive drinks in order to present as the ultimate 'gentleman'.

'The next one's on you,' they always say, the second the card goes through. You walk out together, his hand firmly placed in the centre of your back, guiding you towards the door like a new possession. Will you join him? He's going east, you're west, but somehow you're expected to agree to share a taxi ride home.

I should've left with Jill before the tears and the unwanted fingering. I should've left two negronis down, safe in the knowledge I'd avoid puking the next morning. My mind flicked to what could have been: me jumping on the tube with Jill, both of us laughing, finally able to catch our breath after doing a runner in high heels from a man with a haircut like an Afghan hound.

But I couldn't leave.

Go home? It was far easier to stay in a ridiculous bar filled with people my brain couldn't compute on a date with a man I disliked upon sight.

Go home? It was way easier to let this odd, mean stranger run his finger along the seamed crotch of my tights. (Did I mention I had tights on? Thank fuck I had tights on.)

Go home? It was far better to get smashed on pure liquor, knowing the following day would be a total write-off.

Home? Where's that? No clue. Making my way through the heavy doors of the hotel, I regretted not telling Jill the truth. Regretted not saying . . .

'I'm untethered. I'm not at home anywhere. Not in the rental house, not inside my own body. I'm lonely. I'm so desperately lonely. Lost without my children, I cried all day today. I never should've come out on a date tonight, not in this state. I'm lost. There's nowhere to turn. I hate being alone, I miss my kids. I want to escape my own body. How is it even possible to feel this way?'

Had I told her the truth, she never would've left. Instead, she would've bundled me into a taxi like a kidnapper. Back at her flat, she would've given me a pair of clean-smelling pyjamas, Teresa Tarmey eye make-up remover, a pot of moisturiser and a large glass of water and we'd spend an hour or two laughing about being forty-seven and still meeting weirdos on Hinge. We'd make a pact to never again do a runner in heels.

It was cold that night, but I can't blame the weather for the fact I didn't pull away. As he leaned in, so did his hair, which bobbed towards my face, flicking the side of it with a whip. I sort of kissed him back. A green light. He placed both hands around my neck while pulling my face away from his. With his hands around my neck, holding me at arm's length, he just sort of looked at me.

I have staring competitions with the kids just like this – minus the strangulation. I tried not to laugh. Looking me deep in the eye, his hands gripped harder. A thumb grazed my throat, gentle at first, then firmer. Fingertips pressed at the back of my neck, his thumb plunged into my windpipe. Still staring. His face didn't flinch. Nor did mine.

It was midnight, but busy. People on nights out. Did he presume I'd scream? I felt his other thumb join the party. I was moments away from gagging when he released me, playing with my hair instead.

'Do you like that?' he asked, still staring. 'Do you like a little role play, hmmm?'

Before I could answer, he pulled my hair. Refusing to jolt, I forced my neck to remain strong. No glimmer of lightness in his dead-fish eyes.

The headlights of a passing bus shone a spotlight in my face. A different kind of jolt this time.

I needed a taxi; I had to get away from this boundary-free, lawless freak. Unless that was me? Lawless and freakish, I mean.

Dropping a fistful of hair, he leaned in for another kiss. Thin lips sucked at mine, cold clams in a jar.

Forty-seven years old and being choked by a total stranger outside a posh hotel in central London.

'I need to go home.'

The universe delivered a black cab. A minute later, my phone flashed in my clutch bag. It was him.

'Hello. That was sexy. Next time I see you, I'm going to strip you naked. Would you like that? No fighting back. I'll grab a fistful of your slutty red hair and shove you to your knees. Pulling hair nice and tight, I'll shove my hard cock deep into your mouth until you gag. Do you like deep throat? You're so gonna get it.'

Dating in mid-life? I'm lost. I miss my ex-husband.

PART 2

Marriage

According to the Office for National Statistics, over the past fifty years one third of marriages ended in divorce. Cheery fact, but an important one to note for many reasons. In MARRIAGE, the second section of this book, I touch on a range of subjects, such as the financial rights of unmarried women when there are jointly owned houses and children involved.

I don't wish to come across as all preachy – which means I definitely will, so buckle up – but before walking down the aisle, please, please, please be as well versed regarding your legal rights as you are regarding expensive white gowns and blow-the-budget wedding venues. Knowing how to dress a dozen or so bridesmaids, or finding a location for the most raucous hen party will look fantastic on Instagram for a day. CONGRATULATIONS! But if you don't have your own pot of money and, say, I dunno, the ring comes off, you could find yourself right in the shit. This shitshow is definitely not one for the 'gram, believe me, and I deeply regret not being more prepared for the hell that was my divorce.

As a society, we rarely discuss divorce. We're all about the wedding, all about the romance, and even if there were 'classes' for newlyweds covering finances, would we even listen?

Not for one single moment did I ever consider I'd break up with my ex-husband. As the child of a single parent who went on to marry twice more, I cannot fathom why.

13

Marriage, *Moi?*

Not according to the fourteen-year-old feminist

Presuming all marriages ended terribly, because that's what happened in *Dallas* and *Dynasty*, and despite possessing a raging Cinderella complex, the teenage me never wanted to get married. Not really. Witnessing my parents' generation marry not once, not twice but thrice for good luck, was all the intel I needed. Marriages didn't work, and even if they did, they involved compromise and lots of shouting. And probably no sex. Not that I've ever thought about whether my mum still has sex. Well, not until typing that sentence. *And I don't want to know the answer*, she says, putting a finger in each ear.

As for the admin, I don't *do* admin. I struggle to pay a bill on time, never mind three divorces' worth of paperwork. Change my name three times, then back again? Are you joking?

Baby boomers loved getting married and divorced, then remarried and divorced again, or at least that's the way it seems. I get it, it's called survival. Women had lower-paid jobs back then (many still do), and more often than not, had no choice but to give up work to stay at home with the kids, leaving them financially vulnerable and dependent on partners and husbands.

Although the mere thought of paperwork makes my face itch, I reckon the reason many women my age swerved marriage is, in part at least, down to a marginally increased financial freedom. I say *marginally*.

The pendulum of society and how we're influenced by wider culture and the generations who came before inevitably swings from one extreme to the other. Always has, and I'll wager probably always will. A few years ago, I ran a team of much younger people, which included millennials and women many years my junior. From our conversations, it appeared to me the pendulum had made its way back to the baby-boomer generation once again. The younger people I encountered were seemingly bang-up for walking down the aisle; a few had even postponed their weddings due to the Covid-19 pandemic, preferring to wait for a lavish, in-person BIG event rather than having one of those digital ceremonies that became a thing for a hot minute during lockdown. Zoom weddings never did catch on, thank God. Can you imagine? No, I cannot. Although it's a pretty genius way of avoiding certain family members. Food for thought.

Disney Discourse Analysis notwithstanding (now that's a PhD paper I imagine someone somewhere has already written), I pootled along in life, assuming my prince was on his way – ditto a couple of kids and a comfortable house. Oh, and I'd still have the chance to build my career. But marriage? *Non*. The walking down an aisle bit? *Non*. The party bit? *Oui*. The paperwork? *Non*. Have children 'out of wedlock'? *Oui*. (What a ridiculously old-fashioned term, 'wedlock'. Sounds like an S&M night without the fun.) Going away on a nice holiday, just the two of us? Bring it on. Being 'given away' to a man, by a man? No chance. An engagement ring? Yes – I mean *oui*. A white dress? *Non*, no. Blowing twenty grand on one day? Definitely *non*! Well, maybe *oui* – as long as it's a solo day trip to Harrods. Being together for ever, in sickness and in health, for richer or poorer? Yes, *oui*, absolutely. That last bit, I'm up for.

The world's most reluctant bride, not once have I been tempted to whirl through a bridal department asking to try on gowns, pretending I'm getting married. Saying that, not *all* wedding outfits have me breaking out in hives, breathing into a paper bag like I'm trying to suck the helium out of a balloon at a kid's birthday party (I once caught a mum sucking helium from my son's eighth birthday balloon). Having thoroughly perused the bridal category of Net-A-Porter, compared to even a decade ago, personal style aside, these days wedding 'looks' can be – can't believe I'm about to say this – rather fucking fabulous.

If a 'Stacey's Wedding Day' Pinterest board were to ever exist (which, believe me, it never would), you'd find a mix of glamorously grungy women working a sort of undone elegance with a dash of punk. Rolling Stones wives in white waistcoats, bare arms and huge hats. Joan Didion leaning against a car, wearing a long white column dress on the cover of *The White Album*. Helmut Newton's women standing beneath streetlamps: strict suiting, sharp blazers and even sharper cigarette pants, drool. I'm also seeing Kate Moss in a wide-legged 'pant' suit, or Florence (as in Florence and the Machine) in a long, billowing GUCCI dress that somehow manages to make her look even more ethereal. A GUCCI wedding dress – maybe I *could* be tempted? Not that I could afford a GUCCI gown, considering how much a wedding costs these days.

An industry making profits of, on average, £7.5 billion GBP per annum, getting married is big business. Apparently, the number of couples choosing to get married has been in decline for many years, bar a slight increase in 2014, when same-sex marriages were legalised. As for recent figures (2022), there are, on average, 275,000 weddings per year, with couples and families spending around £14.7 billion. The big day itself is where most money is blown, but nowadays – I'm about to sound like a right old grouch – the run-up to the wedding day is an ever-growing racket, I mean expense. Travelling to stag dos and hen parties abroad is hugely expensive. And how annoying it must be to be in your thirties with three weddings on the horizon. That's a huge amount of money to pay, even as a guest.

Multiple outfits to buy, silly party toot to wear, bail to pay when someone's been arrested for flashing their tits out the window of the stretch while driving past a Greek Orthodox church – all that fandango before the actual big day has even happened?! I'm exhausted just thinking about it. And broke. And disillusioned.

Being introduced as 'Mrs Blah', someone's 'wife', makes my toes curl – and yet there have been many points during my life when I've yearned to feel part of an official coupling, something solid, something bigger than just, 'this is my girlfriend'.

I hope my daughter never feels this conflicted over the role she's expected to play on her so-called 'big day'. Or, rather, I hope she stops to question her motives for entering into relationships and what she really needs from them. Same goes for my son, obviously, but that's possibly a whole other book. Perhaps marriage will be abolished by the time they're eighteen.

Not once did I stop to think, *What is it I really want from my life, from love, from motherhood, from work, from everything?* I just lay down in the road and allowed life to steamroller over me. I actively chose to play a B role in my own life, to be an understudy to the main actor – one I prayed to God would never get sick, because I never, ever wanted to stand on the stage in the god-damn spotlight alone.

Inner thought: whoever's up there controlling the giant spotlight, the one I try to avoid – on my wedding day, please make sure to shine it directly over my head and follow me all day. No more hiding in the dark. As I take tiny steps down the aisle towards my husband, whispers of appreciation filling the room as guests marvel at my minuscule ribcage harnessed beneath the microscopic bodice of my dress, the day shall belong to me. It's my time to shine. Well, for ten hours. And only because I don't have to say or do anything other than look good in a white dress.

Is that why our wedding day feels so important? We finally grant ourselves permission to step out of the shadows?

Having missed countless opportunities – in work, friendships, relationships – I can't help wondering if, had I pushed myself further out of my comfort zone, I could've stepped into the spotlight alone. Capable of shining brighter, bigger, bolder than I've ever dared to,

I've always known I'm capable of far more than I allowed myself to be. No wedding dress required.

But I objectified this mythical 'we', this made-up life partner, long before we met. Not 'might', not 'could', not 'maybe' – a long-term, loving partner WOULD be the safe harbour I needed in order to survive (emotionally, financially, etc.).

In order to steady the rocking boat that was a life lived too precariously, like a heavy anchor thrown into the depths of the sea, a part of me knew the moment I met 'him', I'd tie my boat to the safety of this man.

It wasn't a deeply connected loving relationship I'd spent years looking for, it was a safe place to moor. With huge ropes thrown ashore and tied to metal posts, the choppy seas that had rolled in my mind would become a distant memory.

Safely ensconced in a relationship, I'd grant myself permission to retreat and hide. Being married, or with a long-term partner, would automatically release me from ambitions of playing a role I didn't quite know how to get anyway.

A million miles from Ashton-under-Lyne, I'd taken a very different path to the well-trodden roads followed by my family. I'd always wanted more from life – a career, a future, kids – but only when it suited me. I often told myself I wanted too much, hankering after a life that never really belonged to me in the first place.

14

Brexit Marriage

Stand back, Cinderella – I'll show you how this romance shit works. Be still my beating heart, I can't handle this level of romance. Does anyone have a beta blocker?

At approximately 5am on 24 June 2016, my long-term partner, father to my two children, suggested, rather unromantically, that we get married. I hadn't slept. I was pacing the floor as the Brexit votes rolled in. By the early hours, it was clear the UK had voted to leave Europe.

My wailing must have woken him up. No exaggeration. I wailed. I sobbed. I used the C-word that does not stand for 'Conservatives'. I used the C-word heavily across social media, only to delete everything ten seconds later.

'WE'VE LEFT EUROPE!!!' I screamed at the top of my lungs, waking him up, but thankfully not the children.

I was angry. Incensed at the role the media had played, furious with Farage and his revolting lies, his endless empty promises that had fed newspaper headlines that tore the nation in two. Pure propaganda, a nation divided. Rich and poor, north and south. Most of London had voted to remain; as for the rest of the country, I'd already called it. They wanted out. Not that anyone living within the M25 believed me.

'This is happening,' I'd said to my friends at the pub the previous night. Their smiling faces were etched with sympathy, as though they'd brought out a lovely but elderly aunt for dinner, who was showing the first signs of dementia and needed looking after. 'We're leaving Europe. Tonight. You're ALL living in a London bubble, every single one of you! You have no clue what's going on outside the M25. Poverty like you wouldn't believe. Fourth generations on benefits, through no fault of their own.'

My friends were already laughing, waiting for my usual rant about the coal-miners' strike, or thousands of mines closed without a thought or plan. I stopped short of blaming Margaret Thatcher; I knew it was time to stop. We carried on drinking and I left the pub at last orders, coming home to sit on the sofa and watch the votes come in. I didn't bother going to bed.

Around five the next morning, when my wail had awoken him, I heard a scratching sound as someone entered the room.

'We should get married,' he said looking in the direction of the window, wearing boxer shorts and bed hair.

Eyes sore from being glued to my laptop all night, I took a momentary break from blasting Boris on Twitter. 'What did you just say?' I blinked, and turned to face him, watching as he sat down on the bed in the spare room that doubled up as my office.

'We should get married. We can go abroad, get away from this shitshow,' he said, looking at his feet, possibly wondering whether or not he should cut his toenails.

'That's a proposal, right? To marry you?' Despite a raging hangover, I was now fully awake and very much back in the room.

He ignored the question.

'America's out,' I said. 'Trump will be president come November. I'd rather live in Brexit hell than in a country ruled by that fucking lunatic.' I turned back to my screen, shocked at the discussion of marriage on this of all days.

Marriage had never been mentioned before. His parents were also on second and third marriages, and neither of us saw the point of it. For the sake of what, a piece of paper? I vaguely remember us discussing marriage when we'd first met, both agreeing having children was a commitment bigger by far.

Marriage wasn't mentioned again that day, nor during the week that followed. It was a thought I'd never allowed myself to have before. I wanted to share the 'sort of' marriage proposal with a friend, but instead it hung in my mind, unspoken like a secret. What if he hadn't meant it? What if it had been uttered only as a reaction to Brexit, blurted, but never really meant? An accident. What if?

It was an average Tuesday morning when I finally plucked up the courage and asked. Getting up at 7am to take the kids to nursery and school, three weeks after the Brexit-induced marriage proposal, I decided, despite needing an urgent wee, that now was the perfect time to tackle it.

'Did you mean that thing about getting married?' I asked, making myself comfortable on the throne.

'Yup,' came his reply from bed.

'Can you actually ask me, then?'

Snort.

'Why are you snorting? I'm not joking.'

'Will you marry me?'

My sparkling Disney dream moment: a Brexit proposal made as an attempt to flee Boris Johnson, confirmed as I sat having a pee.

A week after that reluctant, 'Will you marry me?' proffered in the dark, I enquired as to the whereabouts of a ring.

'Do you need input?' I asked, less of a question, more of an order.

He said something I couldn't quite catch, something to do with 'surplus' and 'stock' and 'a mate from school'. I saw red.

As in, 'the Incredible Hulk before he goes into shirt-ripping mode and attempts to tear someone's head off' red.

Enough was enough. I could live without an 'on bended knee' proposal, but as for an engagement ring? *Bitch, please.*

'What's the jeweller's number?'

'Why?'

'Hand over the jeweller's number.'

'No!'

'NOW.'

'OK, sure. Hold on a minute.'

The unromantic proposal, Brexit, rising Trumpism, the polarisation of global politics, and now an engagement ring that was 'surplus stock'. In the weeks that followed, I wanted to curl up, doors locked, fish fingers in the oven, cartoons on the telly, blankets on the sofa, one kid under each arm. I felt utterly destabilised. Even when I rang my mum to tell her I 'might' be getting married, I ended up crying so hard I sent myself into a panic attack.

A wedding would fix it all. Brexit, Boris, Trump, feeling lonely and lost, not fitting in any more at Fashion Month, not knowing who the fuck I was, or how to even find myself. A wedding would sort it all out. It would be fine. We would be fine.

'Hi, Ted? Hi, It's Stacey. Hi. I believe you're making an engagement ring destined for my left hand. Yup, that's me. No, not surplus stock, a new ring. Yeah, I heard. But no. I have a design, and I've chosen the stones. That's right. Uh huh. Sorry, what? How many carats? No. Ha ha ha. Erm, no. Bigger. Nope, bigger. A bit bigger. Actually, do you know what? Double it. Thanks, Ted. Bye.'

15

Marriage Diet

Not medically certified: do not try this at home

Wedding diet

Today's date: 1 February 2018
Wedding deadline: Unknown as neither of us can decide date
Plan: Eat sensibly.
Start date: DUH!!! THAT'LL BE TODAY!!

- 7am(ish) – 45-minute(ish) run
- Breakfast – rye bread, almond butter, black coffee
- Morning – Unlimited amount of black coffee allowed before noon
- Lunch – homemade lentil soup, salad
- Dinner – white fish, vegetables
- No bloody wine!!!
- Lots of peppermint tea!!!

Notes: Wettest February on record. Drank daily, plus occasional lunchtime beer. Feb is fecking grim. Exercising self-forgiveness

for not exercising. It was so damn cold. Coldest Feb on record,
I'll wager. Who the hell diets and stops drinking in February? It's
Fashion Month! No drinkie, no possible.

Revised wedding diet – version 2

Today's date: 1 March 2018
Wedding deadline: I had initially said 4 May, because I really
enjoy saying 'May the Fourth be with you'. Might change date.
Plan: No sugar for three months – apart from sugar found in red
wine, which is good for the heart.

Notes: I FOUND MY DRESS! WELL, not my *actual* dress,
but a dress I love. Spied it at the Preen show. The version the
model wore on the catwalk only has one sleeve, and given my
upper arms look like they belong to a darts player, I'll need a
sleeve. Two sleeves. Two full-length sleeves. Two long sleeves,
due to tattoo-removal marks, plus a longer skirt. Should be easy.
No clue how to ask Preen, and fear if they say no, I may have to
leave the country.

Only one thing for it. Set up a separate Gmail account under
a random name and email them a request, pretending I'm my
assistant. Genius. Why the hell haven't I thought of that before
now?

If I had a full-time assistant, he'd be called Rolf Von Dee-dee.
Austrian royalty vibes, babes.

To: Preen
From: rolfvondeedee@gmail.com
Yeah, it's gonna work.
Anyway, the dress has a beaded bodice, so I need to up the
exercise. Not that I've done any yet, but need to add more to the
plan.

- 45-minute run three times per week.
- Yoga session once per week. Paid for the yoga place up front. Had to go in to do it. Very intimidating. Everyone looking very healthy and bendy (code for 'extremely pleased with themselves').
- Adding boxing classes with a trainer. Wait, do I know any trainers? Gabs Hackworthy will know trainers . . . She has good arms. Call Gabs . . .

Forgot to call Gabs. Blame Gabs for lack of boxing? No. Don't blame Gabs. Could lie and say I called and she didn't call back?

No, Gabs is way too organised to fall for that bullshit.

Revised wedding diet – version 3

Today's date: April-ish, sometime in 2018
Wedding deadline: 22 June 2018 – yes! A date!
Plan: No carbs and that old diet Kate posted on Twitter . . .

Notes: Paid up front for yoga last month, but was too busy so did not go. All sessions now deleted off their yoga-bunny's system. Hate yoga. Hate yoga people. Hate the fact I can't even touch my toes. If one more person says, 'It's a daily practice,' I'll whack them across the back of the head with a rolled-up Stella McCartney yoga mat.

Forgot I *had* a Stella yoga mat. Rummaged for it and came across a Dior hipflask. Never used, only because I reckon I might look like a twat at Glasto carrying a Dior hipflask.

Anyway, Kate's diet looks doable. Not her actual diet – she's a very good cook, which surprises me. Proof even the most rock 'n' roll amongst us have some hobbies. If she fed me for a month, she'd have to roll me down the aisle.

She posted a diet from *Vogue* published in the 1970s that went viral on Twitter. It kicks off with a glass of wine for breakfast, apparently, and you HAVE to drink the rest of the bottle throughout the day (dry, pref Chablis, obvs). It also features eggs and steak – that's it. Three days, five pounds weight loss? Booze 'n' lose? Yup. Bottle of white wine per day will make running more interesting. As for weights, best not risk it, just in case I drop a dumbbell on the cat and kill it. Chance would be a fine thing . . .

According to *Vogue* 'regardless of what the scales say', muscle burns fat and muscle weighs more than fat so there's no actual point in weighing oneself. I'll cross-check that with a fitness expert, thank you very much, *Vogue*. Haven't forgiven you after buying a pair of black suede Isabel Marant knee-high boots with long fringes cascading down the back, as featured in the Feb issue. Almost ended up hospitalised with a broken neck after a wayward lone fringe became entangled in the down escalator at Oxford Circus.

Revised wedding diet – version 4

Today's date: 1 May 2018
Wedding deadline: 22 June 2018
Plan: 5:2

Notes: Five hundred or so calories each Monday and Thursday, 1,200 for the rest of the week. I'll be fine.

One slice of rye bread at 8am, a bowl of soup at 1pm, white fish and salad (no oil or dressing) at 6pm. No wine. No bread. No hummus. A beauty editor once told me that 'hummus is basically lard'. NO LARD. I don't even eat lard. Who the fuck eats lard? Actually, I remember my nanny cooking with lard.

Too stressed to think about complex diets. Have my dress fitting next week. Rolf Von Dee-dee set it up for 10am. Shit. How much weight can I lose in four days?

Revised wedding diet – version 5

Today's date: 18 May 2018
Wedding deadline: 22 June 2018
Plan: Birthday today, no carbs but lots of booze. 500 cals per day for rest of week.

Notes: Gonna get Rolf Von Dee-dee to see if I can join a really expensive gym but not pay. If I'm a member of a big, fashiony gym, I'll be scared into going. Wherever Pippa Middleton got her SUPER-hot wedding bod. Would book a free trial, but can't turn up wearing crappy ten-year-old Nike shit looking like a loser. Eucalyptus-scented towels in the changing rooms; must find something bougie to wear. Will ask Rolf Von Dee-dee to email the PRs.

Revised wedding diet – version 6

Today's date: 1 June 2018
Wedding deadline: 22 June 2018
Plan: Drink rosé all day long

Revised wedding diet – version 7

Today's date: 10 June 2018
Wedding deadline: 22 June 2018
Plan: There is no fucking plan. That's the fucking plan.

Notes: Work out for an hour. Feck me, I'm exhausted. Order one of their new-fangled bullet coffees they make with butter for a 'prolonged' something-or-other to do with getting skinny and not having a big belly. Ask how they make it, and wonder if lard would be a more effective ingredient. Cheaper than butter from cows that've been hand-fed their entire adult lives. Or was it grass-fed? Either or.

Head to dress fitting at Preen studio – and no, I don't want to talk about it.

Revised wedding diet – version 8

Today's date: 22 June 2018
Wedding deadline: 22 June 2018
Plan: Drink champagne from 8am

Notes: Attempt to walk down aisle without falling over.

Actually fall over later on, which is fine, really, considering I survived six months' worth of diet and gym stress. Consider promoting Rolf Von Dee-dee to head of wardrobe for honeymoon.

16

Marriage Vows

*The big day is finally here, and I can't
feel my face or find a nice bra*

22 June 2018

The morning of our wedding, I was a bundle of nerves. I couldn't think straight; who had the remote control? Certainly not me. I'd been on autopilot for years, not that I realised it at the time.

Sitting on the wooden floor of our bedroom, I put my head in my hands, trying to breathe. That's when I noticed a pack of tarot cards. Assumed long lost, they'd been shoved beneath the hairdryer I hardly ever used. Seeking inspiration from another dimension, I shuffled the deck, swooping it across the bedroom floor. *Only angels can help me now,* I thought.

With no clue as to what any of the cards meant, I went in search of the *Everything You Need to Know About Tarot* book that I hadn't set eyes upon for, what? At least a year? It had to be in the crap drawer.

The bedroom crap drawer was huge, deep, wide, cavernous – and full to the brim. One of several crap drawers in a house full of too much stuff: for years, I'd shoved and shuffled things from one place to the next, not ever knowing what to do with them. Bar Marie Kondo, does anyone really know what to do with 'stuff'? Bits 'n' bobs, old keys, pens, broken jewellery, coppers and spare twenty-pence pieces? Where should it all live, if not in a deep, wide, cavernous drawer?

Wedged beneath a pair of pregnancy Spanx – because why recycle them when there's a micro chance you may decide to have another baby in middle age? – I found it. Searching its index for 'P for Pentacles', relief washed over me.

'New beginnings.'

Good news, I thought, going on to pull four more cards. Quickly losing interest in promises of new starts, instead I opted for good tunes in the form of banging house music. It was 8am, and the house was already a bustle of activity. I switched on the radio and danced. Naked, obviously.

For ten minutes, I let rip, tits and ass bobbing around like setting jelly in a bowl. But still, if I'd had to fill out a form at the doctor's surgery detailing levels of anxiety, I'd have been a ten. Ten being 'call an ambulance' anxious. Actually, scrap that – make it twelve.

With 'dancing naked to house music for ten minutes' and 'seeking help from tarot' ticked off, the next obvious nerve-calming trick could only involve a trek to the fridge for champagne. Except *that* would result in chit-chat with the invasion of guests who filled our spare bedrooms. I'd been hiding in our bedroom for two hours, drowning in panic that flooded beneath the door like a horror movie. The wedding ahead had been incredibly badly planned: there had already been three date changes and an argument with best friends who'd tried on multiple occasions to convince me to 'not do it'.

But I was on autopilot, so I ignored them and plodded on with the idea regardless. Locked away in a rusty old cabinet, the remote control was well and truly lost.

I felt absurdly out of place in my own home; I couldn't face anyone. So: no booze. Instead, I swapped house tracks for shamanic ritualistic drumbeats. As you do. I'd just remembered that time in Ibiza when, with no money left to pay for a hotel or buy food, I decided to move into a squat with two Polish DJs. Somehow, I'd managed to 'Om' my way out of a panic attack while lying on a bare mattress in a squat after three days of clubbing. If I could Om my way out of *that* shit, I could Om my way out of anything. Soon, deep, rattling shamanic beats and a vibrating 'Om' (coming from the bloke on YouTube, not me) filled the bedroom. According to the timer running along the bottom of the video, the Om was set to play for the next hour and thirty minutes.

I dreaded to think what the crowd gathered in the kitchen below must've thought. Me, the woman who was soon to be officially part of the family, sitting on the floor upstairs wearing a pair of old M&S big-girl pants, surrounded by tattered tarot cards, with throbbing shamanic drumbeats blaring from her laptop. Whatever they thought, they'd be forgiven. I looked as mad as I felt.

With a head containing two hundred dripping wet hair extensions, I nodded to the beat of the drums. Things weren't looking great. I mean, my hair looked great, given I'd asked my hairdresser to double the number of extensions she usually added to my scalp. Extra-long hair that had once belonged to someone else: I supposed that was my something borrowed sorted. And it was borrowed in every sense, given I'd stuck my fake hair on a credit card. Something old? Well, that'll be me. Something new? The dress. Something blue? I'd found an old hanky.

Panic crept through the gaps in the windows, the woodwork, the plug sockets. Losing it, I decided now was as good a time as any to contact my spirit guides.

'Anyone up there? I need your help, and I'm talking about

Archangel Michael levels of help. I'd be forever grateful if he could assist in the search for my long-lost inner calm, as I'm feeling really out of control. Thank you. Asap, please? Thanks.'

The Pentacles had spoken. The wedding was going ahead, and I was to embark upon a new start. In two hours' time, I'd be a married woman. An 'honest' woman. Everything was sorted: the flowers, the guests, the lunch, the dress. Everything bar that one thing I couldn't remember.

Breathe. Visualise a forest. Breathe. Visualise trees.

I tried, but the only images I could muster were of my favourite TV show, *Absolutely Fabulous*. Updated for 2018, Saffy now identified as Simon. Saffy and Eddie were about to head to church for Patsy's fifth wedding, and Simon, upon finding her mum doing a line of coke in the downstairs loo, began shouting at her to pull her shit together. Simon wore a black suit, as though they were in mourning.

I felt trapped in the bedroom. I could hear our guests laughing and feasting on organic berries, pancakes and black coffee below. They were the kind of family I'd always wanted to be a part of – interesting, educated, peripatetic, intellectual – and yet for some reason, on the morning of my wedding, I couldn't face going downstairs to join them for breakfast. In the weeks running up to the wedding, I'd done nothing but drink myself into a stupor. Rosé, gin, beer, red wine. I don't even really *like* gin. The drinking eased the numbness.

As I sat there with a bath towel hanging loosely off my left tit, I reflected that, with 365 days of the year to choose from, I wouldn't intentionally pick my wedding day to be the day on which I lost it. But something had been brewing. Something didn't feel right. Something I chose to push down and ignore.

In fact, *I* felt ignored. We'd ignored each other – not intentionally, but we hadn't done anything about the chasm growing between us, either.

'Stacey?' The knock at the door interrupted the scene running through my mind involving me clutching a bouquet of fancy flowers and being carted off by an ambulance crew.

Mum poked her head round the door wearing her giant 'going out-out' curlers. 'Alright, luv? What's this crap music yer listening to?' she asked, shoving the door wide open, just in case one of the many houseguests would like to get a good look at my boobs.

Surveying the room like a proper Celtic mammy, I could tell what she was thinking. Crystals, tarot, shamanic drums: 'London nonsense'. Having been married three times herself, she knew the madness that lay before her on the floor was only to be expected. She'd probably been the same – minus the crystals, drumming, shamans, and Oms.

The house vibrated with nerves – mine, mostly. As we were getting married several years after having children, the idea that my husband shouldn't set eyes upon me until I walked down the aisle felt absurd. And yet, highly superstitious of anything deemed to be, well, even slightly superstitious, I switched off the Om, pulled on a pair of jeans and a top, folded the carrier containing my wedding dress over one arm, and braced myself to walk downstairs.

'See you soon!' I shouted towards the kitchen, playing the role of 'breezy bride'. Dead casual. Not having a panic attack WHATSOEVER.

I hugged both kids for a very long time, before reminding my daughter to wear the floral headband that matched my bouquet.

'NO,' she said, grumpily. 'Not wearing it.'

Promising both kids ice cream for breakfast, Mum took her by the hand and led her towards the kitchen.

No dogs were allowed at Marylebone registry office, a daft rule if ever I heard one.

'Shame you can't come,' I said to my Irish ex-husband, before heading to my friend's flat twelve doors down. Justin and his husband had already messaged. 'The champagne's on ice, baby.'

Jimmy Choo golden disco sandals, a small round pouch containing my wedding speech, eyeliner, lip salve, Ventolin inhaler, three Simone Rocha faux-pearl barrettes borrowed from the designer's PR, flowers, plus that thing I'd forgotten – and off I went to get married.

My best mate Kim opened the door I'd passed through many times over the years, mostly late to join a party at 2am. Luc passed the glass of champagne I'd been dreaming about since 7am. Four middle-aged people getting ready for a wedding, all of us wide-eyed with nerves.

I hung my dress on the back of the door frame, then sat in front of the mirror. Justin set to work on my fake hair, drying it off roughly before pinning dreamy pearlescent hair clips to the side of my head until the entire right side of my hair was swished back in a sort of Veronica Lake meets polished punk look. Well, at least that had been my hair brief (no Pinterest board, obvs). I like undone hair. Metaphorically, spiritually, emotionally, physically – undone suits me. I did my own make-up, adding extra lashings of black kohl.

We pulled up outside the newly renovated Marylebone registry office on a boiling hot day for early summer. It was 11am, and I already suffocated in a corset, skin damp from sweat. Mum was there, ready to play the role of stand-in father. The idea of being given away is weird enough at any age, but especially at forty-four. At least we'd managed to break one rule, reject some semblance of Victorian, antiquated tradition.

Then, as we went through some boring formalities in an ante-room, the registrar announced that only my father's name could be added to the wedding certificate. I stopped focusing on intricate cornicing, very much back in the room.

'What? I don't believe you. Only my father's name? That can't be possible. Are you telling me, only a father's name can legally go on a wedding certificate?* A father who isn't here and never really has been? The birth father who made it difficult for my mother to financially survive, so she had no choice but to take on three jobs? The same father who refused to let my stepfather adopt me? The stepfather, by the way – he's not here, either. I haven't seen him in fourteen years, because he disowned me when he met another woman. There are thirty people waiting for me, and half of them have flown in from America . . . '

As I trailed off, Kim tried to comfort me. Mum's hand squeezed mine.

'This is the patriarchy and it's utter bollocks,' I sobbed. My tears weren't from sadness, but anger. 'My mum brought me up. It's her name I want on my marriage certificate.'

Soaking wet from the heat but mostly the grilling, the wedding dress clung to my bare legs. After five minutes, the registrar softened. I read the document before me, written in language so outmoded it would make the Old Testament read like *Fifty Shades of Grey*.

I stared at the marriage certificate I'd just signed, imagining it more suited to being handwritten on an ancient scroll in calligraphy. Rules and regulations made up before women even had the vote, could buy houses, or have a credit card in their name. The whole thing felt archaic. What was I doing?

I'd requested to walk down the aisle to Fleetwood Mac's 'Everywhere'. As I looped my arm inside my mother's, my heart raced. She was wearing a wide-brimmed hat and a floral dress

---

* Too late for my wedding, legislation was finally changed in May 2021, meaning mothers could be added to marriage certificates. On 4 May that year, the *Guardian* reported: 'The reform to the Marriage Act marks the first time the names of both parents of the couple will be included on the marriage certificates, rather than just the names of the father or stepfather of each of the parties, a change that the government has previously resisted on cost grounds.'

from Hobbs, her hair cut into a sharp blond bob. She's always been attractive. I always noticed men looking at her when I was a child.

Mum and I stood behind the double doors of the registry office.

'Can you hear them all?' she said.

Lots of laughter and chatter. I looked at Mum. Our faces were damp, both hot and bothered; we needed face powder to take off the sweaty shine that was on the wrong side of 'get the glow'.

Someone employed by the registry office opened the doors from the other side. I took three steps forward and heard my friend Sara say, 'OMG, she's wearing white!' She clasped both hands over her mouth; she wasn't the only one who was surprised. They'd all expected a tuxedo or something red or outrageous. Still on autopilot, I walked down the aisle towards him. Like walking the plank, but with a smile. I hung on to the arm of my beaming mother, floating somewhere between the cornices of the ceiling and the flourishes on the curtains. How had any of this come about? A wedding date changed several times, last-minute plans made so badly, me in a long white gown . . .

Sara stood up to recite 'He's Not Perfect' by Bob Marley. Her words ricocheted around the room. I so wanted to believe them.

Heart full – or a bit empty. *Is this love? Am I even capable of it?*

I didn't know. What were we trying to prove – to our friends, to our children, to ourselves? Dopamine hits, yes. I can do that. Long-lasting love? Not sure.

I assumed love to be a cottage at Christmas.

Imagining this cottage, my mind wandered. I visualised squirrels making tracks in the snow.

Then our daughter screeched and the squirrels scarpered, bringing me back into the room. She looked as overwhelmed as I felt – no floral headband to match my bouquet. I knew she wouldn't wear it. I stood there, at the end of an aisle so short, Fleetwood Mac hadn't even made it to the vocals. The room fell silent.

I focused hard on the vows, repeating every line with intention. Self-conscious, I could feel myself floating towards the ceiling once again, off to join freshly painted decorative mouldings.

In sickness and in health? I think so. I mean, yes.

'I do.'

17

Marriage Will Save Me (From Abandonment)

Nowhere to turn in choppy seas, the ship sailed on. But not to the big Asda, to Gail's ...

'People with abandonment issues have a persistent fear of rejection or isolation. Characterised by symptoms such as insecurity and codependency, abandonment issues do not constitute a formal mental health diagnosis, says Harold Hong, M.D., a psychiatrist and the medical director at New Waters Recovery in Raleigh, North Carolina.

'Abandonment issues may stem from abuse, neglect or psychosocial stress experienced during childhood, such as divorce, death or illness. These traumatic experiences may have a significant effect on brain development and lead to psychiatric symptoms, such as depression and substance abuse disorders, later in life.'

– LIZZIE DUSZYNSKI-GOODMAN, 'Abandonment Issues', Forbes.com, reviewed by Ziv Cohen, M.D.

People have survived lives way harsher than mine. To say I'm thankful it's not me waking up each morning in [insert name of war-torn country/refugee camp] battling to keep my two children alive, is an understatement. I'm not a refugee who escaped war. I did not lose both parents to be brought up in the care-home system. Born with limbs and organs that work – mostly, bar a couple of things, but nothing too serious – I don't have difficulties with mobility or mental impairment. I was not subjected to physical violence at the hands of a family member.

Today, I do not feed myself and my kids from the local food bank.

I could go on and on and on, but is it useful? Is it helpful to compare myself to those living less fortunate lives, surviving each day in unimaginable circumstances? Sometimes it is. Like when I know I'm being utterly ridiculous and need to get a grip. I mean, I once managed to avoid a panic attack triggered by a PTA WhatsApp group chat (see page 180 by rewatching Turia Pitt's recovery video on Instagram. In 2011, running a 100km ultramarathon in the Australian bush, Pitt was surrounded by an out-of-control fire. Unable to outrun it, she suffered severe burns covering sixty-five per cent of her body. It took medics several hours to reach her, and her unbelievable journey, from hospitalised burns victim covered head to toe in bandages, to learning to walk and eventually run again is beyond moving. Despite major scarring, she went on to have children, launch a podcast, and become an author and motivational speaker. Her Instagram videos move me every single time, and during dark days, her posts provide a light it's often difficult to see when you're emotionally on the floor.

Shoving shame, embarrassment, guilt, white privilege, and all that to one side for a moment, prior to sitting in my therapist's office for four years straight (aka 'Doing The Work'), I had off-the-scale abandonment issues. They affected my career, friendships, money, confidence, self-worth, romantic relationships and even early motherhood. The way in which I perceived rejection was extreme to the point of damaging.

Despite many hours of therapy, abandonment still occasionally comes out to play. Five years ago, an abandonment-induced episode would leave me feeling as though I'd been stung by a thousand wasps. These days, the feelings are far less severe. Less wasps, more like nits. If you've never had nits before, congratulations, I'm very happy for you. I have them on a weekly basis. These days, when my inner abandoned child shows up, I apply a dollop of metaphorical nit lotion and self-soothe her until she's calm again. Is your head itching yet? Sorry. I'll stop with the nit metaphor.

Pre-therapy, though, one sniff of abandonment and that was it: a swarm of angry wasps would engulf my body, and I'd be in agony. A passing comment, an odd look, a terse text would be enough to destabilise me for days. Before having therapy, whenever I encountered rejection, my body would react in such a visceral way. First I'd erupt, then I'd run as fast as I could, as far away as possible.

I know this all sounds very dramatic and weird, but abandonment once felt so violent, it was as though my body was under severe attack.

For example:

1. When I was about thirty, an ex-boyfriend didn't answer his phone. Not just for a couple of hours, but all day. So, I called him 8,920 times and sent so many texts, I reckon I must have filled his inbox to capacity. In a state of panic, I called several of his friends, who, given it was a weekday (and all the way back then, people worked in actual offices), didn't pick up their phones either. At around 4pm, I decided to phone his mum to break the bad news.

   'Hi, it's me, Stacey. Sorry to be the bearer of such terrible news, but your son's been murdered, or involved in a car crash, or fallen into the Thames and drowned. I'm not sure which, but he's definitely dead. One hundred per cent. I can feel it. For sure.'

As I searched for her number in my phone, he rang. From the golf course. Where he couldn't answer his phone. 'What's wrong?' he asked.

'I thought you were dead,' I replied.

'Are you mad?' he said.

'Probably,' I replied.

2.   A firm email from a boss or colleague was once enough to make my heart race to the point of needing a defibrillator. Mouth dry, heart pounding, brain scrambled, for the rest of the day, I'd be unable to think of anything else. Turning their words over and over in my mind, I'd conjure up all kinds of fantastical imagined things that I could've done to upset them. One of these was always simply, 'I'm not good enough' – which, to be fair, is a daily thought that's buzzed through my brain ever since I can remember. Even if a meeting had gone well at work, and I'd been personally congratulated as someone with a 'great idea', still I'd berate myself for not doing enough. For not *being* enough.

Say an editor or a senior member of the team sent an email that was direct and business-like, something to the point. For example:

Hi S,
Really need your copy by 3pm. Subs on a deadline
before the bank holiday and art need to do layout before
E.O.P.
Thanks.

... rather than interpret its tone as, 'Oh, this person seems super busy, better get my copy in before 3pm,' I'd traipse off to the loo, where I'd sit for a good two hours trying to figure out how best to hand in my notice. Ass numb on account of the cheap plastic loo seat, I'd eventually leave the bog and head to my desk to begin typing my resignation letter.

Dear XXX,

Regarding email sent at 10.08am today enquiring as to the whereabouts of copy due to be filed by 3pm: just to inform you I have, of course, written the aforementioned copy, and yes, I am, of course, in the process of a final edit. And yes, of course, I had initially planned to submit the EDITED copy today. However, upon reflection and having now read your OTT aggressive email, I'm afraid I have no choice but to quit.

There'll be no more copy from me from now on.

Want my advice? Work on your tone.

With very best wishes – and hope you have a great bank holiday weekend,

Stacey

On my way back to my desk, or even in the loo itself, I'd inevitably bump into the author of said devastating email.

'Hiya, you alright?' they'd ask, smiling.

'Well, well, well,' I'd want to reply. 'It's you, the person out to kill me. Don't worry, pal, you aggressive git, you win. I quit.'

Nervous system finally settling down to a steady eight, instead I'd say, 'Yeah, I'm great thanks, you?'

3. This one's a goodie and, in a far less extreme way, continues today. It can leave me feeling as though I've been punched hard in the stomach; my head begins to spin

and my face collapses in such a way that more than once, I've resorted to Dr Google, keying in the words 'signs of stroke, contorted weird face, can't feel lips'. My hands would develop pins and needles, and my legs would cease to work. Hell on earth! What is this catastrophe, I hear you cry!?

Upon discovering either one of my children haven't been invited to a birthday party by a child previously presumed to be a really good mate – well, let's just say, all hell lets loose. And it's not just birthdays. Halloween parties, Christmas, Hanukkah – and we're not even Jewish. Upon discovering one of the kids hasn't been invited to something, the red mist descends.

It happened last weekend. A child who has always been invited to my son's birthday parties didn't invite him to his. I wanted to murder the kid's entire family – by strangulation, in the middle of the night, by breaking and entering. I fantasised about having a boxing match with the mum outside the school gate, professional outfit, gloves and all. Seeing my son that upset made me feel sick for two days.

The most memorable non-invite situation, however, happened when my daughter was three. Dropping her off at nursery one morning, I noticed a little girl handing out party invitations. Psychotic, I hung back to see whether my daughter would get one. I counted that little bit*h hand out ten invitations IN FRONT OF MY DAUGHTER without handing one to her. Apoplectic, I rang her father.

'We need to find a new nursery.'
'What? Why? What happened?'
'Oh, you won't believe it.'
'What? Is she OK?'
'No, she is not OK.'

'Oh God, do I need to call BUPA?'

'What? Maybe, God knows how she'll react when she realises. She hasn't been invited to Olive's c**ting birthday party. I'm blocking her mother on WhatsApp, and I've told the nursery we won't be back.'

Remembering I had a job, I then retracted the resignation from the nursery and drove off to work, only to pull over six minutes later intending to block Olive's mother immediately. I parked badly, and adjusted my car seat to horizontal.

Which means I was lying down in my car outside the posh coffee shop in Queen's Park, wearing oversized sunglasses despite it being the cloudiest day all winter, when a police officer knocked on the car window. I was crying so hard it took a minute to locate the button to open it.

'Everything OK?' he asked, when I eventually found the strength to open the window.

'No! Not at all!'

'Aren't you feeling well?'

'NO! I'm bloody well not. My three-year-old daughter hasn't been invited to Olive's birthday party, and I'm so upset I can't breathe. Or drive.'

'Have you been drinking, madam?'

The above examples are the most extreme; most daily worries were far less dramatic.

Years before meeting The Therapist, I realised the daily upset and extreme reaction could be lessened by reducing my exposure to things that genuinely felt like an attack. Seven or so years ago, I left Facebook, and the weeks that followed felt like a break-up. Actual grief; it was shocking. The kids were young, my career was floundering, and I mourned daily connection. Between nappies, teething and potty training, inane updates had provided a welcome break.

*

Somewhere, somehow, in my relationship, I began to lose myself. Coupled with a deep-rooted fear the father of my children would abandon me, I felt too scared to tackle the ever-widening cracks in our relationship. In losing myself, I was also losing him. So, now what?

I'll tell you.

I remember sitting on a large yellow chair in the small snug in the downstairs front room of our house, thinking. His ability to disappear into a new job, a change of career, was admirable; I've always been drawn to men with smart minds who are deep thinkers. Stimulated by his new world – whether he meant to or not – he slowly began to break away from me. Add two young children to the mix, or rather, one baby and one two-year-old, and I felt isolated and lonely.

> 'Perhaps the greatest psychological pain one can inflict on a loved one is to repeatedly ignore them. Attention is our most valuable emotional currency.'
> – JILLIAN TURECKI, @JillianTurecki

It was nothing to do with the fact that, now aged five, our daughter would make the perfect flower girl. A wedding, in my mind, was a way of reconnecting to him, to us, to myself, to the perfect family unit I'd always wanted. The wedding would bring a return to pre-baby romance, and I'd feel part of a couple again. He'd talk to me, want to spend more time with me. I'd be less of a nightmare, less unreliable with dates and timings, and money and finances. I'd sort myself out.

I made a list of all the things marriage would fix:

1. We'll go out more, even if it's just to the pub. We'll hold hands and laugh like we used to.
2. He'll look at me and tell me he loves me. Really look at me, though. He won't just say, 'Love you,' while loading the dishwasher or walking out the door.

3. We'll desire each other again and want to have sex a few times each week.
4. He'll kiss me deeply.
5. I'll kiss him back. Long, deep, romantic kissing that ends everywhere and nowhere.
6. I'll come to terms with the fact I no longer need daring or extra; it's a curled-up, gentle romance filled with warmth and love I crave now.
7. We'll make a vow to be together – in sickness and in health, for richer or poorer. We'll love one another for ever.

I kept the list inside my head. A list of hope that reads as childish babble, a ridiculous fantasy. Marriage is the opposite of a teenage romance; it isn't a bed of roses, it's teamwork and running a home, raising children and making joint financial decisions. Marriage is compromise and selflessness, which sounds a bit boring, but that's the trade-off for safety and togetherness. The fine balance is what keeps it all glued together: keep holding hands, keep the love alive in every way possible.

I went along with the make-believe Brexit engagement. On the outside, we had it all: the house (such a lovely house), the kids (a boy and a girl), the upcoming wedding, a designer who'd showed at Fashion Week making my dress. And yet, I've never felt so alone.

Five years on from the day I had sat in the yellow chair, holding our two-month-old daughter in my arms, listening to his plans for a new career, I assumed we'd be fine. In hindsight, assumption means nothing. Even while pregnant with our second child, we'd already begun living separate lives.

Weekends were the same on repeat. With the kids, but alone, I'd go to the park, buy a strong coffee, and play in the sandpit, or rather, 'snake pit'. A veritable nest of vipers, I'd always have a blow-up with someone over their child stealing my children's special sandpit toys. After the sixth theft, I began naming our buckets and spades, angrily writing my initials with a thick black waterproof Sharpie I carried in the nappy bag. I initialled everything, bar the little sieve thing, because it was impossible to write on; instead, it had its own plastic tag tied to it with a piece of string. I watched other people's toddlers like a hawk observing a mouse, ready to pounce the moment someone dared take off with our tractors, diggers and racing cars. Serves me right for taking so much shit to the park.

We didn't do anything together as a couple, and even if we did, I felt I'd have nothing to say on a night out. 'Wanna hear about the latest sandpit drama?'

My world became smaller as his grew. This shouldn't necessarily destabilise a relationship or a marriage, but there were things I hadn't dealt with, things from childhood that rendered me fearful of rejection. As my world grew smaller, my confidence began to shrink, too. I wasn't happy at home, in the sandpit, at the nursery gate. I couldn't make new friends. I felt awkward and odd, alone and discombobulated. Everything was out of control. I'd lost all sense of agency, and of what I was bringing to the party – the party, in this case, being my relationship.

We never socialised together, never received joint invitations, and we only hosted two dinner parties at our house, after which I vowed I'd never do it again. On the outside, I had the perfect family unit I'd dreamed of. On the inside, I was alone.

Five Thoughts On ... Letting Go of an Old Life by Anne Marie Curtis

Anne Marie Curtis is the ex-editor-in-chief of *ELLE UK*, and founder of *Calendar Magazine*

1. **Take a moment.** The most important advice I ever received was from my life coach, who told me, post

leaving *ELLE* after fifteen years (and spending thirty years working on magazines), to ... do nothing. After three decades working in a fast-moving environment where my focus was always on being on to the next thing, this was the hardest thing I had ever done. It involved a lot of unpacking and working through feelings of loss and grief. But taking that time out to refocus, grieve and figure out where I wanted to go next was an invaluable exercise.

2. **Forge a new identity.** After working in the fashion industry as an editor for my entire career, my work identity felt inseparable from who I actually was and am as a person. This was a tricky one to crack (and remains a work in progress!). Working in fashion is very much tied up with status and peer approval, so unpacking that was complex and, at times, painful. But, in order to grow, you have to let go of the 'old you' and allow the fully minted new version to present itself.

3. **Hold your nerve.** Another brilliant piece of advice. This one was imparted to me by a fellow editor, who was a couple of years ahead of me in the process of reforging a new career post-fashion glossies. The leap into the unknown can feel terrifying, so our instinct can be to stick with what we know. It takes a good while to evolve, with many twists and turns along the way, but now I am out the other side, I can honestly say it's so much better to be brave and take risks, however scary it might seem. Feel the fear and do it anyway!

4. **It's fine to change your mind.** Here's the thing: no one – literally NO ONE – cares about or judges what you are doing as much as you do. Everyone is figuring it

out, so it's fine to make mistakes, fail at stuff and change your mind along the way. My 'plan' from three years ago is actually quite different to how things look now, and they will no doubt look different again in another three. It's important to be open to new experiences and new ways of doing things.

5. **No woman is an island.** Just remember you are not alone. I've been truly amazed by all the brilliant women I've connected with in the past few years, many of whom have gone through a similar journey of change. It's been both an education and a voyage of discovery. Don't be afraid to reach out to people you may not know well, or those who are outside of your 'bubble' or field of experience – you'll be surprised by how open people are to connecting. Just be prepared to be honest about what's going on rather than presenting a perfect image of success.

18

Marriage Over

Knowing when to walk away.
Knowing when to put yourself first

I'd walked the plank. Made it to the end of the aisle. What would happen next, I couldn't have told you; I'd never read that part of the story. Headed to the murky depths below, would I ever make it to the surface again?

He looked handsome in Dior, standing there, at the end of the aisle. Waiting for his bride.

A poem recited I couldn't quite grasp. Spoken, not meant. Heard, not understood. No fathers to hear the words that reverberated around the room. A charade. A pastiche. A story I knew off by heart.

Repeat after me, she'd said.

'I do,' we'd complied.

We'd let it slide. We, or me? Had I let us down?

In the years before our wedding day, we'd bought a house seen and purchased a bit too quickly. I'm not sure he even wanted to move there, to north-west London. I'd offered to oversee renovations: to be in charge, take control. I could do that. I was OK at that.

The house was taken back to brick, and at one point had no ceilings. An empty shell. I liked it like that. No rooms, no door-ways, no kitchen. No restrictions to what life should be and why.

With a twelve-month-old in a pram, I'd started back at work for three months. But there were too many questions – at work, then at the weekends on site. I couldn't make a decision. I couldn't think straight. Post-natal fog. Soundproofing and underfloor heating. Four fashion shoots to organise and plan. Empty-brained, I stared in agreement. At home, at work, at the new house, in my relationship with my ex, I just nodded. 'Hmm, yes, I agree.'

Bland, beige, off-white and grey interiors; I had no clue which colours to choose. I had a baby. I wanted another. The babies, the relationship, the house. I'd asked for a Kenwood blender; I needed to bake a cake.

Bland, beige, off-white and grey interiors – that's what every-one else had, so that's what I chose, too.

I had a baby, and then I had another.

I couldn't think straight. Everything was a mess – inside the house, inside my head, at work, in our relationship. A heavy red velvet curtain had lowered, too heavy to raise, and I was trapped behind it, pretending everything was OK. I needed to bake cakes, to host coffee mornings, to become the polar opposite to the woman I once was. I decided I would have to start sending thank-you cards. Isn't that what you do when you're a grown-up?

Lean into the stultifying state of motherhood and marriage. Bretons and Bugaboos, the armour of middle-class motherhood. Fit in. Go to the baby music groups. Don't mention the irre-sponsible person I once was, a wild spirit since replaced by this imagined opposite. Go to the art club, make wonky pottery. Fit in. Get a library membership.

Not fitting in anywhere, I reached back to find myself, but the old me had left a while ago. I hadn't noticed. Hadn't heard the door slam.

Then I met him.

He saw me first.

PART 3

Motherhood

Only a psychopath would go into the nitty-gritty details of birth with a first-time mother.

'Listen, you're going to birth something very large through a too-small hole, and it's gonna be bloodshed messy.'

It's also messy when both babies are so big, they have to be removed via the sunroof. Too posh to push? Nah, my C-sections weren't an easy way out, something I only realised as I watched my friends with vaginally delivered babies bounce back within a few days. Meanwhile, five days later, I was practically stretchered out of the hospital with a red flashing light attached to my forehead.

As for the weeks that follow childbirth, no woman needs to hear it may not all be knitted bonnets, cupcakes and picnics in the park. Or wait, maybe she does. Should we be more open about the shitshow that's about to unfurl? Every woman is different, but had someone taken me gently to one side and said, 'Listen, love, you're not going anywhere for several weeks, so just get your head into that mode,' I may have relaxed a bit . . .

Instead, gripped by post-natal depression and embarrassed to feel so unhappy during the so-called blissed-out stage of early motherhood, I've never felt more of a failure. A failure not just as a mother, but as a woman. It was a boiling hot July when I had my first child. Other new mums managed to not only carry a floral blanket to the park, but also a homemade picnic – all without accidentally leaving the baby at home. FFS! They were breastfeeding newborns under trees while I was holed up in my bedroom, blinds clamped shut, crying and ordering everything in a size eight from the MatchesFashion sale, despite weighing fifteen stone. I properly lost my shit.

Scared social services would take my baby away, I kept schtum.

Trigger warning: in Chapter 20: Sad Mother, I detail one of my darkest days. I apologise in advance if you find it upsetting or triggering. Please skip ahead instead.

19

Young Mother

Too much too soon . . .

I was high on ecstasy the first time I fell pregnant. 'Fell'. Such an odd way to describe sperm travelling the dark, winding road otherwise known as a fallopian tube in the hope of colliding with an egg. Sperm burrowing deep inside said egg is not 'falling' – but I suppose, in a way, I did fall. I fell into a nightclub. I fell around a dancefloor. I fell into the arms of a perfect-looking creature called Tim. He'd never met his dad, and his mum refused to discuss it.

I lived in a tiny boxroom in Marble Arch. Big enough for a single bed and a small wardrobe. I've never felt so unhappy in my life. Actually, rewind. 'Unhappy'? It was without a shadow of a doubt the most toxic, destabilising, utterly terrifying time of my life.

The boxroom was supposed to be an emergency short-term plan, a stopgap for a couple of months after escaping a psychotic flatmate whose name I won't mention because, twenty-five years later, the mere mention of it still sends a shiver down my spine. I think I met her in a nightclub, I can't remember – perhaps it was a bar. I was so smashed back then, it's hard to recall details, so let's go back to being in bed off my head on E with a stranger, in a boxroom somewhere in Marble Arch.

It was 1996, and I was twenty-two. Tim had excellent dance moves, a beautiful mouth and edgy style. I could tell at a glance he worked in fashion. I have no clue what happened between arriving at the club, meeting him and ending up in bed; I just remember we stayed in bed for a day and a night, drinking vodka and taking E and cocaine. On Monday morning, we both said our goodbyes and left for work. In the weeks that followed, I fell in love with the beautiful, blond, handsome stranger I'd met in the early hours of the morning, and together we rolled around bars and warehouse parties in Shoreditch, years before E1 turned into the Disneyland it's since become.

I knew something about him made me insanely jealous (in his company, I became deranged, love obsessed, insecure and just manic), but I had no idea the rush of feelings was due to being pregnant. While getting ready to go out one evening, I found I couldn't do up my trousers. My stomach was bloated and fizzed inside. I felt mad and teary. I remember going to a nightclub, getting smashed and high, and ending up in a fight with a girl at the bar because I thought she'd looked at my boyfriend.

Even when I missed a period, I remained in a state of denial. I worked for Paul Smith at his head office, earning £13,000 per annum as a press officer. I'd often turn up having had no sleep and borrow something to wear straight off the press rail. The office was in a series of beautiful old buildings with original floorboards and twisting staircases. One morning, not particularly hungover, for a change, I was suddenly aware of the smell of rat droppings beneath the floorboards. As I climbed the stairs, I became short of breath, my asthma worsening with each step. I looked down at my belly, housed in a purple chiffon dress by the designer for whom I worked, and wondered, *Is there a baby in there?*

I rushed to the pharmacy at lunchtime, utterly convinced there was simply no way I could be pregnant. I waited until I got home to do the pregnancy test. My flatmates were out, so I had the place to myself. Just as well, given the scream that escaped my mouth as I doubled over in shock. The blue lines appeared within seconds. Pregnant.

Definitely pregnant.

Within a few days, morning sickness erupted, and nothing felt the same. I called my mum, but she was having her own issues leaving her marriage. Back then, I didn't have the close network of friends I have now, and so, with no one to confide in, I went to the doctor to book an abortion. The night before the operation, Tim said we should go out. I remember the weather being warm, but not much else. Not much else, because after two vodkas, I swallowed the ecstasy Tim had handed me with a smile.

The following morning, I took the tube to the Royal Free Hospital alone. A nurse handed me a blue-and-white gown and prepped me for surgery. With E still coursing through my veins, I lay in a room with a gathering of other women ready to terminate the foetus inside them. I remember a nurse taking me by the hand, stroking the top of it by way of comfort. It was the most love I'd been shown for a while. She whispered into my ear that it wasn't too late, and that 'God would want me to have this baby'.

No, he wouldn't, I remember thinking. *God would be appalled.*

Tim was out on a drug bender when I came out of surgery, so no one came to pick me up from hospital. I lied and said a friend was waiting in a cab outside, and caught a bus home on my own instead. Staring out the window at busy passers-by, I arrived at Marble Arch just before nightfall. As I climbed the stairs to my boxroom, one unsteady foot then the other, I knew I'd always remember this: one of the loneliest days of my life.

Leaving home at a young age, prematurely assuming the role of someone older and wiser, on a mission to be anywhere but festering in suburbia, I'd catapulted myself into adulthood too soon. At the age of twenty-two – not a child, but not a fully fledged adult, either – the abortion shone a spotlight on the disarray: partying too much, having no money, winging it without a plan.

Loneliness hidden behind a façade of fun. I had friends, but not like I do now.

I had a feckless boyfriend, a job I liked, a cheap bedroom in a flat located in the middle of town. Two out of three isn't bad: a starter career in a starter flat, terrible taste in boyfriends, but I guess you can't have it all. A baby, though. That had focused the mind. Half wanting to keep it, half not knowing how.

I could've gone to my family for help, but a deep sense of shame at what had just happened prevented me from visiting them. Keen to avoid endless questions, I stayed in London and crawled into bed, a stiff futon mattress on the floor. Drifting off to the sound of my flatmates cooking in the kitchen, I heard an argument start.

We each had our own cupboards, our own section of the fridge, but through the thin walls, someone was accusing someone else of stealing their food. A packet of pasta and a carton of orange juice. *I think that might have been me. I have to get out of here,* I remember thinking. But where would I go? I had no one to turn to, no family down south – and, having recently escaped a scary flatmate, I knew the dangers of ending up in the wrong house share only too well.

The dangers of the wrong men? Well, that was a lesson I'd yet to learn.

20

Sad Mother

Hide the knives, I'm scared I'll kill the baby

The baby was eleven months old when the card landed on my doorstep. Instantly recognising the familiar swirls, the elaborate cursive I've known since the age of nineteen, I opened the envelope in the stairwell of our flat. I stared at the words I couldn't quite make out, but it was nothing to do with the sender's dramatic handwriting. A fuzzy haze lowered; my stomach churned.

'You don't seem happy. I want the old you back, she was ace,' the card read.

Writing once as familiar as Marmite on toast now seemed to belong to a total stranger. What did I used to be like? And what had made me so 'ace'? I needed to know.

'You weren't happy on maternity leave, and now you don't seem happy being back at work,' the friend continued over text message, after I messaged to thank her for the card. 'Maybe you should see somebody.'

Who, I wondered? Christopher Kane? Miuccia Prada? Marc Jacobs? Should I wear more print? Would that make me jolly? Pass me the spring florals and everything will be OK – oh, wait, designers don't make clothes in size eighteen.

She was right, of course. I wasn't happy. I wasn't happy at all.

I didn't have a 'golf ball' pregnancy, like so many other women I know, whose bodies remained the same shape bar a neat little bump. *Non.* I looked like a bus. Forget randoms on the tube shouting, 'When's the football team due?', even the medical profession appeared baffled by my size. During a routine scan, reading measurements of the baby's femur and skull (which is how the birth weight is predicted), a nurse sucked air through her teeth. 'Geez,' she eventually said, once the shock had worn off.

By the third trimester, I knew there was no way I'd agree to anything but a planned C-section. Especially given my 'geriatric mother' status (aka I was over the age of thirty-five, cheeky bastards). Distraught, I'd spend hours googling 'twelve-pound baby stuck in vagina'. At around thirty weeks pregnant, I stopped sleeping.

On 12 July, I was tired before the birth had even begun. I was instructed to lie down on a bed by an older nurse while she placed a large round silver thing on my tummy and pressed the other side to her ear. Nervous, I did my usual thing and began to overcompensate with inane chatter and friendly banter. How could she possibly have known that with each excitable question asked, I was becoming an increasingly highly charged nervous wreck. Breaking out into a sweat, I could feel myself going. I knew I was about to cry.

'Everything OK?' I asked, body beginning to shake, yet trying to remain breezy and upbeat.

'I'm sure it's fine, I just can't locate the baby's heartbeat,' she replied, at which point, I let out a bloodcurdling scream that caused several nurses to rush towards my bed. The poor woman. One minute she's discussing Florence and the Machine, the next she needs a hearing aid on account of my screeching, 'IS MY BABY DEAD?!'

That's when they hooked me up to a heartbeat monitor so I could hear the reassuring drum of life inside me. Hearing his heartbeat was the only thing capable of keeping me calm.

The drugs did their work, and I couldn't feel a thing – not my toes, my legs, or anything below my neck. I did feel utter elation at seeing his face, though. Although I'd never been told, I knew he was a boy – I just knew – and his name had come to me in a dream two days prior to his delivery. Aided and abetted by the oxytocin being pumped through my veins, hearing his loud scream for the first time induced the biggest high of my life. Weighed, measured and cleaned up a little, the very handsome obstetrician who'd pulled him out gently placed our baby's cherubic nine-pound body upon my chest. Not the twelve-pounder he'd been predicted to be. In the days that followed, I began doubting my decision to have had him by C-section. *Am I a failure, am I too posh to push?* It was the first of many perceived failures to come.

Back in bed, the baby nestled on to my breast, sucking as hard as he could, his little alien face staring up at mine, huge eyes following me around.

'Is anything coming out?' I asked the nurse.

'Just keep going,' she replied. 'This bit's called colostrum; it's full of good stuff your baby needs for his immune system.'

I lay there, staring down at his head, his bird-like mouth sucking as hard as it could, until, worn out, he drifted off to sleep. Each time this happened, I'd lay him back in his crib, where he'd immediately wake up and start crying again. Every attempt to sink into sleep was lost – even when the baby *was* asleep, someone would be checking my blood pressure or a nearby machine would bleep and wake me up. Whenever he cried, I would stretch my catheter as I strained to pick him up, and the endless cycle of breastfeeding would continue.

The following day, exhausted and sore, I asked if I should carry on.

'Yes, yes, your milk will come in,' they all said, between feeling my breasts, pinching a nipple into a point so they could pop it like a funnel in the baby's mouth.

The second night in hospital was the same. As was the third and fourth. At some point around day four, I threw a cup of coffee at the wall. Days blended into night and the baby, yellow from jaundice, was popped into a special heater. I was glad of the break, to be honest. On day five or six, we returned home to our flat to discover a pipe had burst, causing water to flood through the ceiling, so we dragged a mattress from the spare room and slept on the hallway floor. The following morning, all three of us cried.

Visitors came, and we sometimes ventured outside, me wad-dling like a duck, my ass so big my ex renamed me 'bear bum'. Days and nights of trying to breastfeed. The baby eventually lost weight. As he screamed his head off during a routine check-up at a healthcare centre not decorated since the 1970s, I asked what I should do about feeding.

'Keep going with breastfeeding,' they all said. 'Your milk will eventually come.'

Almost sixteen stone, massive tits, no milk. I mean, really? What are the chances?

I checked Facebook daily, looking at other mothers' pic-tures, marvelling at their joy. The pretty back gardens decked with bunting and colourful cupcakes in honour of the Jubilee. Family gatherings, christenings, birthday parties, mummies in pretty floral dresses, smiling babies, Pimms and lemonade, happy summer days. Eventually, I stopped looking; their version of motherhood made me feel like a miserable failure. I went to Westfield to stare through the Prada window. Much better.

On day twenty-eight, utterly deranged from tiredness, I rang my then-boss, remembering she'd had issues breastfeeding one of her own brood. She gave me the number of a woman who might be able to help. Sweet relief came in the form of a staunchly dressed woman who spoke in a no-nonsense tone. Walking across the floor of our flat, she instructed me to 'open' my shirt. Taking one breast in her hand, she gave it a squeeze. 'Absolutely no milk in here whatsoever. If this were the Victorian times, he'd be dead. But thankfully it isn't. Righty-ho, here's how to make up formula milk. And here's a list of everything you need, including the best bottles and so on. It's off to Boots for Daddy. Tally-ho!'

And poof, in a cloud of confident knowing, she disappeared. A huge wave of relief washed over me. Thank God someone had finally given me permission to feed him formula. And thank God it wasn't 1835.

Sometime around mid-September, I remember lying down on our bed, the fading sun tapping at our bedroom window, attempting to entice me outside. *Bother someone else with your golden rays of positivity*, I thought, as I pulled the blinds shut. Bright white stripes of light still managed to sneak through the wooden blinds, shining on the bedding like knife blades.

It was a Saturday afternoon and my boyfriend had gone to the football. I walked to the kitchen to make a cup of tea. Our flat was located at the top of a five-storey house, and the open-plan living space had a small terrace leading off it. I opened the patio doors and stepped outside. Staring at the ginormous tree in the distance, I'd forgotten what I was supposed to be doing. The baby began to scream downstairs.

I walked down to his bedroom in a daze. His face was red from screaming. I felt something inside me snap. I didn't want to do this any more. I didn't want to stay at home. I wanted my old life back. In my old life, I'd had a sense of control. I'd remembered things, I'd had purpose, I'd worn nice clothes as opposed to misshapen cardigans and maternity jeans with elasticated waistbands.

Without realising, I carried him upstairs.

Finding myself standing by the cutlery drawer, I opened it.

The long, sharp, shiny knives my boyfriend used for carving meat reminded me of the irritating white stripes of sunlight that decorated our bed downstairs. I felt comforted and safe. The baby stopped crying.

I don't recall picking up the knife, but I remember thinking how pretty it looked. Neat and orderly, a knife has a purpose – unlike me, a woman who, despite all her best efforts, was unable to get to grips with the baby thing.

Knife in hand, I pressed him gently to my chest and walked towards the open patio door. I reached the high-up balcony and paused. Should I throw him over the railing, or should I jump, holding him? If I threw him first, what if I didn't have the courage to jump? Should I kill him with the knife, then slash my wrists afterwards? What if he survived and I died? What if he died and I survived?

The thoughts were flickering fast. The knife, the railings, the stabbing, the jumping.

Too many options to choose from.

The thought of him dead and me alive pulled me back inside. Back in my body, I put the knife away and closed the cutlery drawer. Then I locked the patio door and held my baby and cried.

In that moment, I understood two things: I loved this child more than anything I'd ever loved before, and I needed help.

I'd been ignoring the feelings of sadness, brushing the emotions under the carpet, fearful that if I said the words, 'I *think* I *might* have post-natal depression,' someone would take him away.

I went to the doctor but didn't tell her about the terrace or the knife. Instead, I said, 'I'm feeling a bit sad.' She gave me a prescription for antidepressants, tablets I never even bothered to pick up. Instead, I began to leave the house more regularly, heading off to places other than Westfield.

I walked the London streets, pushing the pram. Loneliness strangled me, and I wondered if passers-by could see the sadness glowing around me, like a Ready Brek ad from the eighties. *An incapable mother.* Is that what they all thought?

After ten months, I'd grown used to the routine of maternity leave, used to the depression that nipped at the outer edges of my being: a harsh, throbbing frostbite not bad enough to cause me to lose a limb. Used to pulling on an oversized cardigan of tiredness each morning, I liked hiding away.

My pregnant body had grown bigger than I could've ever imagined. Just after the baby was born, I weighed fourteen stone, nine pounds. I felt like an inflated version of somebody I once knew.

Before I knew it, I was back at work. Walking down Carnaby Street one day, I bumped into a friend I'd met at antenatal class.

'Wow, look at you,' she said. 'So there *was* a slim woman underneath all that fat and water retention after all!'

I laughed it off.

Back at work five days a week, I expected life to go back to how it used to be. I'd be *me* again. But I hadn't factored in missing my son.

Monday was great. I'd skip out of the door, giddy at the thought of being able to buy a coffee without a small hand covered in porridge pawing at my shirt. Tuesday was fine, too. By Wednesday, I'd leave the house with small stabs of pain flickering in my heart, and at the end of the day, I'd jam my body on to the tube at 5pm.

Thursday was more of the same, yet harder. As for Friday – well, it was a write-off. Waking up riddled with anxiety, I never wanted to leave him again. Being on my own in a coffee shop felt pointless. My heart felt as though it had been torn from my chest, as though it was attached to my son via a long piece of string, like an elastic band pulled to its limit. By Friday, the string was too short, stretched too taut, and if I ventured too far, it pulled, jolting me back, showing me I didn't want to leave him for this much time during the week. I didn't want to be a full-time mother, but nor did I want to work full-time. And yet working part-time would drastically reduce my income.

I was stuck; I didn't know what to do. So, I reverted to old habits and shopped. Having lost four of the five stones I'd gained, I bought a pair of Miu Miu trousers to celebrate. And a Celine bag, so I didn't have to carry my trainers inside a canvas tote. As for the rest – well, it's a very long list.

I remember the day the haze of post-natal depression lifted. I remember where I was, the time of day, and even what I was wearing. I was backstage at an Oasis concert, wearing a purple jumpsuit festooned with flowers by Isabel Marant. I remember feeling the sun on my face. Walking along a grassy path back-stage, the distant sound of the warm-up band in my ears, my feet comfortable in Isabel Marant wedge sandals, beer in hand, the heavy luggage of the low mood I'd carried around for the past thirteen months suddenly lifted. A heavy blackout curtain was pulled open. It was as though I'd stepped into another realm.

Literally and spiritually, the shift felt so instantaneous, it stopped me in my tracks. I looked for my friends, and then I found my boyfriend. We all stood at the side of the stage, watching Noel play the same tracks we'd heard him play many times before. The weight of depression removed from my shoulders, bones, throat and tummy, I was finally back in the room, ready to get back on stage.*

---

* Not on stage at Glastonbury or V Festival. Not on stage with Oasis; that would be beyond weird, and I don't fancy being pelted by plastic pint glasses. I mean the stage that is my own life. The one I thought I'd never find again.

21

Motherfucker

The schedule 'they' forgot to mention

Dear New Mum,

Before you had your baby, I imagine your morning routine may have looked something like mine?

7.30am: Get up. Moan about getting up at 7.30am. Shower. Brew tea hand-picked by Tibetan monks in limited edition teapot no longer available to buy from Liberty. Read several blogs and online newspapers. Tweet. Eat expensive organic wheat-free toast made by virgins. Tweet. Boil two eggs laid by chickens raised at Buckingham Palace.

8am: Commence beauty routine. Tweet. Check Facebook. Caress limbs with oil imported from Morocco on a bed of petals. Consider doing some sit-ups, but decide there's just no time. Blow-dry hair using several products only available from a salon in Paris.

Moan about never having enough 'me' time.

Apply Chanel foundation. Spend ten minutes on each eye, working the driest Dior mascara wand through lashes first, then the semi-dry wand, and finishing off with the latest, wettest mascara wand in order to create perfect 'backstage' lashes.

8.30am: Try on entire contents of wardrobe.

8.55am: Vow to buy more tops from Net-A-Porter.

9am: Run out the door, cursing the fact there's not enough time in life, and exclaiming you're gonna HAVE to go on a retreat to India/Thailand to 'practise' yoga in order to relax, as it's the only way you can get some headspace, man!

9.30am: Arrive at desk chirping, 'I feel like I've done a whole day's work already; I just don't know how I do it!'

Dear New Mum,

Immediately after delivery, your morning will look more like this.

6am: Get up. Trip over spare travel cot located by bedroom door. Wonder why we have a spare travel cot located by the door? No time to worry about stubbed toe or spare travel cot. Go to soothe crying baby. Vow to pee at some point before lunchtime. Switch on bottle warmer. Feed dog. Feed cat. Get baby from cot. Sit baby in their recliner chair. Look at diary; unable to read own writing, so who the fuck knows what's gonna happen today. Cross fingers.

Feed baby with bottle/tit. Entertain baby. Make baby porridge. Put baby in full-body bib. Take baby food out of freezer while porridge is cooking. Wash baby's bottle. Put steriliser on.

7.15am: Feed baby porridge.

7.20am: Sit shaking garish rattle over head in vain hope it will trick baby into finishing porridge.

7.22am: Make raspberry noises while shaking garish rattle above head.

7.23am: Force dog to wear a trilby in order to entertain baby.

7.24am: Beg baby to finish porridge.

7.45am: Baby finishes eating porridge.

7.46am: Dog licks entire highchair while still wearing hat.

7.47am: Dog is banished to his bed with Dettol wipe attached to his butt.

7.48am: Dettol-wipe cat.

7.50am: Second nappy-change of morning. Wash baby, dress baby, entertain baby.

8am: Empty steriliser, refill bottles for the day, make list of things you need to buy for baby, scrape porridge out of own hair.

8.30am: Lie on floor with baby playing peek-a-boo.

9am: Baby's second nap.

9.01am: Wish Starbucks would relocate to beneath flat.

9.02am: Have two-minute shower. Put on something that isn't covered in sweet potato. Dab a bit of blusher across cheek but don't blend (no time). Whizz small amount of mascara through lashes of one eye.

10am: Notice the blush you didn't have time to blend looks like stage make-up, giving a sort of 'open wound' look to left cheek. No wonder the postman looked at you as though you needed rescuing.

When boyfriend returns home, he may ask, on account of your having applied mascara to just the one eye, whether you've been crying.

Not yet, my friend, not yet. But the party ain't over until the fat lady sings. Or sobs.

22

Guilty Mother

*I feel so guilty about working
full-time, I join the PTA*

'Sorry to bother you with this, I'm not sure you're even the right person to flag this to, but last week's school newsletter clearly states today's bake sale was *card only*. But in fact, it was *CASH only*, which we only found out at the *last minute*! I cannot begin to describe the disruption this misprint caused! I had to call my manny to make sure he went to school pick-up armed with cash, meaning he had to go to a cash machine beforehand – not easy with twin babies and a toy poodle! I had to leave a new business pitch, all so my six-year-old son could buy back his own biscuit? Yes, the biscuits I baked at midnight on Tuesday after three work events. Very stressful.'

Within minutes of joining the PTA, I suddenly found myself starring in my very own series of *Motherland*, except the real *Motherland* is like a harmless episode of *The Snoopy Show* by comparison. Having spent years skittering around on the edges of the school-gate mum-gang, the main reason I worked full-time was to avoid the dreaded question: 'Do you have time for coffee?'

Time for coffee? Who the fuckety fuck has time to go to a coffee shop with a relative stranger to talk about other relative strangers?
NOT ME.

How I ended up on the PTA is beyond me.

First job of the term: organise the Halloween school disco. Sounds easy, but *au contraire*. Imagine the *Hunger Games* meets trying to get into the Celine show in Paris. HIDEOUS. Thanks to limited numbers due to health and safety reasons, not all the kids get to go, and the ensuing carnage and scramble for tickets is reminiscent of trying to get into an early Alexander McQueen show.

The Halloween school disco is not in Paris, nor in a cool London warehouse; it takes place in the school canteen, and *everyone* wants to go.

Pre-pandemic, when it was business as usual, the mums (and one lone dad) who ran the bake sale also got to sell the Halloween school disco tickets. Like drug dealers, they'd cut deals with desperate parents. If you wanted your kid to go to the disco, you'd better be prepared to kiss ass at the bake sale.

I had to excuse myself from a board meeting with the entire team from a luxury French jewellery house, who'd just arrived fresh from the Eurostar.

'It's the school,' I comedy-whispered so that all twenty people sitting at the large, highly polished rosewood table, ready to hear our annual plans, figures and strategy presentations, could hear. 'Won't be a sec.' I flapped apologetically at the person in control of the presentation.

Out in the hallway, I morphed from cool fashion exec to mad, spitting, whispering snake-tongued woman. 'Anna, you HAVE to save two tickets for my kids; I'd leave work, but I can't, they're over from Paris. Actually, hang on. How fast do you reckon an Addy Lee could get me from Knightsbridge to Queen's Park? Anna?'

The boardroom doors swung open. 'They're ready for you,' said an assistant.

'Sorry! It's urgent – can you delay my part? I'll be there in a minute . . . *Anna* . . . Do you have the tickets? What do you mean you've been told you can't bulk-buy for more than twenty families? OK, I'm coming, I'm going to book one of those motorbike passenger couriers. Sorry? What? You *do* have the tickets? Two of them? Are they physically in your hand? Take a pic and send it to me as proof. OK, OK, thanks. I'll collect them tonight. I know they're two pounds each, but I'll bring a Fortnum & Mason hamper and fifty quid.'

I re-entered the boardroom, interrupted the entire presentation and forgot my lines when it was my turn to speak. But fuck it, my babies were going to the school disco, and I was triumphant.

Cut to two years later, and I'd lost my job. Not on account of leaving important meetings with fashion VIPs to spit down the phone at mum-friends manning bake sales at school, but because there was a global pandemic and shit happens.

I may no longer have been a fashion executive sitting comfortably (albeit harassed) in a boardroom any more, but I was still suffering from Halloween-school-disco-related PTSD.

On this particular morning, this little ole single parent, who was minding her own business and just trying to get two kids to school on time, one of whom had to be at maths club at 8.30am, had seriously lost the plot.

A bowl of bran flakes had been 'accidentally' tipped into the cutlery drawer – milk, flakes, the lot – during a ten-year-old's midnight snack attack.

The day before, my mate Kate had sent a text doling out her latest doggy wisdom, which went something along the lines of, 'Go to the Halal butchers on Kilburn High Road and get the puppy a lamb's heart.'

What she'd failed to mention was, A) probs don't give the entire heart to a puppy in one sitting, and B) you might want to c**nting cook the heart first to rid it of blood, guts and gore.

Arriving in the kitchen at my usual time of 6.45am, I'd assumed there'd either been a murder, or the puppy had somehow caught its tail in the door, thereby squirting blood everywhere like a scene from *Carrie*.

All of which led to me hastily typing out the following WhatsApp:

'It's not fair on parents who work and therefore can't possibly make it to the bake sale, to miss out on the opportunity of buying Halloween disco tickets. Oh, and there's also the minor detail of having to actually *know* someone "manning" the bake sale stall in order to buy Halloween school disco tickets.'

Ignoring the kitchen stained with lamb's heart blood, I ferociously tapped my phone so hard that my nail beds hurt.

'It's akin to insider trading,' I went on, despite having bribed Anna in previous years with the promise of a hamper. 'It's wrong, it's corrupt and it's very middle-class to think ordinary working parents can just leave a meeting willy-nilly to sort out disco tickets.'

I shall for ever regret not turning up to the bake sale on a motorcycle courier, not that I mentioned *that* in my PTA WhatsApp rant.

As I pressed send, my phone bleeped: 'Just a thought, don't give Poppy the entire heart, it might upset her tummy.'

Oh, cock off.

At least I'd sent the out-of-character (PTSD-loaded) rant to the PTA WhatsApp containing only six people, rather than the larger PTA reps group of thirty, which is where all the real *Motherland* shit happens. A resounding wave of WhatsApp return messages flashed across my phone – 'Agreed!'.

I hadn't been expecting that.

Fuelled by a puppy's runny tummy, a kitchen covered in lamb's blood and a cutlery drawer filled to the brim with bran flakes and milk, I'd finally nuked the bake-sale mafia. Take that, suckers.

Later that day, the sensible man on the PTA found a website that hosts a 'lottery' system for situations like this kind of war. All parents who wanted a disco ticket had to pre-apply, and a week later, the lottery site would inform you whether or not you'd been successful. Paging Katniss Everdeen . . .

Enraged parent no.1: Dear PTA, what is this random website we are using for the Halloween disco? ALL the parents in my class are very confused as to why tickets aren't available at the bake sale as per usual. Thanks, Sarah.

Me (I wish): Dear Sarah, because it's a literal bunfight. Bye.

Enraged parent no.2: Hi PTA, obviously everyone is very upset and disappointed regarding the draw for the Halloween disco tickets. Some parents have asked what happens with the resale tickets? Some parents think numbers must've been cut by half. Some parents have already written to the head and want answers – now!

Enraged parent no.3: Hi PTA, so some parents are suggesting that maybe they should have just worn costumes to school instead of having a disco? Why are so many children missing out?

Enraged parent no.4: Dear PTA, there are several Halloween disco splinter groups happening! Parents are arranging their own parties because so many children didn't get tickets for the disco. And those that did don't want to go because their friends aren't going. This really is such a mess.

Enraged parent no.5: PTA, can we have several shorter disco sessions to accommodate more pupils? So reception and year one for thirty minutes, then another group from the same year group, then the same, right up to years five and six? Does that work? Things are looking really desperate ... My Frank has been in tears all day.

Enraged parent no.10,560:
Hi, can someone from the PTA tell me, as lots of parents from year three are very upset, regarding the 'random' ticket lottery, was the lottery per class, or was it random throughout the year, or perhaps the entire school? This is a joke.

PTA reps: Although I understand the disco ticket lottery system is fairer on working parents, there will be a breakaway class disco, and frankly, you can't stop us. We're considering having it sponsored by Party Wishes. She's donated a zombie.

PTA reps: Why didn't you consider spreading the disco across two nights to increase overall numbers!? It's never going to be a smooth run with a forty-nine per cent chance of getting a ticket, so this increases the capacity. We're going to the breakaway disco anyway . . .

From PTA reps: As the Halloween school disco is

completely PTA-run, why
don't you consider doing it
at an alternative venue, if the
school is opposed to having
the disco on more than one
day or splitting the times so
more kids can go? Everyone
is so upset. Kids crying.
WhatsApps blowing up ALL
night long.

PTA reps: THIS DISCO SHIT IS
SO UNFAIR.

PTA reps: The local cinema
is hosting another break-
off Halloween — how cool
is that? The local pub is
providing beer (go!). Seems
the school disco will be the
afterthought party rather
than the main gig!

Dear PTA reps,
    This will be the last Halloween School Disco for the
foreseeable future.
    Best wishes,
    THE ACTUAL PTA

The PTA hot chocolate fiasco

Susan: Hi, sorry to be a pain, but the sugar content in hot chocolate is SUPER high!

Me: Headteacher says no alcohol. No mulled wine at a Christmas fair is a bit of a downer, I reckon. Hot chocolate feels like the obvious 'Christmassy' alternative?

Deborah: It's not sugar I'm worried about, it's my Matilda's milk allergies – dairy AND nut milk. IT'S A NIGHTMARE! Plus, I can't bear the idea of soy milk destroying ecosystems.

Me: Ecosystems?

Deborah: Agrochemicals? Water-system pollution?

Me: Ah, OK. Let's go for dairy and a non-dairy option like oat, then? If people need to know ingredients, I'll make sure we have all the info uploaded to our phones.

Deborah: Dairy!? Hope you mean milk from a cow-friendly supplier?

Me: Sorry? There's a farmer who talks to cows?

Deborah: LOL, no. The guy, oh what's his name, good-looking, runs a cow-positive milk van from the kerbside outside Queen's Park farmers' market each Sunday. We don't need cow pus in our hot chocs! You know about infected cow teats, I presume?

Me: I was just gonna buy a load from the small Tesco next to the overground station. Will the cow pus be visible? Is there anything I should look out for? Will I find 'contains cow pus' on the label?

Deborah: Ha ha! You're funny! Go to the Positive Cow Man. Honestly, it's worth the extra pennies.

Me: A pint of milk from the small Tesco is £1.05. I'm rubbish at maths, but with the chocolate being supplied free-ish, I reckon we're at an eighty per cent profit margin. How much does Positive Cow Man (sounds like a Marvel character – lol) sell his cow-friendly milk for?

Deborah: It's £7 for two pints.

Amy: Alarm bells! Free-ish chocolate? Is it organic? From where are you sourcing the chocolate, Stacey?

Me: The big Asda by Brent Cross.

Amy: And the brand?

Me: Asda own-brand.

Amy: I don't mean to be difficult, but could we check the supply chain? Did anyone else read the piece in the weekend papers about cocoa-bean provenance? Structural poverty, human slavery, child labour, etc. We consumers really have to start voting with our money, it's SHOCKING!!!!! We should write to Gail's!

Me: Gosh! I did not know that about infected cattle teats, and, honestly, thanks so much for highlighting the disgrace that is this vile, allergy-provoking, zero nutritional-value, social-injustice-causing hot drink. Oh, by the way, sorry to change the subject quickly, but how are you sourcing your cruelty-free cocaine at the mo? Any women enslaved during production, sex trafficking, etc? Anyone have a number for a cartel-free, non-violent cocaine supply chain? With the amount of cocaine that enters vegan bloodstreams around here, I'm surprised anyone gives a shit about hot chocolate and infected cow tits. Fuck off. Bye.

In the days running up to the fair, I fantasised about driving my car into the dead of night in search of houses mid-renovation. There are hundreds of skips sitting in driveways in this neighbourhood. Wearing a set of overalls, thick gloves and balaclava, I'd climb into one in search of a discarded bath. Preferably lilac or something gross and eighties. I'd clean it with a chemical-heavy detergent, plonk it in the playground and, while everyone else was faffing around with Christmas trees and homemade decorations, I'd fill it with the cheapest vodka I could find from big Sainsbury's, then add fifteen bottles of Irn Bru. I'd decorate the bath sides with a homemade sign reading, 'Eco-Juice for Cunts (PS No known allergies)'.

Although I didn't send the message, inwardly I vowed never to run the hot chocolate stand at the Christmas fair again.

23

Guilty Mother II

*The shit no one told me dot com, dot co
dot uk, forward slash dot org*

There are so many crucial bits of information 'they' left out. The
mythical 'they' being my mother, society, *Mother & Baby* magazine, the woman up the road who told me I was pregnant before
I'd even taken a pregnancy test. OK, so yeah, I admit it, I was a
total fool for thinking I'd spend my maternity leave doing the
stuff I did pre-baby (PB), i.e. faffing around on a monumental
scale. *Je suis le* queen of faff. I have a master's degree in 'faff'.

Yes, of course I thought I'd be tootling off for 'fancy' lunches
within a couple of weeks of delivery. Out to lunch mentally? For
sure. Actually going for fancy lunches in town? IN TOWN?
Dressed FANCY? Cock-a-doodle-doo!

OK, maybe 'they' *did* tell me, but perhaps I had my previously
well-manicured fingers in my ears. Or maybe I thought it would
be different for me, this baby malarkey. I mean, how hard could it
be? Stick the nine-pound mite in a swanky, overpriced pushchair,
pair with sensible yet fashion-forward footwear (possibly Lanvin
trainers in several peppy colourways), add large sunglasses, *et*

voilà! I am Gwen Stefani-lite (if you squint and are very short-sighted and have lost your glasses).

I thought I'd be the ultimate culture vulture. 'What are you doing today?' my boyfriend would ask, to which I'd reply, 'I'm off to the V&A for the day, darling.'

Needless to say, I did not make it to the Leonardo, Degas, Twombly, Emin or Corinne Day shows, nor did I go to any gigs, have dinners out, see anything on TV, read a newspaper or have a conversation about politics. If you're interested to know about the destructive properties of a breast pump, I'm your woman. Want to know what's happening at the V&A? No clue.

I did book a huge, comfy seat in the fancy bit at Westfield cinema once. My boyfriend suggested I seemed a tad 'emotional' and perhaps needed 'time out'. No shit, Sherlock. I ordered a ginormous glass of wine that might as well have been the entire bottle and watched the film in what was essentially an armchair with a side table. I ordered a huge box of popcorn and scoffed it all a bit too quickly.

I had thought maternity leave was supposed to be like taking a really long holiday, during which I would get paid to lounge around and read books or look at Italian masterpieces. Instead, I just about managed to read about Amy Childs' tits spilling out of a too-tight dress on the *Daily Mail* website.

The biggest thing 'they' forgot to mention was the guilt. Yes, that's right, GUILT. I'm not talking about mild guilt, like when you've overspent on the old credito card because a voice inside your head shouted, 'You must buy new season!' fifty times over before you eventually relented and took a taxi to Bond Street. I do love that voice – well, until the endorphin rush wears off and panic floods your body, and before you know it a bunch of drunken butterflies are partying in your tummy.

No, *this* guilt is the Big Daddy of all guilt; I'm talking about 'mothers' guilt'.

Let me break it down:

1. I felt guilty for moaning about being tired to friends who didn't have children. They didn't want to hear it; they were just nodding politely, wondering when their friend would be back in town.

2. I felt horrendously guilty for moaning about being tired to friends who'd had children before me. I wasn't there for them when they were going through the early stages of motherhood, and that makes me feel really bloody GUILTY. What a shit friend I was (beats self with over-priced shoe).

3. I felt guilty for admitting I wanted to go back to work, because surely that's easier than being a full-time mum? By the way, I was the only woman willing to admit this in my antenatal group. I mentioned it at one of our coffee meetings and exited before social services were called. Funnily enough, there wasn't another coffee morning after that. Thank God. I hate coffee mornings.

4. I felt guilty about *not* wanting to go back to work. I had moments when all I wanted to do was stay at home and play with my children and brightly coloured squeaking plastic objects – and I'm not talking about RuPaul's collection of handbags.

5. At one point, I hired a nanny for two afternoons a week, and I felt guilty about that. The first time she came, I stood at the bottom of the stairs, semi-spying on her, foaming at the mouth with jealousy. Oh, that's normal. Not.
   IS THAT NORMAL? HOW CAN IT BE NORMAL?

The whole experience made me feel terribly guilty. Clearly, she was a nice person and I was not, and my baby would prefer to be with her.

Play 'Insane in the Membrane' as backing track here: I FIRED HER, FROM THE BOTTOM OF THE STAIRS, TEN MINUTES AFTER SHE ENTERED THE HOUSE.

(I did not. Well, I did, but only inside my mind.)

6. I felt guilty because, instead of utilising nanny-time wisely and sitting down to write, I fannied around in Westfield (again!?) and stared longingly in the direction of – yes, you guessed it – the Prada store. Everyone else was at Paris Fashion Week, and it was pissing me off. I made voodoo dolls of the front row from cotton buds (because yes, they're that thin) and fashioned faces and hair from Aptamil and spit. I needed help.

7. I felt guilty because nobody else in my antenatal group had part-time help. *Shoves head in GUCCI nappy bag the press office gave me that everyone at the antenatal class thinks I'm a wanker for carrying.* No one actually said, 'Duguid, you're a wanker.' I just KNOW it.

8. I felt guilty because I wondered if I breastfed for long enough. Everybody in my antenatal group was competitive about breastfeeding. I decided I'd pass them the number of a good surgeon when they were done, which would probably be in four years' time, knowing that lot. I BREASTFED FOR FOUR WEEKS AND ALMOST DIED FROM DEPRESSION. So everyone can just fuck off with their 'bitty'. (Bitty as in, the character David Walliams once played. You know, he's an upper-class gentleman and is still breastfed by his mother. LOL.)

9. I felt guilty because I had 'write a novel' on my to-do list, but it wasn't really happening. Which is why I got the part-time help, but then the sales are on, and, and, and ... well, you know. That voice inside my head made me order three huge boxes of stuff from MatchesFashion, and then I sent it all back on account of none of it fitting ye olde bear bum over here. I had ordered everything in my usual size ten, but *NON*! None of it fit. I couldn't even get the heavily discounted Erdem pencil skirt over my knees. How the mighty had fallen. I didn't let my boyfriend see, obvs. I changed in the baby's room. That poor child has seen things no child should bear witness to.

10. I felt guilty for having fantasies. Maternity leave was supposed to be me pushing an expensive pram around Bond Street, wearing over-the-knee Jimmy Choo high-heeled boots, a Max Mara belted trench and possibly even a fedora. Can you picture me swishing through reception at the Connaught as the head barman ushers me to my special table, where an already poured French martini awaits? This, my friends, is called being utterly delusional, and is a possible indication of a serious personality disorder.

11. I felt guilty for feeling depressed.

12. I felt guilty for wanting my old life back.

13. I felt guilty for feeling guilty.

24

Dog Mother

My first child was born in Ireland . . .

When I was thirty-three, something very odd happened. One February during Milan Fashion Week, a sharp pain ripped through my lower stomach.

'I think I have a ruptured appendix,' I announced, making myself comfortable in the back of the fashion van, readying myself for the day ahead. With fifty-five fashion shows, showroom visits, a call with the office to discuss the next set of shoots, plus dinner with the Burberry team in my diary, I added 'No time for that shit, though!' while secretly hoping I might be carted off in an ambulance at some point between the Max Mara show and a meeting at the Loro Piana showroom.

I find that when a potential hospitalisation is on the horizon, it's best to dress up. You never know, a hot Italian junior doctor may be poking around my pants by teatime. For the sake of my future junior doctor husband, I wore a navy-blue miniskirt by Chloé, a pair of ACNE ankle boots, a V-neck jumper by Uniqlo, thick navy-blue tights and an oversized checked coat by Marc Jacobs. Although the sharp pain around my tummy was weird, I pushed it to the back of my mind, knowing Fashion Month can do weird shit to my body.*

So, ignoring the tummy pain, I carried on as usual, drinking all the wine in an attempt to recover from sensory overload, which only added to the burnout. When Milan Fashion Week ended, I came home for a couple of days. A boyfriend had moved in with me, after knowing each other for the sum total of, oh, two months. I wasn't sure I particularly liked him. He never made me feel good about myself, and our sex life was crap.

To spice things up a little, one Saturday afternoon, I appeared at the living room doorway all trussed up in black lace. I was even wearing heels and crotchless knickers. He was watching the football, so I coughed a couple of times in order to get his attention.

'Well, well, well. Helllooooo there, big boy,' I said, practically purring, right arm caressing the doorframe as if it were a ginormous, hard penis. 'Looky looky over here, cutie pie.'

Eventually tearing himself away from the footie, he turned around to see what his beloved had in store this time. 'What the hell are you doing?' he said.

'Oh, I just thought we could, you know, have some Saturday afternoon fun,' I said, trying not to let the fear show in my voice.

'Oh God, stop it,' he said, smirking, and turned back to his shit Second Division (or whatever it's called now) football team. He didn't so much as glance back. I tottered upstairs to get changed, feeling deeply ashamed. I've never felt so vulnerable. Openly mocked, I vowed never to allow myself to feel that way again.

Anyway, after Milan, I was home for a short amount of time. I repacked my bags, and a few days later went to Paris for five nights. By the end of Paris, the Chloé miniskirt, which I'd worn only fourteen days prior, no longer fit. Nothing unusual after a

---

* Case in point: the time I cut a fringe in New York using nail clippers after seeing Karen Elson with a newly cut fringe at a party. Sadly, it was 3am, I was drunk and alone, and waking up with hair all over my face the next day was nothing short of alarming. I had to wear a hat for the next six months.

month on the road; I'd often return from Paris in March having gained just under a stone in weight from hotel living, no exercise and late dinners with clients.

A week or so later, I threw up. A week or so after that, a pregnancy test confirmed I was – yup, pregnant. Sara, who was around six months pregnant at the time, suggested we meet for lunch to talk about it. We met at Nobu. She was past the puking phase and looked radiant. I asked the same question in multiple ways. Essentially, I wanted someone to tell me whether I should keep the baby, knowing I didn't love the father. I wanted a baby, just not with him.

The crucial piece of information I didn't share was that I had absolutely no recollection of having had sex, and was therefore in total disbelief that this was even happening.

Alone with my diary, I spent hours trying to figure out how it had happened. Not the penis going into the vagina and cumming (coming) part. Our sex life was almost non-existent, so how could I possibly be pregnant? Not remembering having had sex with my boyfriend yet finding myself up the duff layered on top of the crazy hormones and shock. No wonder I began to lose my tiny mind.

I discussed it with him, my boyfriend, but no one else. Instead, I turned inwards, spending hours staring at dates in my diary, trying desperately to figure out what the hell had happened. Paging baby Jesus: could this be the second immaculate conception?

If I could only remember how I'd got pregnant in the first place, I reasoned, maybe I would be overjoyed. But this phantom of my imagination, this baby inside – none of it felt real. I felt disconnected from the pregnancy, from myself, and from my boyfriend – who, by way of explanation, had simply said, 'Well, we must've had sex.' The pregnancy felt like it was happening to someone else.

Knowing the baby wasn't real, I figured a scan would finally prove it. So, I forked out £250.

'Take a seat,' said the gynaecologist. 'How many weeks, do we think?'

I shook my head. 'Not sure.'

'Date of your last period?' he asked, rolling a condom down the ultrasound wand, an act that never ceases to make me feel like a twelve-year-old girl in a sex-education class. Titter.

'First of February,' I said.

'OK, so roughly, let's say if conception was between the twelfth and fourteenth, that makes, um . . . ' He checked a piece of paper with numbers on.

'I'm not sure when we had sex,' I said, embarrassed.

'Hmm, well, let's see. So implantation would have been roughly around the sixteenth of February.'

'I was in Milan,' I said, remembering the pain in my stomach. 'I *felt* it.'

'Yes, some women can feel implantation,' he said, wafting an ultrasound wand around my vagina. 'And – there we are. Your baby. Just let me measure here, and . . . OK, you're around seven weeks, I'd say.' Then he turned up the volume and the foetus's heartbeat filled the room. 'Nice and healthy sounding! Do let me know if you'd like to come back for your twelve-week scan.'

I went home on the tube in disbelief. A baby! Inside me! With a heartbeat! Without even having had sex! Impossible. Stressed, and with no real answers from my boyfriend, I declined mentally, unable to get out of bed. I called my boss at *ELLE* and said I had to take a week off sick.

During the week off, I left bed on just one day. I wandered through a graveyard – because that's what you do when you need cheering up – and then set off on a long walk, ending up in Notting Hill. Before I knew it, I'd found a pub, ordered a glass of wine at lunchtime, and got out my diary to run through the dates again. So, 12 or 14 February – I'd have been in London, packing for Milan. Then 16 February – in the van in Milan, feeling that strange, stabbing pain. How had it happened? Pregnant, with a man I didn't love or see a future with.

I called a private clinic and asked for the price of an abortion, then I booked it using my credit card.

The days that followed the abortion were horrendous: Sara, still pregnant, wearing Alaïa leggings with cute baby-doll dresses over the top; me, no longer pregnant, also wearing leggings on account of having gained fifteen pounds. I felt alone and unloved by my boyfriend. I felt bereft. I had wanted a baby, but the confusion around how I had fallen pregnant had made me lose my mind.

A few weeks later, I decided to get a dog.

I first saw Bo online. I remember the first time I saw him on the Mayhew's website: a look of pure contempt evident in his eyes, he was staring at the camera, neck pulling at his taut lead as if to say, 'Erm, this is a terrible mistake – take me home.' It's a look I still search for when looking for males online – deranged, dangerous and daring. Just my type. I can take or leave the leash and collar, TBH. A terrier cross with white, wiry hair and black markings, his energy was pure 'I may look scruffy, but believe me when I say I'm bigger, better, bolder than any of the other mutts in this joint.' It was love at first sight. I had to have him.

After a proper grilling in my own home, during which she checked the garden fence for holes in the manner of a forensic police officer searching for a dead body, the woman at the Mayhew suggested I take Bo for a walk as a 'test run'. I picked him up from the rescue centre in my car. I'd read somewhere young dogs ought to wear a seatbelt, so I clicked him into the newly purchased harness, which attached to his collar, and then somehow clicked into one of the seatbelts. With Bo securely fastened in the back, I set off driving. Within two minutes, he managed to chew through the dog seatbelt. He then launched himself towards the steering wheel and stood proudly on the handbrake, one paw on my shoulder, his head looking forward as though he himself were driving. I vowed to buy a stronger seatbelt.

At the park, unlike most dogs, who use all four legs to walk, he did an entire lap of the park on his hind legs. I laughed so much; I knew this was the dog for me.

He'd arrived in England via a boat from Ireland, having narrowly escaped being euthanised in a council pound. Aged just one, with a broken rib and big scratch across his nose, he'd been so badly treated. Knowing he was home, and with zero plans to leave my side, he lay on my chest for hours that first day, letting out several huge sighs. Feeling his heartbeat next to mine with his nose placed directly beneath my chin, I felt scared to move for fear of disturbing him. As the hours passed, his sighs lessened and I could feel the anxiety of his epic journey leaving his little body. He was home at last, and he knew it.

He lived for a further fourteen years. He was the same age as Sara's eldest child, and 23 March was his 'rescue' birthday. 'Rescue' is a loaded word. I didn't rescue him. Bo saved me. My twenties were a bloodbath, and although my thirties were a little less hideous, there were thunderstorms, nevertheless. When, a few months later, I broke up with my boyfriend, Bo slept in my bed. Spooning him, I'd cry into his fur.

He saved me, because having an animal at home meant leaving nightclubs on time. I couldn't and wouldn't stay out until 5am, wouldn't have another wrap of MDMA or whatever hors d'oeuvres was on offer. I had someone to go home to, a body to hug in bed. There were so many nights when I could've easily stayed out for longer or gone home with the wrong guy, had Bo not been waiting for me.

Having Bo was a reason to get up in the morning, and as our paths crossed those of other dogs and their owners, owning him made me talk to strangers, a bit like my mother does up north. Despite the bad breath and fur shedding, he was my perfect online find: a male I could depend upon, someone I truly loved. Someone who was there for me every single day, without fail. Bo always walked into a pub on his back legs, and was for ever stealing shit, such as packets of biscuits from the bottom of prams.* Chaos always.

Not once did he growl or bark at my children. Quite the opposite; he'd sleep beneath their cot by way of protection.

A year after having my second child, I started running, and eventually ran a marathon. I had several long runs to tick off before race day, but I became aware of something that was troubling me. It was nothing to do with endurance – I have plenty of that – it was a harsh internal voice. Step by step, I tried to overcome it – to literally outrun it – but then, during a twenty-two-miler, running along the river close to the Tate Modern, I remembered the important thing I'd forgotten.

As I hit twenty-one miles, the memory came in thumps.

Thump, thump, thump: from nowhere, I remembered how I'd 'fallen' pregnant all those years ago.

Thump, thump.

We'd been out, had a big night, drugs, drink, the usual.

Thump, thump.

Addicted to sleeping tablets, I took them every night. I remembered waking up the following morning wearing only my pyjama top.

Thump, thump, thump.

Remembered finding my pyjama bottoms tangled up with bedsheets; remembered looking down at my naked lower half, feeling confused. I'm northern. We don't go to bed naked.

With each step, the memory became clearer. Eventually, I collapsed on the pavement by a busy road, my back against the wall of a bridge somewhere in SE1, sobbing. It wasn't my fault. He'd fucked me while I slept; that's why I couldn't remember getting pregnant. *Would this be classed as rape?* I wondered, sitting on

---

* Erm, sorry about that. Actually, I'm not. I'm too busy laughing at overpriced organic snacks being scoffed at high speed.

the ground, sweaty from the run, so upset I didn't know how I'd make it home.

For years, I'd blamed my 'stupidity' for that pregnancy.

In Bo's final year, he couldn't eat, and I made regular trips to the vet to pick up antibiotics and arthritis medication. He developed a huge tumour the size of a large fist on his side, that meant he could no longer sit down with ease, and we made the difficult decision to euthanise him in the comfort of his own home – the family home I'd already left. Surrounded by those who loved him most, as befitting for a beloved pet considered nothing short of a family member, he left this earth knowing he was loved.

My ex took the kids out, and I rested my head on Bo's bony ribcage. Then I opened a beer and said my private thank yous.

1. Bo, thank you for not mauling the babies when they came out of hospital (a relative who shall remain name-less convinced me you would).
2. Bo, thank you for the time you rolled in a ginormous cowpat at a cricket match, then immediately entered a tent to violently shake your cow-crap-covered body ferociously all over men and women dressed in head-to-toe white. A decade on, people are still talking about it. The look of horror on everyone's faces is something I'll never forget.
3. Bo, thanks for all the times you demolished bowls of steaming hot pasta straight off our kids' highchairs.
4. Bo, thank you for ruining school mornings by climbing on to the kitchen table to hoover up everything in sight, including the butter. Which reminds me: thanks for all the butter you've puked up in the back of the car.
5. Bo, thanks for the time I took you to a 'new mums' coffee morning after having my first child. I was so depressed, it was a miracle I'd made it out dressed,

with a baby in a pram and you on the lead. Thanks for deciding to dry-hump a toy rabbit one of the mums had brought along to the coffee morning. I'll never forget the look on your face, your crazed eyes, that hard-on that looked like a pink Chanel lipstick, as you fucked an expensive stuffed toy rabbit on the floor in front of three mums from Brook Green. 'Oh my God, it's from Harrods!' screamed the mother.

Ending a life is an uneasy feeling. When the vet laid Bo down on his side on the living room floor, we put our hands on his sedated body and thanked him for all he'd given us. We were crying so much, I thought we'd never stop – the children, me, my ex-husband – a family already split down the middle, and now the dog had died. The sadness of divorce felt magnified. The dog was now gone, the furry baby my ex-husband and I had cherished like a child before we had our own. It was the culmination of too many losses, too much to bear in one year, and our hearts smashed to bits. I held the children for hours that day.

After his sedation, the vet had prepared two injections. 'He'll pass just shortly after the second,' she said softly. Ten minutes after Bo ran across the rainbow bridge, the vet whispered, 'They're here to collect the body. When you're ready, of course.'

Holding a huge plastic dog bed, a man appeared in the doorway. 'Does Bo have a favourite blanket?'

My ex ran upstairs to fetch it, then covered his body, leaving only Bo's head uncovered.

The man responsible for the cremation looked solemn. Reaching into his pocket, he brought out a sheet of A4 paper. 'As a way of remembering your beloved pet, there are a few things we can offer.'

Unprepared for a shopping list of dead dog merchandise, we all stared at him.

'We can dip the dog's paw in ink to create a paw print, framed. It's twenty-two pounds.'

Slightly taken aback, we both nodded. 'Yes. We'll take two, please.'

'And would you like his paw cast in clay?'

Oh, erm, no. No thank you, that sounds really fucking weird, I wanted to say. 'Yes, yes, two of those, please,' I heard myself say.

Was he going to carry on?

'And how would you like the ashes? Single cremation in a scatter tube?'

I wanted to ask what happens in a multiple cremation. Would the scatter tube contain the ashes of several other dogs? Would you get to know their breed and names? I stopped myself. 'Yes, that's great. A single cremation.'

What next? How about band T-shirts? Instead of tour dates printed down the back, how about it detail a list of Bo's favourite haunts, walks, trees, areas to pee and snacks? Was this man going to offer up scarves, calendars, pens and mugs? Dog deaths – big business, apparently. Although I'd say the band T is a missed opportunity.

Apologies to the innocent workers at Gail's, Queen's Park, aka the first people I saw several hours after the dog had gone. Once I'd peeled myself off the children, sadly it was the poor souls of Gail's who bore the full wrath of Bo's death. Sobbing over cinnamon buns and olive bread, I argued, 'No, I cannot leave my bike outside! I don't have a lock.' It was kind of the staff to pass several napkins as I sat in the middle of the shop on a bicycle, wearing dark sunglasses despite the dull weather. Weeping, soaking wet from the pissing rain, I'd set off on a bike ride to the Mayhew. Standing outside, wailing, I decided to retrace our first walk from the Mayhew to the house I'd owned pre-marriage, pre-kids, pre all the grown-up stuff.

Seeing my old house, the grief rolled in. I missed my family. I missed my ex. I missed being a family of four, plus a dog and a cat – now just a cat. Too many endings in one short year. I went back to my rental house alone. I thought of my ex and the man in charge of dead-dog merchandise loading Bo into a van, leaving the family home for a final walk.

Before I'd left, I'd reached down and kissed his forehead. I'd felt his ear. It was cold. Gone for ever. A part of me had, too.

25

Single Mother

*Or, diary of a white middle-aged
Craig David on HRT*

Monday, mid-January 2021

New me, new life, new diary, new intentions. Manifest a new life, they said. Alright then, I replied.

9am: Begin plans to conquer world.

9.01am: Consider writing in new diary, but don't. Never once have I managed to keep a diary for more than a few weeks, not even when splashing out on a £170 Smythson job. Posh diaries scare me. I end up just staring at them for a while before sniffing the pages like a dog.

9.02am: Realise zero-childcare situation for next ten days may scupper world-domination plans.

9.13am: As part of world-domination planning, must choose between two commercial agents. Can't decide, so WhatsApp Natalie and ask for psychic channelling. She beams her energy rays from Edinburgh, hitting a scrap of paper upon which I've written both agents' names. I mean, choosing an agent on the basis of how nice their Instagram looks just makes me sound mad.

Natalie channels my 'future projects' and tells me which agent to choose. What a perfect start to the day!

She is usually right – although, saying that, she was very very wrong about the bloke I snogged on NYE. My so-called 'soul angel'.

9.45am: New agent now hired, am a fully fledged entrepreneur! Make a large pot of coffee to celebrate. Suppress desire to open front door and shout, 'I have a commercial agent!' at whomever happens to pass by. Talk to the dog instead.

Open packet of expensive coffee a jewellery brand kindly sent me as part of a Christmas hamper. Now I'm gonna be rich, I'd better get used to drinking posh coffee at home. Might even be able to pay my gas bill this winter without calling Mum or Sara to borrow money. Excellent progress. Not bad considering I'm only forty-seven.

10am: There's something unwanted in my knickers. Unrelated to Tinder.

I hope.

Google 'itchy bum' followed by, 'adult with itchy bum, child with itchy bum'. Self-diagnose threadworms. Trudge to chemist for tablets. Over-zealous pharmaceutical assistant interrogates me for five minutes. Re: itchy ass, she appears to be convinced I'm fibbing. I mean, of course I'd lie, in public, about having an itchy arse.

'How many people in your immediate family?' she asks, removing her reading glasses.

'Is this a trick question?' I ask.

She just glares back at me through thick plastic sheeting.

'Three. There are three people in my family. Oh, wait, no, four. Well, three.' I'm now stuttering like a fool, thereby confirming her suspicions of *fake itchy-ass-itus*. What if I *don't* have an itchy ass? What if she's right? OMG! Could it be Munchhausen syndrome? Am I actually just seeking attention by making up an itchy ass? Consider calling psychiatrist but become distracted by assistant pharmacist handing over meds in what feels to me to be an unnecessarily aggressive manner.

'Err, can I have another box? For my ex. He's still my husband. Well, in name, legally, etc. But not actually my husband.' I'm glowing red like a sunset.

'Is he your husband or not?' asks the assistant pharmacist, while looking at me as though I'm some sort of NHS scammer.

'Err, yes, he is, but we don't live together. But the children go to his house each Wednesday and Thursday. Oh and Sunday, and alternate Saturdays, which I realise sounds SUPER confusing, but actually, it's way better than the four days on, three days off he initially proposed. I have ADHD. I couldn't keep up with the ever-changing days, and no mother should be without her child for four days in a row. Don't you think? Anyway, we get along now. I mean, gawd, I don't care if he has worms per se, but I'd hate him to have worms and pass them on to someone else.' At this point I let out an actual guffaw. 'I'm such a lovely ex-wife. Fuck's sake. I feel like a cat at the vet. Please can I just have one more box of worming tablets.'

'No need,' says the assistant pharmacist. 'There are four in a box.'

The interrogation/possible new Munchausen syndrome diagnosis makes me doubt my threadworm self-diagnosis. Seriously, what if I go home only to work out the itchy butt isn't threadworms after all, but an old pregnancy-related haemorrhoid flare-up? Which reminds me . . .

'Oh, excuse me, sorry.'

The assistant pharmacist lets out a small noise before turning her battery-operated eyes towards me. I swear to God she's a robot.

'Can I please have a tube of Anusol? Erm, no, not that one, the one further along, along a bit, down, yes! Does it say "soothing relief" on the box? Great. Ooooh, I see you've just received a delivery. I think that might be my favourite nit lotion behind you? In that unopened box? Oh, fantastic. Four packs of nit lotion, please,' I ask, with the enthusiasm of a woman shopping the latest exclusive Loewe capsule collection from Net-A-Porter.

I'm aware I'm being weird, but I can't stop myself. I'm on an illness roll.

'Do you have something for thrush?'

Without any further questioning, she hands over the thrush-loot. 'Is that it?' she asks, furiously tapping at the till with her bionic robot forefinger.

One tube of thrush cream, a Diflucan tablet (just in case the thrush cream doesn't hit the spot, literally), a tube of Anusol 'soothing relief', three boxes of my 'favourite nit lotion' (because, apparently, I'm not allowed to 'stockpile' four), and two packs of threadworm tablets – sorry, one. She glares at me from behind the plastic screen erected to protect her from nits, worms, sexual intercourse-agitated thrush, pregnancy-weight-gain-induced piles, and even, perhaps, COVID-19. She shoves my medication through the small gap in the screen.

Shit. I don't have a bag.

'I didn't bring my canvas tote! Soz! I always forget,' I say, to a woman who's no longer acknowledging my existence. 'Don't worry about the bag, I'll manage.'

I came to regret those words the moment they left my mouth. Like a flea-ridden game of Jenga, my medical purchases fell to the floor with a clatter.

'Let me help you,' said a manly voice close by.

'Thank you so much!' I said, sinking to my knees – not in a sexual way – and turning my head to the left, only to face a man I recognised from Hinge.

So, erm, what now? As someone, somewhere once said (possibly RuPaul), 'Own it, girl.'

We'd matched the week before, but were still at the 'Hi, how's your weekend going?' level of comms, aka deathly boring. I yanked the Celine sunnies resting on my head down towards my nose, got up off the floor praying my knees wouldn't click, and attempted to stand up as straight as possible.

As I flashed a huge smile that screamed 'mama mania', all that was missing from my pile of decrepit healthcare products was a bumper pack of Tena incontinence pads. And my herpes meds. Well, at least handsome Hinge man now knows I have nits and haemorrhoids, plus thrush in my poonani and threadworms nestling between my butt-cheeks. The early stages of relationships can be *so* awkward. Best to get things out in the open sooner rather than later, I reckon.

Gosh, what a Monday, I think to myself, as I pootle out of the chemist carrying my festival of doom in a damp swimming cap.

Tuesday

Wake up with a terrible head cold. Poppy enters her first 'heat', which, from out of nowhere, renders me a total hot mess, poring over puppy photos and wondering whether I've been a good enough mother. A *heat*? It's a bloody period, and that's what I plan to call it. Her vagina is swollen like an orchid or a Georgia O'Keefe painting – or like that time my cousin Keeley whacked me in the mouth. My third baby is no longer a baby. I resist the urge to cry.

Rush kids to school. Glance at my to-do list, which, despite spending several hundred pounds per annum on stationery, is written on the back of an old tax demand. According to the scribbles, I'm due to start working with a new tech client today. I'm a fashion-genius tech whizz. A couple of Nurofen Plus, and I've got this.

Phone rings. It's 9.35am. 'Can you come for your son? He has a terrible cough.'

Drive to pick him up. Spend rest of day running up and down stairs, offering endless mugs of hot lemon and honey, hugs and an assortment of basic beige food.

Pick up youngest child at 3pm. Tech start-up woman calls. No time, so don't answer. Too busy fighting the three dogs trying to gangbang Poppy.

Wednesday

Both kids off sick. I'm sick. Cancel all plans, including recording a podcast that's been in the diary for eight weeks. File *Telegraph* column. No clue what I've written. Go to bed having not got dressed. Whatevs. Poppy's humping all the soft toys she can lay her furry mitts on. Especially the unicorns. Gives a whole new meaning to 'mama's got the horn'. She somehow manages to get hold of a large stuffed beaver, tearing it apart at the seams.

Thursday

Open eyes and question whether I'm actually in the room. Yes. I am. Alive. In fact.

Lie in bed for thirty minutes discussing youngest child's fear of earthquakes. She goes to school; eldest does not. Work on new client project: a bag brand with a woman I'm not a huge fan of. In other words, she's a bit of a twat. That's not nice or PC. Cancelled . . .

Youngest arrives home from school complaining of a bad-smelling bottom. We stay up until 1am. She has a UTI. Dread seeing the assistant pharmacist again tomorrow. At least our arses have stopped itching.

Friday

8.30am: Ring doctor.

'You are number three hundred and fifty-two in the queue.'

The three of us jump in the car – all non-itchy asses, dog now in full-flow period mode. Drive to a local emergency hospital that's not quite an A&E, but somewhere you head if the emergency isn't a blue-flashing-lights emergency.

Park the car, pay for a ticket and head towards the hospital. A scrappy homemade sign on the door reads: 'No walk-ins. Ring 111.'

I call 111, who tell me to call my GP. I call my GP (have I mentioned how freezing it is?) as we stand outside the non-emergency emergency hospital doors, waiting for the GP's receptionist to answer. In hindsight, we should've waited in the car, but after twenty minutes, someone answers. I blurt out the words 'urine', 'infection' and 'eight-year-old girl' as fast as I can before the receptionist can hang up.

In a brusque tone, she replies, 'Call 111.'

I stare at my iPhone as though I've never seen one before.

'Mum? You OK?'

Released from my trance, I call back, and someone answers within six minutes.

'Hello? Hi, hi. Before we start, just to say, A) it's freezing, B) we are all sick, C) we're standing outside a hospital we're not allowed to enter because we can't get an appointment to see a GP and we don't want to bother A&E, and D) thanks to the dog being on her period, plus us three humans catching worms, I'm gonna blow.'

The GP's receptionist asks the doctor to call me urgently.

Doc calls within forty-eight seconds.

'Can you please come to the surgery, Ms Duguid? We'll prescribe your child antibiotics, but I'll need a urine sample first.'

I drive like a bat out of Hell. Take youngest into GP surgery, dump eldest into newsagent's, chuck credit card at shopkeeper, leave son browsing *Pokémon* cards. This ain't gonna be a cheap ride. Grab sterilised pot from receptionist, run to loo with youngest. Dying for a wee, child pulls down her trousers, sits down on loo. I roll up my sleeve, shove my hand inside the toilet bowl, ready and waiting to catch her pee in the pot. Hand hovering somewhere beneath her vagina and her butt, I'm focusing so hard, I just know I have a full pot. We laugh, we whoop! What a morning!

Pull hand away to discover the pot is completely empty and my arm is soaked in pee. Refusing to leave defeated, I pee in the pot myself, hand it to the woman on reception, who waves us off with a prescription.

CIAO FOR NOW!

Eldest is outside with pockets stuffed full of dud *Pokémon* cards. Well, at least that's what he's claiming, because we all know 'dud' equals returning to the shop in order to spend another £28. Poppy, still very much on her period, appears to be surrounded by male dogs, two of whom are howling towards the sky like deranged werewolves as they're driven so mad by her 'heat'. I suggest we make a run for it before an Alsatian tries to shag my leg.

Saturday
Book to watch *Sing 2* at the local cinema. And, despite it being only 11am, I order two bottles of wine. As the haze of booze begins to soften my mood, I vow to add 'global domination' to *next* week's to-do list. That's if I can find all my expensive stationery. If not, a cardboard box will do.

NHS app flashes to tell me urine sample is 'all clear'. I google 'what can you catch from putting your hand inside a public toilet bowl?'.

Halfway through *Sing 2*, which the kids say is babyish, before telling me I'm a humiliating embarrassment on account of being the only person in the cinema singing, laughing, whooping and slapping their thigh, I remember I forgot to call the tech client back.

Shit.

PART 4

Money

I hate talking about MONEY, so we might as well do it. Come on, then. Let's be having you. Once upon a time, during my decade-long tenure at *ELLE* magazine, projecting a perfect image was a full-time job. When I returned from maternity leave still a stone or so over my normal weight, I was able to justify buying a stupidly expensive Celine tote because – and I quote myself – 'it covered my bottom'. What an arse.

To my financial and emotional detriment, I now know the true cost of attempting to maintain an out-of-reach perfection on a par with Kim Kardashian.

Debt, huge swathes of it. I recently found an old diary in which I'd penned in flouncy cursive how much debt I was in. I was stunned to read it. We'd never had much money when I was growing up, and yet still Mum managed to save up, and buy and upgrade houses. She is good with money; I am terrible, and so wish I'd been taught finances at school. I learned how to touch-type instead (admittedly pretty handy for writing this book).

Let's also talk about the fact that women are more likely to be in debt than men. Targets of consumerism, women are 'sold' unnecessary products via social media algorithms. Women also have to fork out hundreds of pounds per annum on beauty products. And as for sanitary products, well – bravo, Scotland, the first country within the UK to recognise periods are not a choice. We'd rather not spend our already stretched budgets on Tampax, thanks.

26

Maternity Money

*The bit where you need to pop some money
to one side for the actual baby*

To: Laura@financielle
Subject: Maternity leave (the conversation I wish I'd had)

Hey Laura,
You well?
　Apologies for emailing you out of the blue, but when you get a minute, can we please chat all things money and maternity leave?

Stacey

To: @staceyduguid
Subject: Maternity leave (the conversation I wish I'd had)

Hi Stacey,
Sure, what do you need to know, other than the usual sinking funds, pension contributions, etc?

Laura

To: Laura @financielle
Subject: Maternity leave (the conversation I wish I'd had)

Hi Laura,
Um, 'sinking' fund? Is that like a pub kitty? And pensions ...
Oh God, I knew I should've listened to the bore in the grey
suit who came to *ELLE* that day ...

Stacey

To: @staceyduguid
Subject: Maternity leave (the conversation I wish I'd had)

Hiya,
LOL. No, a sinking fund is nothing like a pub kitty; it's a
pot of money you pay into each week or month towards
something big like buying a house, or, as in your case,
having a baby.

Laura

To: Laura @financielle
Subject: Maternity leave (the conversation I wish I'd had)

Hi Laura,
Oh! God, I'm mad. Of course. Um. Christ. Do women
really have a baby sinking fund in place? I feel properly
overwhelmed. Having a family is sooooooo stressful!

Stacey

To: @staceyduguid

Subject: Maternity leave (the conversation I wish I'd had)

Hi Stacey,

Yes, lots of women save up for maternity leave, and given the drastic drop in finances during this time, it makes sense to do so. OK, don't panic. Let me explain.

Recognising the gap in financial literacy between men and women, my sister and I came up with the idea to launch Financielle. Regardless of income, via engaging content, our app aims to empower women to make the best financial decisions they can. We cover everything from how to save on a low salary to how to save to buy a house. It can be done!

I can go into all the other stuff, such as savings, ISAs, pensions, etc. later, but with regards to maternity leave, we've recognised that women are spending their statutory maternity pay on items that ought to be paid for jointly. Things such as nappies, formula, new babygros, bibs, socks, baby and parent groups, etc. These are essential baby expenses that really shouldn't fall solely on the mother, especially given her reduced income.

If bank accounts are separate, to ensure all costs associated with children are fairly divided, steps should be taken ahead of time to ensure expenses such as car finance, petrol, food and bills can be met. Bills don't suddenly disappear when you have a baby, but being on statutory maternity leave, three-quarters of your wage does!

None of it makes mathematical sense, hence why it's important you and your partner go over the numbers together. It will feel so good to get your shit together, *together*. Often partners don't realise how much all the baby stuff costs, as it's something they've never had to consider or think about before. Don't sit back silently, feeling too embarrassed to talk about money. And definitely don't wait angrily for your partner to offer, either. Take control and plan.

By planning, you'll also protect your mental health — and let's face it, having children impacts our mental well-being enormously, so the less we have to worry about finances during this time, the better.

Hope that helps?

Laura (BIG HUG)

To: Laura @financielle
Subject: Maternity leave (the conversation I wish I'd had)

Hi Laura,
It's very, very grown-up isn't it, this baby stuff? I'm now wondering if, in addition to the joint account we set up solely for paying bills, we ought to set up a separate account for baby expenses. What do you think?

I hate the idea of him suggesting we go out for dinner or away for the weekend, and I can't pay my share.

Stacey (aka a wannabe grown-up)

To: @staceyduguid
Subject: Maternity leave (the conversation I wish I'd had)

Hi, oh, grown-up one,
While running the numbers together, the priority (after the baby is clothed and fed!) is to ensure pension contributions are maintained for the one whose salary has dropped.
This is really important — more important than a gift for a friend's birthday, more important than a new beauty buy, and

definitely way more important than eating out or a weekend away. A pension shouldn't stop for one parent just because they're caring for a baby.

Last point! Do a baby-prep budget by listing all the items you think you will need. Cost up those items and begin saving as soon as you're thinking of starting to try for a baby.

Good luck!

L

To: Laura@financielle
Subject: Maternity leave (the conversation I wish I'd had)

Hi L,
Me again. So, wait. Should I have figured out costs for baby items before even TRYING for a baby?

S

To: @staceyduguid
Subject: Maternity leave (the conversation I wish I'd had)

Hi,
Yes, ideally.

So, in your 'trying for a baby budget', would be a cot, nursery items (such as nappy-changing table), a car seat and clothes. Cost everything up as 'brand new', but also be open to buying second-hand items and anything you can grab from free-cycle marketplaces. This will help reduce the amount you have to save in total.

All that's left then is to gather the costs and build your

'baby sinking fund'. Money shouldn't limit us from trying for a baby!

Any specific questions that would be helpful to answer?

Laura,

To: Laura@financielle
Subject: Maternity leave (the conversation I wish I'd had)

Hi,
Gosh, it's not very sexy, is it?

Thankfully, I'm already seven months pregnant, or I might have suggested he have a vasectomy. Jokes ... lols ...

I think I'll go for a long lie down now, with the curtains tightly closed ... despite it only being 2pm. I have a million questions about pensions, but my eyebrow just started to twitch, and I can no longer see out of my left eye.

Anon,

Stacey x

Money Energy, by Lucinda Gordon Lennox

Lucinda Gordon Lennox is a mentor, coach and trauma therapist, and author of *Nobody is Broken*.

We have been fed a tremendous amount of untruths about money. Stories, if you like. This is just part of society, and is no one's fault. Essentially, though, just like everything else in this world, money is energy. It is not good, it is not bad, it just *is*. We are taught all sorts of things about money: that it is greedy to want it, vulgar to spend it, stupid not to save it, impossible to earn it; that it is difficult to come by, and only available to some people; that debt is bad, spending is bad, saving is bad, having money is bad, losing money is shameful – and the list goes on.

Everyone will have different belief systems around money that they have either been taught directly or have had embedded in them through their families and society. And it's not just women who find it difficult to cope with finances, debt and planning; men do, too. It may be that women find it more challenging because of the past patriarchal systems that have been in place, which perhaps position men as earners (think hunter-gatherers) more than women.

But again, these are just systems and stories. We have treated them as if they are true, but this does not mean that they *are* true; it just means that we made them so.

If we can simply grasp that money is energy, and that if we want to be good with money, we first need to understand that everything we were taught about money was part of a system and not necessarily the ultimate truth, and if we can then start to disassemble those beliefs, then we can start to see ourselves as being worthy of having money, capable of earning it, strong enough to hold it when we have it, and brave enough to release it, knowing more is available. Whatever we choose to do in order to make money, we know that we are able to do so; this is a great first step towards having a much better relationship with money. This applies both to men and to women.

We are raised and conditioned to believe that money is a scarce commodity. Our minds and belief systems have been trained to think this is true. Therefore, we project a scarcity mindset out into the world. For example, we see something we like, and we say, 'I can't afford it.' Or interest rates go up and we say, 'I'll never be able to make my mortgage payments.' Or we engage with other people in conversations that have negative connotations about money: 'We can't afford a holiday,' or '"X" is so expensive.' We might even tell ourselves we are hopeless with money. If we watch ourselves talk about money, we will undoubtedly be amazed (and hopefully a bit shocked!) by the negative projections we have around this subject.

If money is energy, imagine how we are repelling money by talking about it so negatively. If we change our language and start to say, 'How can I afford it?' or 'How can I make my mortgage payments work?' or 'How can I get more money?' or 'How can I save/plan better?', then things will begin to shift.

27

No Money

The ELLE *years*

I shopped when I felt sad. I shopped when I felt happy. I shopped to fit in with the tribe. I shopped to travel to Milan. I shopped to carry the right handbag. I shopped because I was stressed. I shopped because a boy dumped me. I shopped when I got a new job. But mostly, I shopped because the Halifax upped my limit on my credit card to £20,000. I mean, why *wouldn't* I load my credit card to the limit? It's free money, right?

Aged twenty-one-ish and pretty much alone in London, I needed a pair of black Kookai trousers as though my life depended on it. It was more than just an item of clothing; if I could just own this particular pair of trousers, I knew I'd be able to access a life currently unavailable to me. A life filled with riches and cocktail parties, dishy men and expensive perfume; a life of shiny Notting Hill door knockers, and late nights in bars where the bill never came. Wearing the Kookai trousers, I'd be invited into a world that was the opposite of mine, given mine was currently living off one packet of Ryvita per week, along with a box of Cup-a-Soup sachets and, if things were flush, a pot of full-fat cottage cheese with chives. Living in a one-bedroom hovel in a shit part of London, those perfectly cut trousers were my only hope of escape.

The Kookai trousers in question were mannish and long, like tuxedo pants. I was already a fan of boy-cut trousers, of which I owned three pairs.

I'd bought the old-man Farahs for £2 in a charity shop in Edinburgh. Coming from a generation that never wore jeans, Grandad would've called this kind of trouser 'slacks'. It would seem, according to photographs, that from the 1960s onwards, all he wore was a pair of biscuit-hued, straight-leg trousers. A veritable one-stop style solution, he wore them everywhere, whether he was tinkering in the garage or heading out wearing a neat driving shoe with his pals from the RAF. Some asshole in the early noughties named this type of dressing 'smasual', as in smart-casual.

Anyway – I spent the latter part of the 1990s wearing light tan, low-slung Farahs with either trainers or heels. The Kookai trousers would be a major upgrade from those vintage Farahs, slacks that, to me, represented an old life in which I was a total Cup-a-Soup-drinking loser. But no matter how many times I tried them on, I couldn't afford to pay £80 for a pair of trousers. On my fifty-fifth trip to Kookai in Oxford Street, I saw a white, fluffy, off-the-shoulder jumper, which I tried on with the afore-mentioned trousers several times.

Either worried I'd wear out the zip given how many times I'd tried on the trousers, or just sick of the sight of me, eventually the shop assistant spoke up.

'Hi, you like the trousers, yeah?' she said, swishing her thick, black ponytail in mild annoyance.

'Yup. I do. But I can't really afford them.'

'Can't *really*?' she asked, emphasising the *realllllly* in a way that could be pure mockery. I couldn't tell.

'No. Not at all,' I fessed up, remembering there was only one Cup-a-Soup left – and it was minestrone.

'Take out a credit card, then. That's what everyone else does. No one can actually afford to buy all this nice stuff.'

So I did. I took out a credit card with Morgan Stanley. It was silver with a rainbow hologram. Whenever I removed it from my wallet, it sparkled as brightly as the clothes I planned to buy. The card looked expensive, and with it in my purse, I was less of a loser.

The following week, I set off to face my old pal, otherwise known as the Kookai shop assistant. I bought the trousers – and also the jumper. A week later, I snaffled a pair of boots from Warehouse. Five minutes after leaving the shop, as I walked down the steps of Oxford Circus tube station, I did an about turn and went back for a coat I'd tried on for an entire hot second. When the bill came in a month later, the numbers made no sense. Without enough money in the bank to pay off the bill in full, I popped it back into the envelope it had arrived in and never opened another.

I was earning £12,000 per annum working as a press office assistant. The credit card company seemed to like me – and so did the bank. My frugal mother had always drilled into me that renting was a waste of money, and I should get on the property ladder as soon as possible. With that in mind, and with no money to my name, I went off in search of a flat to buy, which is how I ended up living in a (then) *very* bleak part of the East End – but that's not really my point. After viewing the place once, I fell in love with its dank, dark basement interiors, and made an offer that was accepted. Back in 1997, before the world's economy crashed thanks to dodgy mortgage lending, you could borrow pretty much anything. God knows why, but HSBC agreed to loan me £60,000, so all that was left was the small matter of a deposit.

'You don't need much,' said the mortgage advisor. 'You can easily secure a mortgage with a five per cent deposit. So that's three thousand.'

Hmmm. Where to find three grand . . . ? *Oh! I know!*

A heady mix of credit and an overdraft.

Eureka. Man, I'm good at this money shit.

In my next role working for Paul Smith, my salary increased to around £17,000 per year. Still, I didn't pay off more than the monthly interest on my credit card, and threw all the bills in the general direction of the cardboard box in my bedroom where I 'filed' my financial paperwork. Now that I had a mortgage, other credit card companies began to write, telling me how much they loved me. So sweet. Nearing its credit limit, my Morgan Stanley card had begun to lose its rainbow-enhanced shine, so I opened up two more credit cards. Halifax first, then American Express. Halifax really, really loved me, and gave me a whopping credit limit. American Express less so – but then, to confuse shit even further, they gave me two different cards, one gold and one blue.

As the interest owed on the three cards increased, the direct debits plus a mortgage left me in deficit. Even on the first of each month when my salary landed, I was still past my overdraft. That's when I had the idea to remortgage. In the year since buying the flat, its value had almost doubled. Boom! And can you guess what happened next?

It doesn't take a genius to work out what poo-storm came rolling in from the west, but here goes.

No one seemed to want their money back in full, but paying off the monthly interest rate was a killer. Despite my monthly income not balancing with my monthly outgoings AT ALL, I continued to shop. I shopped and I shopped, and I blew my house down. Not literally; I remortgaged. I went from a £60,000 mortgage to a £90,000 mortgage, and cleared off my credit cards. With all gleaming white credit cards, all shiny and new again, I went to Selfridges, where I basically camped out, leaving only to sleep and work and get high.

Wearing nice clothes, I felt part of something – part of the gang. But soon enough, I was back in debt. Remember that diary entry I mentioned in the introduction to this section? This is what it said:

I'm in debt. I'm in £35,000 worth of debt.

Going to various Fashion Weeks was a big part of my job, and to hide my social anxiety I shopped, and I also drank. Sitting at around ten shows per day, I had to look and act the part.

Picture the scene: it's one with which anyone who's ever had an extreme hangover will be familiar. At 5am, the alarm on my iPhone explodes, the force of the vibration sending it tumbling to the floor. The first few seconds of post-drinking waking are mildly euphoric, something like I imagine an out-of-body experience to be. Then, as memories of the night before come flooding back into my consciousness, there's a minute of staring at the light fitting in the hope that the dull pain building above my right ear might go away. A pat of the hand to the left or right confirms nobody else is in the bed. I find I am able to start breathing again at this point, as I'm still not over the time I woke up next to two drag queens I'd let crash in my room after a very late night in downtown New York.*

After conducting a mental body scan, thereby ensuring all parts are present and correct after a big night, I notice the Balenciaga shopping bag strewn across the chair. I register sore feet – a Louboutin injury – and one almost-closed sticky eye thanks to an eyelash-glue incident. A tightness around my tummy confirms I am still wearing my Spanx.

---

* Gusty Wind and her sidekick Coco were big girls who'd ordered an astonishing amount of food on room service. There was no way I could get away with six man-size portions of pancakes on my meagre daily expenses account. Some woman in the accounts department told somebody else in accounts that I'd had a 'visitor' in my room from the look of the room service bill, which, within days, evolved into me going to New York Fashion Week to organise a gang-bang. Gang-bang? I know you think the fashion department just swans off to NYC for a 'fun' time, but I'm way too busy for that kind of sex, Pamela. Plus, I hadn't waxed my bikini line in a while.

It's mid-February. It's dark, it's rainy, it's ridiculously early, and all over the world, fashion editors are making their way to airports, dragging behind them overstuffed suitcases full of borrowed new season. We don't earn enough to buy a whole new wardrobe of outfits every time we go to a Fashion Week, unless you're one of the girls who have a private income and a husband who works in finance. (Yes, that does make me cross, but anger-management therapy is helping.)

After several days of packed shows and schlepping around in the rain, London Fashion Week ended last night with the usual end-of-week blow-up at the Burberry head office. London's favourite design house knows how to throw a good party; it was wild, even by my standards. Filled fit to burst with ad-campaign beauties, freelance stylists and my gang, the magazine editors, it was like an early Primal Scream gig, all Kate Moss-lites in vintage Chanel and smoky eyeliner.

Partying in the same room as models is not a good look when you're over thirty. The more pissed they get, the sexier they look; their bedraggled hair becomes 'salt-spray styled', their sweaty brows become a 'glow'. The rest of us mortals just look pissed and a bit peaky.

And now it's on to Milan Fashion Week. At Heathrow, everybody will be wearing enormous shades, everybody will be wearing the highest heels they own, and everybody will pretend not to notice one another. Nobody will eat, but they will mainline black coffee. Some editors take yoga mats, others carry bottles of Rescue Remedy; one even travels with her personal trainer. Short of taking a hot, naked travelling guru with me, I decided a few years back, after a particularly challenging season, that a bucket of red wine every evening is the only way to get through it. That, and strong Italian painkillers, bread, pasta and occasionally screaming out of my bedroom window 'WHY ME?'

And, of course, shopping.

Five Thoughts On . . . Talking About Money with Children, by Gemma Godfrey

Gemma Godfrey is a money expert who has appeared on *ITV News* and *Good Morning Britain*

1. Children build their money habits as early as five years old so it's never too early to set them up with skills for life. The best way parents can talk about money with their kids is through play and seeing how money works in action.

2. For younger kids, this could involve setting up a play shop with toys, price tags and fake money to exchange.

3. For older kids, earning pocket money can help teach its value. It can also show the power of saving up money in order to afford bigger toys later. Adding a few pennies to pocket money saved each month can show how earning interest is a reward for good money habits. This can also help explain how there is a cost to owing money that can spiral over time.

4. While money can be a very emotional topic, discussing it openly in a balanced and factual way can help children build the knowledge, confidence and skills they need to navigate the working world later.

5. By letting them make money mistakes early, a penny lost now could save a pound later on.

28

ADHD Money

Beta blocker, anyone? I'll take the whole fucking box, thanks. Making sense of a tangled mind

Ignoring the poor squire who tried to talk 'pensions' at the *ELLE* offices many moons ago, single-parenting in my mid-forties sure brought all money-related things into sharp focus. Without any back-up in the bank, unless trading ACNE blazers suddenly becomes a commodity on a par with gold, after a lifetime of financial fuck-ups and never considering how I'd financially survive in old age, well, you do the maths.

Old age? That shit happens to other people, not me, Stacey Duguid, ever youthful, carefree and wild. Ignoring future financial planning aged thirty is one thing, but it's defo not so fine when you're knocking on the door of fifty without a plan.

To be clear, I am not afraid of getting older. I am, however, scared witless and shitless about my lack of future planning. Not the type to stand around feeling scared witless and shitless, the moment our marital financial settlement was arranged, I had an idea that was bound to secure my future wealth. Ta-da! It came to me in a flash. I shall not die alone surrounded by empty crisp packets and white wine bottles, fifteen cats licking my face clean because the water has been cut off. When it comes to staying in London, for the next ten years or so I don't really have a choice. I can't buy a much cheaper house up north and be nearer Mum while the kids are this age. Hence my ta-da! Idea. Ready for it?

Drumroll . . .

ENTER THE IMPULSIVE IDEA TO BUY A HOUSE IN A STATE OF DISREPAIR WITH A HOLE IN ITS ROOF IN — MENNNNNORRRRRRCAAAAA!!

I don't speak Spanish.

Erm, hola.

Si, I did! Why? Because after a tumultuous two-and-a-bit years of upheaval, I needed a plan; needed to feel 'home'. Why Menorca? I've always wanted to buy somewhere small for us as a family to return to each holiday. Writing this in full knowledge and acceptance of an ADHD diagnosis (autism diagnosis pending stage left), I now fully understand why I like the idea of returning to the same place each year. It boils down to the simple fact I don't like change; don't like arriving somewhere unknown; don't like being in a hotel room I can't quite get comfy in. I could go on to include long-pile bath mats and those bed covers that don't get changed along with the bedding, but I'll stop. If you know you know.

Aware that to many, the idea of returning four times per year to the same place may sound alarmingly odd and, not to mention, a tad fucking dull, I hear you, I see you, I just don't want to join you backpacking through South America.

Why Menorca, you ask? The first house I wanted to buy was in a village in Scotland where I'd spent many summers. Located in the Cairngorms, not only is it stunningly beautiful, it's also deeply calming. One day in 2019, unbeknownst to my ex-husband I took a flight and made an offer on a house in a village called Braemar. Working full-time, I'd already secured a mortgage (also unbeknownst to my husband), but in order to buy said house, I needed to release around £60k equity from our family home. You can probably guess where this is going . . .

Quiz time. On a scale of one to ten, ten being 'ultimate shit show', one being 'meh', please rate how badly you reckon it went down when I announced my flying to Braemar, making an offer on a house in the hope of buying it using a mortgage secured in Secret Squirrel mode plus equity from the family home.

TEN!!!

It was a bold move, to go ahead and make that kind of decision without discussing it with my ex. I knew the property was set to increase exponentially in value and, for ever more, would have rental appeal thanks to the clever people behind the mega-brand Hausser and Wirth buying the local shitty hotel. Located two minutes from the house I intended to buy, the Fife Arms, now dead fancy, having undergone the facelift to end all hotel overhauls, had become a destination for famous folk and those with epic taste (and deep pockets). Gorgeous food, incredible art, yes it's MEGA expensive but name somewhere else you get to eat your dippy egg 'n' toast seated beneath a REAL Picasso? I knew I could undercut their room rates on Airbnb, given my house was a 1950s bungalow. Even so, located minutes up the road, my guests would have full use of The Fife Arms' restaurant and bar. You see, I am a pension planning genius. Oh yes I am.

Revisiting Braemar with my ex the year before, staying at the Fife Arms for my birthday, remembering summers spent in my uncle Gordon's caravan, I felt nostalgic and began yearning for a slower pace of life. Having lived in London for so many years, craving a quieter life came as a total shock. Walking through hills with my ex on my birthday, we happened upon a random hillside croft with a sign outside saying, 'teas and coffee'. Except the sign was made-up, the electricity-free house wasn't a cafe at all, hence how I ended up walking straight into someone's front room.

Two men were seated fireside with their dog. 'Good morning!' one of them said. 'Dram?' asked the other. They'd fashioned a homemade sign and hung it on the door to entice (lure?) passing walkers to knock on the door. Having hung back, and not given my safety a second thought, my ex walked through the door to quite a scene – me at 11am drinking whisky with two random men and their dog. 'Sit doon,' they both said, turning to look up at him. I knew they didn't intend to kill two Londoners up a mountainside. I also knew I was home. Minus the caravan.

Everyone in Braemar can pronounce my surname. Duguid is from nearby Aberdeen. Not pronounced du-gid, doo-good, doo-goid, or nay-good, as the kids used to call me at school, the Scots pronounce Duguid 'Jew-git'. Five minutes after arriving in Braemar, I envisioned myself wearing tartan dresses working as a full-time painter. The fantasist had it all worked out. I even had a Pinterest board and opened an Instagram account called The Scottish House. (Twit.)

I finally had a plan but I hadn't considered it might not be actionable. In order to put down the cash deposit, I needed my ex-husband's permission to remove the money from our joint asset – our house. As to be expected when your wife heads off to the wilderness and makes an offer on a house unbeknownst to you, a few disagreements are exchanged and the house sale collapses, taking with it our marriage. It's odd what sends you over the edge in a relationship and, for me, this was it. The idea I had to ask permission to do something I knew would be met with a 'no' was infuriating. Although, to be fair, it wasn't a resounding 'no'; after the initial shock subsided, it was more of a normal, 'OK, shall we discuss this?'

Background noise – it had always been there: me knowing that I didn't have an equal share in our family home. The exact reasons for this are so unusual, they are not worth explaining in detail. I'll just say this. During the earlier years together, I regret not being stronger of mind and believe that had I 'done the work', I would've been able to discuss finances, both current and future, in a way that is 'normal' and grown-up. Pre doing the work, I was trapped in a childlike state, especially when it came to money. I was reluctant to talk about perfectly normal things, such as being on the deeds of a family home, planning a pension to live off in old age, saving up for holidays, what the scenario might be if we ever split up. Why? A: I didn't believe it was worth it (due to my financial situation), B: to discuss the future felt so abstract I couldn't fathom it (time blindness and how it relates to ADHD) and C: to contemplate splitting up felt like standing on the precipice of a deep ravine on a windy day.

Unable to find the emotional inner strength to *assert myself*, I shoved my fingers in my ears and donned a ginormous Versace visor so I couldn't see, hear, feel what was happening before me. Wearing a Versace visor, it turns out, was an expensive mistake.

Protecting yourself goes both ways, by the way. Whether you're financially independent or not, this is my ten pence worth. I HEAR YOU – of course we wish and hope and dream for the happy-ever-after romance, but given that almost 50 per cent of marriages break down irrevocably, surely we ought to prepare for the worst? I know, right, bloody Debbie Downer over here. They don't tell you to prepare for money Armageddon when you're buying a ginormous blow-up cock to decorate the hen-night hotel. Cock-ageddon, yes . . . but that's the next book.

While the details of my situation were probably unique, I know from others' experience that dividing family property is almost always a minefield. It's OK for marriages to end and for people to move on, but do not for one second think your mild-mannered partner – male, female, other – shall remain Mr, Mrs, Ms, Mux, Mix Meek Mike when it comes to the green stuff. From filing Form E to all the other fun divorce-related paperwork I couldn't get my head around, when it comes to discussing money, expect the unexpected and prepare for things to get seriously fighty. I'm not suggesting this was my situation, but it wasn't exactly pretty. Money *often* brings the worst out in people and in divorce, money often represents power. Perhaps wielding money-power over someone is a form of control during one of the most uncontrollable situations a person can find themselves in, so I guess any human would grab hold of what they can to make themselves feel less mad. I'm being generous. The person you once loved may one day be unrecognisable. I hope you never find out the hard way.

When we separated, it was me earning the big corporate dollar and even though my net worth was hysterically non-existent and my savings matched my empty pension pot, based on my income there was a chance I could end up being liable to pay my ex child maintenance. I will never know what a court of law would have decided, given I lost both my mind and my job shortly after separating.

Although I have plenty of female friends with a clean bill of financial health, for many women, broaching the icky 'money conversation' is unimaginable. I'm only half-joking when I say put away your wedding Pinterest board and get the spreadsheets out. Says the woman who, in a new-born-baby stupor, agreed to an arrangement that left me owning 4.6 per cent of the family home. At the time, I knew it was odd and, in later years, it began to really bother me. Am I a lodger in his house?

When getting divorced, the first lawyer said, on repeat, 'Thank God you're married!' After the third time, I asked, 'Why?' She laughed so hard, her grey bob whizzed backwards and the wheels of her office chair moved. 'Why!? Because you'd be entitled to NOTHING! The house is in trust!!! Hahahaha ... '

Five Thoughts On ... ADHD, Women and Money, by Dr Samantha Hiew

Dr Samantha Hiew is the founder of ADHD Girls,
a social impact company aiming to empower women
and girls living with ADHD to thrive in society

1. Women with ADHD go undiagnosed because of the naughty white boy stereotype perpetuated by the media

and gender-biased research, which often accentuates the worse cases. As girls, we were expected to be good, to do as we are told, to give people what they want, to know better, to be better. Often, with nowhere to express our thoughts and feelings, we internalise them instead, sometimes finding unhealthy outlets to channel the turbulence within, at the cost of our self-esteem.

A late-in-life diagnosis can make you re-examine your entire life, questioning why you were missed, the choices you made, the relationships you had, the kind of life you lived, and who you are. It opens up the investigation into our authentic self underneath the masks we wore and the archetypes we assumed to fit into society. We learn that, in order to move forward, we have to heal the wounds within.

2.   Oestrogen indirectly regulates dopamine, which is often at reduced levels in the ADHD brain. This is why ADHD presentation in women is likely to fluctuate across the month, and during periods of hormonal transition, such as puberty, pregnancy, after birth, or pre-menopause, when hormones are in flux. Hence the rise in many people in their late thirties, forties, and fifties being diagnosed, when their coping systems no longer work in the face of declining oestrogen.

Due to a lack of research, the understanding of women's hormonal health is dire. This means, for example, that women with ADHD who also experience Premenstrual Dysphoric Disorder (PMDD) (often accompanied by reduced serotonin), may experience more severe mood swings and increased suicidal thoughts, but instead of getting the support they need, they might get slapped with a personality disorder label by their healthcare professionals. Education is necessary for change.

3. We are more than that one label or diagnosis. The sum of how we show up in the world is an expression of our beginnings, what we've been through and are going through.

    Some of the factors that either create or exacerbate how ADHD presents in our lives are:

    - Genes you inherited
    - Trauma just by living in this world
    - The archetypes you assume that impact your quality of life
    - Things that happen to you or the life stages you're in (intersectionality of physical health, social class, race, culture, parenthood, divorce, etc.)
    - Chronic stress (a disease of modern society)
    - Less time to look after ourselves (lifestyle and nutrition that isn't where you need them to be)
    - Dysfunctional relationships (brought on by unhealed wounds)
    - Addiction (self-medicating)

    To really support someone, you need to look at the context of their lives, allow them to tell you what they wish they had if there weren't any obstacles.

4. The ADHD brain has stronger 'bottom-up' signalling (where our senses are stronger) than 'top-down' signalling (where the rational brain runs the show). As a result of this, we navigate the world through how we feel first, before our thoughts can interfere. This also means we have stronger instincts than most; however, making a decision can be challenging if we run into decision paralysis and chase our own tail. It helps having someone hold the space, to deconstruct what we truly need and want in our lives.

5. As women in society, the roles we are expected to assume may become more overwhelming as we become parents, juggling work and raising little people. It can be very demoralising for an ADHDer, especially if they are compared to other women who also have to perform the same roles and seemingly are able to juggle better. This can lead to increased anxiety, depression, heightened OCD traits, reduced earning potential and generally losing their shit.

I say 'Fuck it' to needing to fulfil female roles in society. We make our own rules.

Five Thoughts On . . . Money, Money, Money – and Divorce, by Ceri Griffiths

Ceri Griffiths is a financial advisor and founder of Willow Brook Financial Planning (@willowbrookfinancialplanning)

1. **Due diligence**: Your due diligence isn't finished unless you can agree with the following statements:

   - I really understand what my ex earns (including bonus, benefits in kind, long-term incentive plans, and so on).
   - I have a document that lists all the joint and sole savings, investments, properties and debts (otherwise known as a schedule of assets), along with supporting docs. (Ideally this should be a list that you both agree on!)
   - I know why I might need specialist reports (e.g. business valuations, pension reports), and I've attained them.

2. **Negotiating**: You're not ready to start negotiating unless you can agree with the following statements:

- I have worked out my income and outgoings post-divorce.
- I know how much I need for a home, and how much I could borrow.
- I know my projected income in retirement.

3. **Settlements**: You're not ready to sign a settlement unless you can agree with the following statements:

- I know what my income and outgoings will be as a result of this settlement.
- I know what my income in retirement will be as a result of this settlement.
- I know what my housing will be as a result of this settlement.

4. **Post-divorce finances**: These are the top three statements you should be able to agree with in terms of your independent post-divorce finances:

- I have a clear understanding of my current income and expenses, and have created a budget that reflects my new financial reality.
- I understand any future shortfalls I might have in savings or retirement income.
- I have a financial plan that shows me how I could meet any shortfalls in future years (through downsizing, inheritance, future savings or earnings, and so on).

5. **Managing investments** If you can agree with the following statements, that means you've got the foundations in place to manage your investments post-divorce:

- I know what income and/or growth I need any investments to produce.
- I know what investment risk and diversification are.
- I understand how investments produce an income or
  growth.

———————————————

PART 5

Mayhem

Another hit hurls me against the ropes. Slipping between gaps, I tumble off high buildings towards uncharted seas. No lighthouse, no search party, no silvery moon dancing across watery surfaces to find me. A torch at midnight? I need one.

Miles away from shore, I imagine my mother, my grandmothers and all the women who came before. In dark silence, I tell myself this fight won't last for ever; it's not a world war.

It's a divorce. No one will die. I stay quiet, remaining small and silent. Too tired to fight another round.

I'm broken.

It will be over soon.

Foolish woman.

Another blow, worse than the last. Three years spent scrambling to standing, and then: ten, nine, eight, seven, six, five, four, three, two, one . . . I'm knocked out this time. Zero fight left.

A death toll of one. The war is won.

I don't want to live any more. I've thrown in the towel. You win. Rock bottom.

I'm done.

29

Marital Mayhem

I do . . . I do want a line and another wine . . .

23.06.18

It's 4am. I'm awake before the alarm. Hardly slept again last night; not sure I've slept a full night in months. The line of coke I said I wouldn't do might have had something to do with it. A forty-four-year-old bride, wedding dress hoicked past her knees, sniffing lines in her middle-class downstairs loo. Even Farrow & Ball's latest hue can't save me from myself.

A few people, mostly my mates, came back to ours for a drink after the wedding. You told everyone to leave at 9pm, turned off the music just as the party was getting started. I was embarrassed to be chucking everyone out.

I'm trying to avoid a crumpled heap of white fabric on the floor, previously known as 'my wedding gown'. Aunts, uncles and grannies are fast asleep in spare bedrooms. Upstairs, our children are out for the count. Although I'm tempted, it's far too early to wake them. Bags are packed, only because you made me do it, otherwise I never would've bothered. I prefer 'panic packing', i.e.

total carnage: clothes flying all over the place, screams, tears, a taxi driver calling several times asking whether I'm still coming before driving off in a plume of pissed-off-ness. This chaotic approach invariably means I arrive on holiday with one half of a bikini and a single sandal. Having learned this about me the hard way, you insisted I pack my stuff in the same suitcase as yours at least twenty-four hours before we were due to depart. Wise man.

I can't believe we're off on our honeymoon. A flight to Sicily via Germany, then a boat out to the islands and a taxi ride. Pantelleria.

Now, the morning after our wedding, I wish we weren't going today. I'd far rather stay here, cosy in the bosom of my old and new family, huddling with my kids. Even the thought of family makes me feel safe. Feeling safe. That's new.

Yesterday was a blur, apart from Kate having to decipher my table placement, which was scribbled on the back of a napkin. Ever canny, she found a biro and wrote everyone's names on gross yellow Post-it Notes. The flowers looked great, though. The food was good, too. The speeches were out-of-control funny.

But today, now, you aren't yourself. Not much sleep for you, either. The sound of a taxi engine outside indicates it's time to leave the house – hopefully without waking anyone, especially the kids. The dog is awake. My Irish ex-husband, Bo, busy looking for food.

We're both quiet on the flight.

'Yesterday was fun,' I say, 'Despite the lack of childcare and food, and name cards on the table, and also a few other fuck-ups.' I'm trying to make you smile.

The Italian harbour is bustling and noisy, but it's the colours I notice most: orange, white, denim. There's lots of sing-song shouting, huge dramas over nothing, foggy cigarette smoke. The bright sunshine lifts a heavy tiredness. We didn't speak much on the plane, so now I break the silence with: 'Would you like a beer?'

I head over to the bar to flex my limited Italian. Having spent years coming to Milan, I've mastered the intonation, and was brought up with Scots who roll their 'r's like the Italians. Cold beer on a sunny day; I already feel better, more awake. You spy the ferry and head towards it with your new wife in tow. I follow. I always follow; my dire sense of direction is legendary. I grab your hand in mine. It feels soft and comforting. Unlike me, you have elegant hands.

The boat is busy and hot. Flicking through Instagram, a picture of me from yesterday takes a second to process. Our wedding photographer has posted yesterday's pics to her account, tagging Preen, the designers who made my dress. They've already re-posted the picture to their account. Hundreds of messages of congratulations. I wanted to savour the images, to pick over them with wine on our honeymoon. We'd paid a couple of thousand quid for them, the photographer's day rate, so why am I seeing them for the first time on somebody else's social feeds? I start to shake.

'What a fucked-up way of working.'

I know you don't really mind; you don't get the whole social media thing.

'Look at this picture,' I continue. 'I look so fat.'

I hate everything she's posted, but most of all I hate the fact I forgot to tick the box that would've prevented her from posting anything in the first place. I never get it right, the details. The small, massive-deal details.

We sit downstairs, and waves crashing against the window scare me. Fighting tears, I'm flooded with anxiety. Leaving the kids, yesterday's wedding, the photographer, the accidental line of coke, the total disarray. The childcare, the pizzas, the everything. I'm the problem.

'Need anything from the bar?' I ask, hiding my face behind the ginormous straw hat we both know I'll never end up wearing. You shake your head. I stumble off in search of alcohol and fresh air.

Everyone onboard is very well-dressed. Tods loafers, ironed trousers, crisp white shirts from Prada; not my vibe, but still, I can appreciate it. Thank God I didn't pack this morning. I'd be wearing my 'Ibiza' rave look. Not the time, not the place. Not the holiday.

Out of the window, I see the hotel, clinging to the side of a cliff. Bright pink bougainvillaea seduces its way up the walls. To the left is a rocky beach. The hotel is Slim Aarons perfect. When I get out of the car, I notice several women with insanely toned, worked-out bodies lying next to paunch-bellied husbands on sunloungers. Deckchairs covered in wide yellow stripes pepper the shoreline, fabric stretched to max, supporting the weight of the men's asses. These out-of-shape bodies look even stockier next to the slim limbs of their perfect wives. I pull back my hair to get a better look.

Have I forgotten I have children? Only briefly. Rushing upstairs to our room to call them, I'm jolted back to reality. 'Hi, it's Mummy.'

The enormity of the day before hasn't sunk in for them yet. How could it? They had no clue what was happening, their parents getting married then disappearing. Perhaps we should've waited until they were teenagers.

We head to the hotel terrace for dinner. Wearing make-up and heels, I attempt to liven things up a little. It's our honeymoon, after all, the perfect time to put on a show. I am a seal balancing a bright red ball on the end of my nose, chitter-chattering away, hands dramatically flapping. I'm funny and witty. Your long, Pinteresque pauses make me feel nervous; they always have. Butterflies erupt in my stomach. Your intellectual inferior at the best of times, I feel even more idiotic tonight.

I'm talking too loudly, too fast; I'm drinking all the drinks too quickly. Although I'm annoying even myself at this point, I carry on regardless. When I finally run out of steam, after an hour or so, I'm exhausted.

I allow a theatre curtain of heavy silence to engulf us. Sorry folks, show's over. We head upstairs to bed.

27.06.18

I feel so unattractive today. I've never liked the way I look. The bend in my nose, a square jaw, my thin hair and crap nails. I resent the way I agonise over clothes, but somehow never like what I'm wearing; the way I act either too loud or too awkward, too cocky, too shy. The chaos that follows me around like a bad smell, the stupid things I say, the dumb way I can't answer the simplest question. The getting things wrong and upsetting people. Talking over everyone.

A chaotic fucking mess.

On our extremely expensive Italian honeymoon paid for by you, I feel even less attractive. Compared to the French and Italian women, I'm too much, too obvious. I need to be less, be smaller. I should've packed a suitcase of only black, white and tan. No point googling 'what to wear on a chic Italian holiday' now.

Staring off into the distance, you don't notice how I'm feeling. I want to go home. Desperate to see my kids, my friends, I'm sick of watching honeymooners by the pool, stroking, kissing, giggling beneath towels. Naughty hands rummaging their way into swimsuits. Did we ever do that?

I make an arse of myself at the wine tasting we go to. Uncouth, I 'forget' to spit out the wine as instructed. I swallow, then ask for more instead. Rip-roaring drunk on white, rosé, red, sherry, white, red, repeat, at 3pm, I stagger back to the room to lie down.

Scrambling through luggage, looking for Nurofen, I find a copy of *Red* magazine I'd bought at Heathrow. Flicking through it, I see an article by an ex-*ELLE* colleague: a veritable ray of sunshine in soft, silky blouses and 1970s-inspired flared jeans. Although we were the same age, next to her, I always felt like an unruly teenager. She was a proper grown-up by comparison, with her perfect marriage, the kids she'd had young, the career she was so loved for and good at. It all felt so intimidating. While she was building a life, a career, a family, and buying a house outside London, I was rolling around nightclubs getting high.

Now, I'm gobsmacked to read about her husband's affair, stunned to discover she's chucked him out after instinctively going through his phone one morning. She'd asked his password; he'd blithely handed her his phone. Reading Rosie's world has fallen apart immediately sobers me up.

I message her on Insta. 'Rosie. Just read *Red* magazine. Fucking hell. What a powerful piece of writing. Meet up?'

People's lives, eh? Never what they seem.

25.07.18

I've booked a house in Northumberland for a week via Airbnb. Mum, Mike, my mother-in-law and her husband, David, the dog, the kids – we're all due to meet there today.

Driving down the winding farm track to the holiday home, the sight of a rusting old trampoline in an unkempt front garden is all the information I need as to what's about to unfold. I've done it again. Another holiday howler.

You'll have to get us out of this holiday shit I've landed us in.

The house I paid top dollar for is filthy and badly equipped. Trying to make it 'fun' upon arrival, given the sun is shining, I open a bottle of wine. For a moment, it's kinda funny. Not so funny at nightfall, when the shitty little lamps refuse to switch on and the bath taps turn out to be set to thimble speed, meaning it takes an hour to run the kids' bath.

With the kids finally in bed, I head upstairs to our floral-festooned bedroom.

'Jesus,' I hear you mutter, pulling 100 per cent nylon towards your chin.

At around 5am, the entire household is awoken by an overly enthusiastic cockerel. I decide to pull on my running gear. Might as well be the first up and out.

Distracted by my phone, I forget to go for a run. Now the kids are up, and Mum's shouting, 'Oh my God, what's that!?'

I find her in the kitchen, jabbing a finger manically towards her grandson's head. His hair is abuzz with flies; so is his sister's. Weirdly, so is mine. The three of us have had nits for so long, they've grown into full-blown adults and sprouted wings.

'How was I supposed to know this was why our heads were so itchy? I've never had nits before!' I yell at the top of my lungs, before heading out for a fast run. Slamming the door of the shitty farmhouse behind me, I run down the winding farm track and across a field full of cows. I cross over a stile and keep running. Past sheep, past cows, past no one.

Dopamine, serotonin – running provides them in spades. Boosted by chemicals, upon my return I demand a full refund from the grotty cottage's owner. It lands in my bank account within the hour, and I check us all into a nearby hotel, one I know well on the borders of Scotland. On the way, I ask you to pull over, so I can ransack the local pharmacy, buying every bottle of nit lotion I can get my hands on.

26.07.18

'Hi Stace, fancy a job?'

'Doing what?'

'Fashion, content and art direction. Reimagining a whole new look for an old-fashioned brand.'

'When?'

'Start next month? I'll get HR to reach out.'

Marion's well-spoken voice has never exactly been quiet, hence the whole family staring at me across the hotel breakfast table.

'Go on!' says Mum, eyes on stalks. 'Who was that and what did she want?'

'Looks like I'm back in fashion!' I say, slamming down my iPhone.

06.08.18

Our northern summer holiday is almost over, give or take a couple of days. Having driven up from London, we're not beholden to any particular train on any particular day. Suits my kind of planning.

I've made everyone come to my favourite beach in the UK, an unpretentious place on the Northumberland coast called Lower Newton. Too small for a shop, four rows of traditional houses line the hillside. Down towards the shore, nestled in the corner of a small square, is a pub with its own microbrewery. Too small for a shop, never too small for a pub. Welcome to Great Britain.

It's slightly overcast today, the grey North Sea bold and blustery. It's illegal to wear a coat in winter up north; in August, it's also against the law to wear anything other than shorts, despite the rain and cold.

The kids begin digging a massive hole on the beach. Heaping spare sand in a mound towards the middle, I help them carve out a little moat. Dunking red plastic buckets into seawater, the kids dash back and forth, refilling water into an ever disappearing moat. We watch in wonder as the water disappears, before running back to shore for more.

After a ploughman's pub lunch, we go back to the beach

to find our sandcastle half-destroyed, like Warkworth Castle. It's been taken out by an incoming tide. We rush over to fix crumbling walls. Glancing over my shoulder, I see our mothers comfort you. I keep the children focused on the moat. Four lives changed for ever.

08.10.18

Marion's promise of a 'big' job came true: my first full-time role in over a year. I take the tube to work and, despite everything that's happening at home, I manage to arrive twenty minutes early.

My new schedule means getting up at 6am and getting dressed before waking the children. I make breakfast, get the kids dressed for school, and someone else takes over the school run. My mother-in-law's still here, on hand to help. After herding the kids into their clothes, I run to the tube. I'm a sweaty mess before the day has even begun, but I don't care. I've missed the solid structure of work.

The excitement in my stomach is soon replaced by fear. Bond Street. My stop. *Deep breaths. Find something solid and run your finger along it.* That's what I remember someone suggesting I do, should I ever find myself on the brink of a panic attack. A zip, a button, a watch. By running a forefinger along the pink sapphires of my engagement ring, I try not to dissociate.

I'm sitting four rows back in a large amphitheatre. Within an hour, the man in charge of staff training has the entire room gulping company Kool-Aid. I'm in – totally sold. This is going to be the most exciting job of my career so far. Not to mention the best paid.

After being given a swipe card that lets me access all floors, I tap the door of my new office. Various people I met during the interview process flock to say hello. I'm immediately bombarded by questions, demanding immediate solutions. I try to take it all in. On day one, I don't even make it to my desk.

I say 'yes' to everything.

22.10.18

You go away on business, and I don't know when you'll be back. I tell the kids not to worry: 'Granny's not going back to New Zealand any more, and will live with us instead.'

My top lip buzzes. In order to avoid fainting, I sit down on the kitchen bench.

My head is fit to burst. The job, the kids, you away. I feel sick and abandoned, again. My safe harbour has been overtaken and is now inhabited by crocodiles.

05.11.18

At work, people ask me to do things without any explanation. They talk in acronyms I don't understand. Three-letter words I google during meetings so as not to be 'found out'. I'm panicked and totally out of my depth. Between the kids and work, and with you away, I shut down. I'm numb and I feel cold inside, yet I know I'm on fire.

I've been asked to present my strategy. A fucking strategy? After a month of being here? How can I build out a strategy with virtually zero information? What the hell have I done, taking this job, a job without a job description? A job that's not really a job at all. You would know what to do.

Not enough questions asked. Not once did I step back to consider the consequences of not being fully informed. And now, I'm due to present this mythical 'strategy' on stage in front of – who? Editors, press, buyers, brands, the CEO? For fuck's sake, who knows?

At the end of each day, I climb into bed with the children, the only place I want to be. The only place where I feel calm. At the weekend, I now fully understand what it means to be a fully present mother. I'm theirs and they are mine.

I've been awake since 4am, still trying to figure out what I'm going to say on stage in front of 200 people. I'm supposed to be presenting a subjective vision of a brand I've been employed by for the sum total of a month: a vision underpinned not by marketing, not by stats, not by facts, but by what? Intuition? How will I do this? By ad-libbing soundbites and bullshit? Talking crap about something I don't believe in is the very definition of pure hell.

The minute I walk on to the stage wearing last season's Marni, a dress bought from Bicester Village, I've already lost the crowd. Bluffing my way through the presentation, with key members of the leadership team sitting in the front row, I witness their faith in me draining from their eyes.

I've never been able to look at a screen and present. Never been able to remember words or read anything off by heart.

I imagine them to have buzzers like Simon Cowell. Three red 'X's plus a loud, unpleasant sound. One month in full-time employment, and it's all over. I'll be singing for my supper from now on. Better learn to dance, rollerblade, and ice-skate my way into the boardroom after this. What an absolute shitshow.

Mid-November

Work is a blur. Life is a blur. The only things that are not a blur are my kids, as all my energy is focused on them. I still, somehow, have a job, and have been asked to make a film. The woman who needs it sends across an image by a digital artist, which she asks me to replicate. She also needs high-end films of models wearing new collections. I fire off a dozen or so emails to contacts I've worked with in the past. Pulling together a team, I ask about the budget. She, a younger, very good-looking woman, just looks at me and giggles. 'Oh, I don't know, work your magic!'

What with filming and shooting, work is beyond busy. It's all going pretty well – until I realise the woman in question has zero budget. I've spent weeks on a project that's taken me away from my day job. Whatever my actual day job might be. Who knows.

December

I don't know when the kids' school term ends, never mind when the end-of-term concerts are. The plays, the charity donation day, own-clothes day, the Christmas jumper day – I turn up late for everything, at the wrong time, or on completely the wrong day.

Determined to not get the Christmas jumper thing wrong, I leave work, late as per usual and in a hurry. I forgot to order jumpers on Amazon, so I head to the Kilburn High Road, aka the only place on the planet I imagine has Christmas jumpers this close to the end of term. In Claire's Accessories, I go all out. Tinsel, stripy elf tights for her, light-up Christmas glasses for them both, antlers, hats featuring Santa legs as though he's stuck down a chimney. I drag the haul back to two excited children. The following day, they're the best-dressed kids at the gate. If not the most flammable.

End of term

You're still away. My therapy sessions are so full-on, I sometimes throw up afterwards. Sometimes, I don't bother going at all. I've started rearranging furniture because it feels good. Cabinets, bookshelves, plants, tables, sofas – these, I can control. Nothing else. I've had this idea to smash the kitchen island with a hammer. I'm considering repainting the white hallway jet black.

23.12.18

Today I'm informed because I didn't fill out the company documents I was given when I first joined, HR has denied the big fat pension I signed up for. The documents came in a swirl, and what with your trip away, the kids and this difficult job, I couldn't keep up with it all. The disorganised PA the company assigned me is, in fact, a creative person like me. Both of us are caught in the same wind tunnel, two disorganised creatives with a lot on their plate. Each time I ask her for help with my admin, neither one of us quite knows what we're supposed to be doing. It always goes wrong. But missing out on a company pension blows a last stab at future financial planning straight out the water.

At least you are home.

25.12.18

Having had shitload of wine, Mum spies an errant gift lodged beneath the Christmas tree. On her hands and knees, she crawls on her stomach, commando-style, to grab it. The tree topples over, trapping her beneath.

Back when I'd assumed I'd never have children, I'd started a Christmas ritual just for me: buying otherwise out-of-my-price-range decorations in the January sales. Now, they're all smashed to smithereens.

You go away again. I resist the urge to smash down the kitchen island on Christmas Day; I'll wait until the kids are back at school.

06.01.19

Without imprisoning someone from IT and forcing them to open the spreadsheets under the threat of losing a finger, I have no clue how my boss managed to get hold of the budget to send me to Fashion Month, but she has.

The millennials can keep their three-letter acronyms; I'll take Fashion Month any day. Old territory for an old diva. At least I know what to do at the shows.

And, having just grasped the meaning of BAU (business as usual, of course), this morning, I set off to work with a glimmer of confidence.

Back home, once everyone is out, I take a hammer and smash the fuck out of the breakfast bar. It's smashed to pieces, but still too heavy to carry. I call a rubbish collection van, and for £200, he takes it away. The room is big and empty, and there's a small hole in the floor with wires coming out. I hadn't factored in the fact I'd be removing the double electrical sockets.

February

I love the grey streets of Milan when winter meets the cusp of spring. The early spring air is a warm welcome after months of English winter. I'd forgotten the pace of Fashion Month, and the sensory overload of one show after another. Burning out a little more as each hour passes, I keep myself going with shots of coffee and wine.

Being non-stop busy takes my mind off everything going on at home – and, of course, at the office. Seeing my editor colleagues makes me remember my value and my worth; my sense of both has been battered out of me by company politics.

Old shopping habits die hard. I've bought way too many

clothes, bags and shoes. Stuff I can't afford, whacked on the ole credit card. I'm dressing for my job and I need to fit in with my colleagues.

I like going to bed alone in a hotel room.

07.03.19

At 10pm, my train rolls in from a very long Paris Fashion Week. The industry I've worked in for decades has changed, and brands no longer court magazines – it's all about influencers. The game has officially changed.

After working three weekends in a row, I'm overloaded and need time to decompress. In the cab back home, I check my work phone, hoping to clear my diary tomorrow morning. All I want to do is take the kids to school and swap heels for trainers.

'*8am: Stacey to present trends – breakfast meeting, hotel conference room 4, Kensington Plaza.*'

Staring at my work phone, my breath quickens. A full day of presentations I haven't prepared for. I message my assistant: 'Hi there, what's this?'

'Trends presentations with senior teams. And then a VIP shopping event the following day.'

30

Marital Death

Until death do us part

04.04.19

I still don't have a job description. HR still won't agree to my company pension. You go away for a few days. When you return, the hallway's painted jet black.

I am nostalgic for when the kids were little. Rain, shine, snow, sleet, every weekend you were studying, the three of us would head out to the sandpit opposite our house. It's easy to look back with a sense of longing, I suppose. Now that they are older, it is easy to say I miss the days when the kids were toddlers, days that felt as though they'd never end, the backbreaking work of dressing, cleaning, playing, cooking, bathing two small humans. How the longest days turned into the shortest years, I'll never know.

I miss trips to buy all-in-one waterproofs, knowing the colour of a rainproof all-in-one would be the biggest sartorial decision I'd make that season. The little wellington boots, the tiny gloves on strings. Endless runny noses, all bright red at the end. A low mood, a loss of identity, their physical smallness seemingly a reflection of my ever-shrinking world.

Snacks. Always carrying snacks. The dog licking the bottom of the pram clean. Trips to the zoo. Just us. Hours and hours of them without you.

I've started crying in the car, playing the same song on repeat. The last-ever tune played at the closing of SPACE, a club I loved in Ibiza. We'd been out all night. The following day, at around noon, after twenty-four hours of clubbing, Carl Cox played Angie Stone's 'Wish I Didn't Miss You'. The place erupted.

Every single word breaks my heart. By the time I pull into the office car park, I've listened to it six times over.

But today, I'm not in my car. I'm flying to NYC, so I dragged a small suitcase on to the tube at 7am instead. After hosting a breakfast event at 8am, I'm due to fly to New York mid-morning to interview a celebrity. I'll be in and out of NYC within the same twenty-four hours. The much younger me would've kicked off, accusing the commissioning editor of 'pushing me to my limits'. How little the thirty-something-year-old me knew about 'limits'. I have no plans to see friends in the city on this flying visit, on account of my body and mind being on separate planets.

I'm wired. I'm wired from hosting the breakfast event (public speaking, not mentioned in the non-existent job description, drains every ounce of my energy), but I'm mostly wired from three nights of no sleep. I used to sleep like the dead, now I lie in the dark, staring at the ceiling, wondering if you'll lean over and touch me ever again. I should reach out to you, a hand on your back at the very least, but I can't. I'm frightened.

On the plane, I do my usual thing of ignoring the pithy advice I myself have trotted out in countless beauty features over the years. Under headlines such as 'How to Look Good After a Long Flight', or some other bollocks, I go on to lecture the reader about why looking their best upon arrival is crucial to their well-being.

'You must hydrate by drinking lots of water. Don't wear make-up, add extra moisturiser, eat fruit.' Yet here I am, as per, drinking all the wine, eating all the crisps, asking for more wine.

I don't sleep on the plane. Even in the car on the way to the Standard hotel, another surge of adrenaline hits. It's as though my body's decided it doesn't need to sleep any more. I've packed one white shirt, which I plan to wear on tomorrow's shoot. It makes things far easier: one outfit choice, no faffing around at the hotel, changing outfits.

The hotel has twenty-one floors and my room is almost at the top. As I pull apart gauzy privacy curtains, the setting sun bounces off a thousand skyscrapers, sending the city skyline into rapt applause.

I step inside the glass shower, body lit soft orange by a sultry setting sun.

Is this the life you signed up for? Lost in motherhood, a wife in a lonely marriage. A grown-up now, but only half a woman, playing along with life's plans. What do you want? Where are you going? Who are you?

Tomorrow's white shirt hangs in the wardrobe. Ignoring the creases, I pull it on and head to the rooftop bar. I sit alone, sipping a cocktail. This bar, this scene, this vibe, is something I would've enjoyed a decade ago.

Well-dressed women with incredible bodies talk to men who lap up their every word. I wish I'd had their confidence at that age.

Observing the room, I am unaware that I too am being observed: a man my age, wearing a matching white shirt, pulls up a stool close to mine. He's from Lebanon; he looks expensive and well-educated. He shows me pictures of his wife and teenage kids as an icebreaker. I tell him his wife is very pretty. She is. Way prettier than me. A yoga teacher, she is petite, muscular, tanned, brunette. The opposite of the pink, northern sausage skin I inhabit.

'Fancy another drink?' he asks, while simultaneously getting the check and paying. He's bossy, dominant.

I'm unused to this kind of manipulation, turning to putty in his hands. I don't fight it.

'Shall we go?' he says, taking my arm without waiting for my reply, a sleazy hotel scene from a film the bartenders at the Standard have watched one too many times.

We meander through the Meatpacking District for a while. Inwardly, I reflect on how much it's changed. Naff, cheesy, commercial: not the edgy place I remember when I used to come to New York in 2002, booking cheap flights just to go to an all-day club on Sunday called Body and Soul.

We go into a bar I never would've frequented back then. It's packed with drunk kids in their early twenties. Two white shirts in a sea of band Ts. We don't belong in here. Shoving his way to the bar, he orders two bottles of beer. I notice he's shorter than my usual type. Not my type at all.

Regardless, it's clear what's about to unfold.

His mouth meets mine. A different taste, a new smell. I close my eyes, inhaling the type of slow, deep kissing I'd forgotten about. Lost in cocktails and chemicals, the grotty club wall against my back, I'm pushed against it, my one white shirt now covered in club grime. No one notices his fingers opening the buttons of my jeans.

I like his short, stocky body. It's different. But I don't want to have sex with him; straightforward penetration is not what I need. There have been times over the past five years when I've felt so alone, my skin has ached. On days like these, I book a massage, but it's not the same as feeling the heaviness of someone's body lying on top of mine, mouths glued together, climbing inside one another.

I don't want to let him climb inside me. I don't want to have sex with him. I don't want to have an affair.

He walks me to my room. Worrying he'll linger in the hope

of sex, I quickly close the door. Thank God I remember to set the alarm.

When the alarm sounds at 7am, it's already sunny in New York. I've had just a few hours' sleep in four days, but I'm no longer tired. Last night someone wanted and desired me. The hand of a stranger on my neck; a chemical collision of dopamine and serotonin. I'm more than awake.

I'm awakened.

15.04.19

One of us suggests couples' therapy, and the other one agrees. He must feel as lonely as I do.

18.05.19

I'm forty-five today, and it's a shock to not feel dreadful. Turning forty-one was a confusion of grief: grieving for the woman I'd been before motherhood, heading into my forties with a four-year-old and a two-year-old, the previous years had been a monotonous blend of illness, physical labour and loss of identity. Forty-three was the worst, though. Lost in my career, self-esteem on the floor, along with my relationship, I'd had this idea that at this age, women were either supposed to be at the peak of their careers or slowing down, ready for the next stage. I was neither.

Waking up today, though, forty-five feels like a new beginning. A life that's more than halfway through, yet there's still so much to aim for.

On my hen night last year, I wore a paisley-print, floor-length, high-necked, long-sleeved cotton dress from H&M. From head to toe, every inch of my body was covered – well, apart from my head. I hadn't meant to wear it; I randomly pulled it out of my cupboard, giving little thought to what I was wearing on what was, I suppose, a big night. That modest dress was a sartorial symbol of a mind and body disconnected. Motherhood had shut off any notion of feeling sexy.

But at my birthday dinner tonight, I wear a tight-fitting mini-dress, black eight-denier tights, black patent high heels and a biker jacket. And at the restaurant, I feel seen. Seen by my friends, seen by the room, seen by the waiting staff – male, female, other.

Seen by myself.

19.05.19

I book a babysitter so you and I can go out for dinner. We head to a local Italian restaurant so we can walk home if there's an emergency. Not that there'd ever be a child-related emergency; it's just you and I don't really *go* 'out' out. We sit in silence; we've become that couple who don't talk to one another. A few times, I start a conversation, but I feel self-conscious.

You know everything. You read everything.

I'm losing my confidence around you.

08.06.19

I hate couples' therapy. I'm always late. An act of aggression, apparently. Am I angry? I don't know. My own therapy sessions are also a shitshow. The other day, seeing me pushed to my limit, she asked if I wanted to scream.

'Yes,' I said.

'Go on, then,' she said.

So I did.

I screamed and screamed and couldn't stop. My throat hurt for two days.

14.07.19

Kate Spicer turns fifty today. Classic Kate, to be born on Bastille Day. Lunch started at 2pm, and at around 2.30pm someone asks if I'd like to try Peyote.

'Coyote, as in the Road Runner? OK, go on then.'

'Sprinkle it into water, like this, then down it. Tastes foul.'

It's hallucinogenic, and comes from a cactus. Given the effects can last ten or more hours, I take half the amount suggested. About twenty of us are sitting around one table. A hot sensation sweeps across my skull like a sparkler.

I look across the table at you.

Are we done?

You leave around six. I stay for the duration. Kate's my mate, after all. A bell rings last orders, and someone hands me a one-for-the-road glass of red.

He sees me first.

Our friends are on the pavement outside, talking to a group of newcomers, guys who've been on the lash, watching the cricket.

He makes the first move.

'Where are you from?' he asks, curving away from the men he's spent the day with at Lord's Cricket Ground.

'Edinburgh. You?'

'No way, me too!'

'Really?' I ask. Our Notting Hill surroundings feel suddenly incongruous.

'Hang on. How old are you? You look familiar.'

'Forty-six,' he says.

'I'm forty-five ... wait, are you Steven?' I ask. 'Oh my god, I had the biggest crush on you when I was a kid! Do you know who I am?'

Without giving him time to reply, I say, 'I'm Stacey Duguid – and YOU were my first love!'

'WHAT. *You're* Stacey Duguid? Shit, shit! No way! So come on: kids, married?'

'Yes, two kids, married. You?'

'Same. Two kids, married.'

It's odd, seeing someone you haven't seen since childhood. He's older, different looking, but the eyes remain the same. On the surface of his gaze, we replay memories.

'Can I take your number? Stay in touch? Maybe go for a drink? I'd love to catch up!'

A million miles from Edinburgh, on a pavement in Notting Hill, a handsome man just asked for my number. What's the worst that could happen?

It's midnight, and there's talk of going back to someone's house, but I don't want to go. I want to be alone with this feeling, now that the world is hung with fairy lights. I won't remember the Uber ride home. I'm ecstatic, joyful, smiling to the point of having to put a hand over my mouth to stifle the happiness that must be exploding from my face. I'm relieved to find the house in darkness.

Removing my make-up in the mirror, my reflection knows bumping into him was meant to be. Crawling into bed, my phone flashes. It's him.

'So good to see you. Can I call tomorrow?'

He started it.

'So, how are things?' My therapist's opening line, the same every single week. Bet she says it to all her patients.

'I'm great, I feel alive!' I say, resisting the urge to sing for fear I may actually leap to my feet and ask her to join me in the conga.

Her eyes – neither green nor blue, but a sort of cloudy grey – widen.

'Oh, OK. Any reason for this sudden change in mood?'

'Yes. His name is Steve.'

31

Marital Adultery

A woman walks into a bar and . . .

17.06.19

We message non-stop for days, then agree to meet at Soho House.

Feeling sick from nerves, I try on everything in my wardrobe, eventually going with my usual uniform of jeans, shirt and blazer. He's sitting towards the back of the restaurant. As I walk towards him, I can tell he's as nervous as I am. It's 1pm on a Thursday, a 'work' day. I order a large glass of white wine, then he orders a bottle.

For four days, we've been exchanging fast-fire WhatsApps. Messages I wake up and immediately look for, turning away from the family breakfast table to hide my deranged smile. Now I'm in front of him, I don't know what to say. My mouth won't work; my brain has frozen.

We order lunch, but neither of us eats. We swap stories of our marriages and how unhappy we are. United in feeling a deep love for our children but not our respective spouses, we bemoan the drudgery of marriage, and how misunderstood we both are, how ignored, how abandoned, how unloved.

He moves his chair closer to mine, and we share a first kiss.
'You're so beautiful,' he says. 'And fucking funny.'

In the last therapy session of the summer, I tell her I'm in love.
Like, totally and utterly in love. 'I've never felt this way before.'

Fixing her cloudy grey eyes on mine, she asks if I've ever heard
of the term 'Limerence.'

Happy I won't be seeing my therapist until early September,
I skip out the door. When I switch on my phone in the car, he's
sent seven messages in an hour. I smile all the way home. After
pulling up outside my house, and only for the sake of curiosity, I
google 'Limerence'.

This woman knows jack shit about Steve.

I'm in LOVE. The end.

End of August

'Meet at the bar around 3pm?'

'Sure! See you there!'

'OK. I'll check us in.'

I head up to the room first, to make sure it looks right. I'm feeling so nervous the ends of my fingers tingle. We've been apart for
three weeks, after spending most of August with our families. I'm
desperate to be held by him, to be fucked by him, to wake up with
him. I bury the web of lies I've told to make tonight happen in the
farthest recesses of my mind. I'll deal with the guilt tomorrow.

After various faffs, mostly involving hair, I head to the bar,
where I sit at a corner barstool. Touching the surface of the cold
marble bar keeps me rooted in the room. I'm 'working' today,
so every few minutes a message pings in from a team member. I
don't care about anything – work, friends, family. All I want is
him. I only want to see him, to be with him, to talk to him.

He's late.

'Hiya,' he says, flustered, carrying no overnight bag. 'Office is mad, kids are back tomorrow. Sorry, I had a lot to sort out.'

'Where's your bag?' I ask, panic lashing from the soles of my feet up towards my chest.

'I don't need a bag,' he says, nonchalant, like we haven't been arranging this night for the past few weeks via 5,000 messages per day.

'What do you mean? We're staying the night. Surely you need a change of clothes?'

'My wife's arranged for the cleaner to come in at seven tomorrow morning, and I have to be there to let her in.'

'She what?' I'm holding back tears. *The Krypton Factor* has nothing on the kind of arrangements I've had to oversee to be here. I've lied to work, to my husband, to my kids.

'The cleaner doesn't have a key. She needs me to let her in.'

'Why at seven?'

Well, well, well, a voice from above pipes up. *His wife doesn't trust him. He's clearly done THIS before* . . .

The atmosphere changes. I down a vodka and order another. *Fuck*. This can't be happening. I reach for my personal phone and order a gram of coke.

Warmed by vodka, I smile and pull him close. As my arms dangle around his neck, I can feel his shoulders stiffen. Watching him glance around the bar, paranoid and on edge, the excited nervousness I felt on my way here quickly turns to something else.

This person from my past, this man intended to be my *actual* safe harbour, isn't being straight with me. The rescue mission hasn't even been fully launched, and already the boat is beginning to sink. This can't be happening. This man is – *was* – my life raft. I need him to be the goddamn life raft.

Up in our hotel room, I've already drawn the curtains. Ringing room service in a familiar Scottish lilt, an accent I was brought up around, and one I miss dearly, he orders a bottle of vodka. I head back downstairs to meet the dealer.

Roughly three or four vodkas down, I'm not a middle-aged mother having an affair in a hotel room, I'm a teenager enacting what should've happened years ago. In the bathroom, I change into the Agent Provocateur black lace body I bought specifically for the occasion.

When he removes his shirt, his body is muscular, beautiful and tanned. He goes to the gym. I don't – hence the lace body with clips in the gusset. Covering my mum-tum, the good-quality lace is powerful enough to hold it all in. I have zero intention of removing the damn thing, especially not when being fucked from behind.

In the dark, I play a part I presume has been written for me. First-time sex with Steve isn't exactly spectacular, but there's plenty of time to work on it tonight.

'Shall we go out?' I ask, already feeling claustrophobic in the confines of the hotel room.

Soho is rammed. We bump into a million people I know, and his mood slips further. Back at the hotel, somehow it's already 2am. Very high on coke, he can't get an erection.

'Who are you ringing?' I ask, now totally naked on the bed, black lace body cast aside, along with my body shame.

'A hooker,' he says. 'A woman.'

I'm very high and can't really speak. The combination of his hanging limp dick and my AP lace body strewn across the floor while he's using the hotel room phone to call a sex worker at 2am makes me feel as if I'm on the set of fucking *Scarface*. A threesome? With a sex worker? Not exactly how I imagined the night going.

She doesn't call back. High, we twitch around in bed, neither of us able to sleep. At around 5.30am, he suddenly appears, fully dressed, in the bathroom doorway.

'Where are you going?' I manage to say, images of a cosy break-fast in bed smashed to smithereens.

'Like I said, I have to let the cleaner in.' The door slams shut behind him.

I know he'll come back for me. He has a key. If I lie here, he'll be back. He'll be back to hold me tight. Wild-eyed, I watch bright blue numbers changing, until the digital clock flicks to 7am. I start to cry.

He's never coming back.

I'm a middle-aged woman, abandoned in a hotel room, amid a seedy scene of empty vodka bottles and cocaine debris. Next to the expensive lace body, discarded on the floor, he's left a pile of cash. He said he'd pay for room service. I suppose he can't have it come up on his card, in case his wife finds out.

Who's the sex worker now?

He's not my safe harbour.

'Kate.'

'Stacey, what's happened? You OK?'

'No, no, no. I fucked Steve. In a hotel room. And – and he's gone, he left me here. I'm high, I haven't slept. Can you come for me? I need someone to pick me up?'

'I can't. Hold on, I'm calling Claire.'

Now sobbing to the point of screaming, I shove the lace body back inside the secret compartment of my suitcase. Drenching a towel, I scrub white lines off every surface: the toilet seat, the sink, the bedside tables. I flush rolled-up notes down the loo. My mobile rings.

The fourth emergency service, otherwise known as Claire.

'Right, I've booked a car. It's outside. All you have to do is pack your bag, put on your sunglasses, walk out of the hotel and get in the car. We'll deal with the rest when you get to my house.'

I take the money.

*

The car pulls up outside Claire's house, and she's already at the door. Grabbing my suitcase, she quietly takes me upstairs to her bed. Heavy velvet curtains already drawn, she tucks me in like a child. At the sight of her holding a bottle of Rescue Remedy, I open my mouth like a baby bird. A bottle of sparkling water, two headache tablets, and a cup of mint tea are already lined up by the bed. She strokes the side of my hair. 'It's OK. It's going to be OK.'

I wish I believed her.

32

Marital Trauma

Two days later

We head to Richmond on a family walk. At lunch, you notice I'm not eating. I down a pint and order a large glass of white. I'm remote, distracted, heartbroken; you see it written across my face.

We haven't slept together since my one-night-stand disaster. Even though it's Saturday night, and we'd usually spend it watching TV together, tonight, after the kids' bedtime, I just shout downstairs, 'Goodnight.'

Exhausted, I fall into a deep sleep. I only know this because you shake me awake at midnight. Groggy, it takes a few seconds for my eyes to see your face.

Holding a glass of wine, you calmly tell me you've found Steve's emails, read all the text messages, and that you've taken photos of the bar and hotel receipts. I'm still lying down; you're standing above me. I hadn't changed the password on my computer. I never thought to.

Do I understand everything has been sent to lawyers as evidence?

'Yes.' I nod. 'Yes, I do.'

*

A few weeks later, I drive to work listening to Angie Stone. An unopened letter sits on the passenger seat beside me. It's dark in the office car park, especially in the corner where I leave my car. It's the only place I feel safe enough to read what's inside.

You told me to 'expect something', and, well – here it is.

' . . . filing for divorce on grounds of adultery'.

Five Thoughts On . . . Preparing for a Divorce (Actually, Make it Twelve Thoughts), by Sara Davison

Sara Davison is a divorce coach and author of Uncoupling: *How to survive and thrive after breakup and divorce*

1. Get your Break-up Support Team in place. It's easy to get overwhelmed with the break-up process from a financial, legal and emotional perspective. So it's vital to get experts around you who can help answer all the questions you have and give you the best advice. For example, if you are concerned about finances, then find someone who can help you create a financial plan for your situation that will give you the clarity you need to move forward.

2. Get clarity on what you spend each month so you can understand your spending patterns and how much money you need. Create a budget spreadsheet of your weekly and monthly expenditure. Take ownership of this, so you feel more financially independent and in control.

3. Agree with your partner what to say to the kids about the break-up. The ideal scenario, if possible, is to sit down and tell them together. Reassurance that they are loved and that this is not their fault is key.

4. Treat each other with respect and kindness. You are bound to disagree over matters at some point, so make an agreement to treat each other kindly and respectfully, and this will create a strong foundation, helping to keep things as amicable as possible while minimising tension. If your ex is toxic or abusive, this will not be reciprocated but it's important to always do the right thing and take time to think before responding to nasty comments. Breathe and even sleep on your response to ensure you maintain your dignity and avoid pouring fuel on the flames.

5. Pick your battles. In the heat of the moment, it is easy to get worked up over the little things. Take a step back and work out if you will really care about this in a few months' time. This will help you to get perspective on what is important and when emotions might be getting the better of you.

6. Don't talk about your break-up to everyone you meet. Share your feelings with close friends or family, but don't get sucked into a world where the only thing you talk about is your split. It will keep you stuck and you will be constantly reliving all the negative emotions.

7. Don't bad-mouth your ex to others. It may well get back to them and make things worse. Of course, you can be honest with your inner circle of select friends and family, but avoid openly discussing your ex in public.

8. Self-care, eating well and exercising are crucial to keeping a strong mind and enabling you to make better decisions. Exercise is a great way to instantly boost your state of mind. Even a brisk walk around the block will make you feel better and help you stay in control of your emotions.

9. Write a list of all the things you weren't happy with in your relationship as you take off the rose-tinted glasses. If you are heartbroken and finding it hard to let go of your ex, this is a great exercise. When we reminisce about our partners, it's easy to focus on all the good bits and romanticise things. But this will keep you stuck in the past, and it isn't always reality – as your list will prove.

10. Spring-clean your life. Create a plan for the life you want to live and the person you want to become. Out with the old and in with the new. Try new things, do things differently and make small changes that add more sparkle to your life. Detox your home of anything that doesn't make you feel good and replace them with things that do.

11. Create some fun in your life. Break-ups bring with them a roller coaster of emotions, so make sure you find ways to laugh and connect with those you love. Break-ups are an opportunity to rediscover yourself, and, while you may feel like curling up and hiding away from the world some days, making an effort to see a friend or try something new will help you feel stronger. It's so important to have fun things in your diary so you are not consumed with your break-up. There is more to life than relationships, and you need to maintain a healthy balance in other areas of interest, too.

12. Research the best way to get divorced to suit your situation. While a legal advisor can explain what to expect from your split and manage the process for you, you can also get divorced online at a fraction of the cost.

33

Taxi to Mayhem Central

Why have one therapist when you can have two

Hearing the usual, 'So, how are things?' from my therapist, I immediately begin to dissociate. The skin on my face buzzes, the air tightens around my brow, the calming candle lit to create serenity burns hotter than the gates of Hell.

'Put both feet on the ground,' she says, while gently counting to ten. 'Feel the ground beneath your feet.'

'It's over,' I eventually say, after asking permission to lie down on her sofa. 'With Steve.'

'Oh, I see,' she says, her cloudy eyes staring into mine. When I look at her, I sometimes feel I'm hallucinating.

'It wasn't love; it was infatuation. Limerence. You were right.'

'Yes,' she says. 'And no wonder.'

'No wonder?' I say, body pulling back into the room, bracing myself for a lecture.

'To live without touch must have been very difficult.'

I've been dreading telling our couples' therapist about Steve, especially because, during the months we've been seeing her, I've managed to convince myself she hates me. So it's *her* reaction to the news of the fling that surprises me most.

'I could've bet my entire career on Stacey having a sexual encounter; it doesn't surprise me one bit. Let's not refer to this as an affair, though. It was a four-week fling – a reaction to what's been going on over the past several years.'

I want to leap to my feet and hug her.

I've been forgiven, or at least acknowledged.

By her, I mean, not by you.

34

Fashion Week(s) Mayhem

D is for Dolce & Gabanna, but also David

Mercedes Benz has supplied a chauffeur-driven car to take us around London Fashion Week. No matter the city, no matter for whom I'm working, I've noticed the same thing: when we're sitting in the back of a car, several hours per day, endless days per month, women open up to one another. Unless you're travelling with Anna Wintour, in which case I imagine you might not say a word.

It's Sunday morning. I sink into the expensive tan leather bucket seat. 'My marriage is over,' I say, words hanging in the air like burned toast. 'Married for just over a year, and it's done. I feel sick.'

The woman next to me reports to me, and although she's quite used to my spectacular lack of boundaries, she seems unsure as to what to say next. Lightening the mood, she says, 'You should date again, now!', she says, whipping out her phone and showing me a random dating app. 'Oh, go on, join, JOIN!' So I do.

A week or so later, at Milan Fashion Week, I notice several emails from the app. Jesus, I'd forgotten about that! The emails take me to the site, where a message from a man called David catches my eye. A quick glance at his photo confirms he's hand-some, but then the Dolce show music starts and I put my phone away for fear of being chucked out of my seventh-row seat by the PR. Rumour has it, some designers film the audience, to check who's paying attention and who isn't. Allegedly, after an Armani show several years back, one editor even received a snarky letter instructing him to focus on the show instead of chatting to the person next to him. LOL.

Later, safely away from the show and any prying eyes, I check my messages. A C suite executive, it's clear David is used to get-ting what he wants. I'm not interested, not after the Steve disaster, not with so much to sort out at home. I'm sleeping in the spare room; I'm not exactly dating material.

'When are you free to meet?' his message reads.

'Saturday?' I reply, distracted. I already know I'll cancel, which is frustrating for everyone involved, so why lie in the first place?

When the day comes, not only do I forget I am supposed to meet him at a pub in Maida Vale, I turn off my phone and have an early night. It's a red rag to a bull. He spends the next day pursu-ing me even more.

What I might wear on a first date
if I had my act together

1. A black skirt suit. The skirt would be knee-length and tight-fitting like a pencil; the jacket would be longer and nipped in at the waist. Essentially Dior's 'New Look', but probs from eBay.
2. Vivienne Westwood heels, platforms, spike heels, or the black patent pumps from Saint Laurent that require foot surgery to walk in.
3. A hat. Maybe an enormous black fedora.
4. Fucking HUGE sunglasses by Celine. If you can't find Celine, switch out for ski goggles/visor. Same same.
5. Underwear-wise, I don't tend to wear anything other than my M&S four-for-the-price-of-three or whatever the deal is. Thank God for Rosie Huntington Whitely.
6. A white silk blouse that's a bit see-through. You know, Charlotte Rampling vibes. All bouncy tits and scruffy hair.
7. Wolford tights. Eight denier.
8. Malle's famous fragrance, Portrait of a Lady. Perhaps that's not me.
9. That Bobbi Brown black eyeliner that, once applied, you only have a few seconds to smudge, after which point it won't move. Not even should you find yourself at a foam party in Ibiza.
10. Massive gold circular earrings. As in, the ones John Lewis sell, but without irony. Sort of Chanel meets Monet. Clip on.

I've just described what my mother used to wear in the 1980s. Just add fifteen cans of hairspray and blue eyeliner.

35

Separation Mayhem

Fun fact: dating strangers while midst-nervous
breakdown won't make you feel better

Mid-October

The spare room feels increasingly claustrophobic. I miss my marital bed. The one we chose together, when I was heavily pregnant, waddling through Heal's. I miss looking at the trees through the window. I miss being in love with you.

I've started to gather my belongings around me, boxing things up. The kids seem not to notice.

End of October

You hate the black walls in the hallway, the huge, cavernous kitchen. I move the furniture around until midnight. I clean out the cupboards for hours, yet nothing feels clean.

'This is a very clean house,' you tell me, which I know to be true, but still I can't describe this feeling of dirt.

November

The game of cat-and-mouse with David is entertaining. I've cancelled on him five times, but today, feeling lonely in my own skin, my very existence ignored at home – or at least, it feels that way – I am craving attention, so I relent and ask him to meet me at Soho House in Notting Hill. The kids are at school, and I'll only pop out for a quick coffee.

He's late. I watch him walk in from my seat at the back. He's working the same C Suite off-duty look as in his photo: too-tight jeans, too-neat trainers produced by an Italian brand to look intentionally scruffy. This, in my opinion, is ridiculous – why these guys don't just stick to the classics such as Nike is beyond me. Perhaps this intentionally scuffed trainer is the modern equivalent of the jazzy comedy sock? Perhaps the tight jeans worn at C suite level serve to show everyone how big their manhood is.

Although he's badly dressed, he's sharp. Very, very smart.

'Listen,' I say, in a way that suggests bad news. 'I'm not actually who I said I was in my profile. I just needed to get that out there, you know, quickly.'

'Your actual name comes up on your WhatsApp, so I put my tech guy on the case. Nothing you have to say will surprise me.'

'Wait, you googled me?'

'Ha! Way deeper than that.'

I'm creeped out, but admittedly intrigued. After an hour, I have to go.

'Can I drive you home?' he asks, which I don't really understand, given no one has ever offered to drive me home during the day before.

Outside, a small crowd is gathered around his car. Some rare Bugatti. I have no clue what that means, other than it's loud and brightly coloured.

Embarrassed, I asked him to drop me half a mile away from home. I can't bear the thought you might see me, us, in this monstrous car.

And you.

Truth is, it's you I'd rather go for coffee with, or for lunch, or cocktails, or whatever. Not some random guy I met on a website who seems to not care I lied about my background. I have nothing in common with him.

Mid-November

It's done. We're done. I told you I'm done. Are you done, too? We *say* we're done, but are we? I'm not sure I've been listening. The spare bedroom walls close in; water reaches the tops of walls. Weird things pull me under, with no Chewbacca to protect me. I need you to pick me up and run.

We share a house, children, but not a life. Separate friendships. Your friends don't really like me, and I'm not a huge fan of them. This posh public-school thing, the way everyone talks *at* me without asking a question. I feel unheard by them and their old-fashioned partners and wives, who look at me as though I've landed from Mars.

Now it's done, this short marriage of ours. And we're together in this house. This house with the black hallway you hate, and the kitchen I ripped apart. I'm sorry. I don't know why I did that without asking. You've always called me impulsive.

In an odd way, knowing that we are done has released me. I no longer feel this seething anger towards this empty hollow of a thing we call a relationship.

I feel lighter. I feel freer.

Do you?

Top ten songs to listen to when going through a divorce

1. The Cure, 'Boys Don't Cry'
2. Prince, 'Purple Rain'
3. Frankie Goes To Hollywood, 'The Power Of Love'
4. Dolly Parton, 'Jolene'
5. Massive Attack, 'Teardrop'
6. Wham, 'Last Christmas'
7. The Bangles, 'Eternal Flame'
8. Every single song written by Coldplay
9. Sinéad O'Connor, 'Nothing Compares 2 U'
10. Bruce Springsteen, 'The River'
11. Sorry, it has to be eleven – Elton John, 'Sorry Seems To Be The Hardest Word'

* WAILS INTO THE ABYSS. NO ONE COMES. DRINKS WINE. TAKES A NUROFEN. STROPS OFF TO BED WITH THE DOG.*

December

The month passes by in the usual manner. The kids' end of school concerts haven't been noted down. Nor has their Christmas jumper day – no clue when that is. I miss PTA requests for the bake sale;* they must have been in the newsletter I never read. By way of self-protection, I've well and truly alienated myself from the pack that is the 'mum club', hence why I arrive at the school gate wearing expensive clothes, ginormous sunglasses and high heels. I'm like a caricature, a sort of Patsy Stone meets Jessica Rabbit. Dressing up has always been my way of survival, of keeping everyone and everything at arm's length. It's something I've always done, wearing outfits that say, 'Leave me alone, fuck you.' I picked it up from Mum, who learned it from her mum, although their approach was less 'fuck you', more, 'Look at me, I might not be rich, but I can put on a good show.'

The end of term comes as a surprise once again. My therapist asks why I'm not turning up to sessions. I'm still packing to leave the home we have together. Small things packed into small boxes. A pot our son made aged two; a collection of doodles supposed to be paintings I cannot bring myself to throw away; the schoolbooks everyone tells me to shove into the recycling bin. I've kept their baby clothes. Too many of them housed in boxes marked 'Memories'.

Late December

'I'm sending a car for you. Eight o'clock, Friday.'
     Audacious, considering we've shared only one coffee and

---

* Bake sale top tip: decant two boxes of sugary doughnuts bought from the little Tesco into a large Tupperware box. Kids will marvel at your baking prowess, and you get five hours of your life back.

a loud drive home in a fancy car, a journey cut short out of embarrassment.

'A car? Where to? The last time a man sent a car to pick me up, I ended up at Donatella Versace's house with Kevin Bacon.'

'Oh, this will be way more fun.'

'Car's outside,' David informs me over WhatsApp.

I peer out the window to see a chauffeur wearing a hat standing on the kerb by a blacked-out car that looks like all the other blacked-out chauffeur-driven cars in the world.

I open the front door, making up some bullshit about going to a fashion dinner. No questions are asked. No questions are ever asked. I've left the house on countless occasions, and no one seems to mind where I'm going. Is that normal?

'OK,' you say, without looking up.

'Good evening, Ms Dooogood,' says the chauffeur, opening the car door.

'Hi. Stacey. Nice to meet you.'

Sitting in the back, unsure as to whether the car is bugged with some sort of microphone David or the driver may have planted, I don't utter a word. We rattle through the streets. Or rather, we glide, it's the inside of my head that's rattling. The driver stops outside a restaurant in Mayfair: a small, discreet place I've never noticed before.

I'm assuming we'll join the diners seated in the room to the right, but the waitress turns left, opens a door and walks down a set of very old, dark oak steps. Paintings of noblemen adorn the walls, which are decorated in flocked, dark green wallpaper. I've lost count of the number of steps; there are so many.

'Here we are, Miss Duguid.' A huge door opens from the other side to reveal David sitting alone in a private dining room. A large table designed to seat twenty is set for just the two of us. There is low lighting, with plenty of candles. I imagine the Jacobites holding secret meetings, plotting to bring the Stuarts back to the throne.

I check my phone for a signal. Zero bars.

'You look insanely beautiful. Champagne?'

'Yes please,' I say, relieved I chose the tight, mid-length, off-the-shoulder cocktail dress I'd bought in the MatchesFashion sale, as opposed to my usual casual blazer, nice top and jeans.

'Now listen,' he says, in a way that gets my adrenaline pumping. 'I want to get something straight.'

'OK,' I reply, thinking I don't remember this man looking quite this handsome last time we met. Unless it's his obvious power that's changing things: the fast car, the big watch, the discreet staff in the background tending to his every whim without requiring instruction.

'I like you,' he says. 'I really like you.'

The flattery flies to my head and my stomach flutters to attention. 'OK, go on,' I say. 'There's a but . . . ?'

'That's it. No but,' he says, sitting back, observing my face. A satisfied look I can't quite decipher stretches across his own. 'My ex-wife and I are good friends. We co-parent the girls very well. I'm happy. Even happier, now I've met you.'

My mind goes into overdrive. This man is offering a rescue mission. This strong man who knows how to swim.

Here's a man who won't let me drown.

36

Paris Fashion Week Mayhem

I blame Saint Laurent

February 2020

I only just make it out of Milan. Turning up at the Dolce show bang on time, only to discover the show has started early, is the weirdest thing to ever happen in fashion. The show is usually at least an hour late each season, given how many celebrities take up the front row. I just stand there on the pavement outside, totally and utterly shocked. Something strange is going on. The Dolce show never starts early. A cold tingle runs up and down my spine. Looking around, I realise something's wrong.

At the airport out of Milan, everyone is carrying luggage and a manic energy. People are wearing face masks; so odd. Landing in London, though, it's as if nothing has happened.

The next morning, I repack my suitcase and take a mid-morning Eurostar to Paris. I'm working on an 'influencer' shoot for Dior, and the press office has sent over a long, floaty, terracotta-hued dress for me to wear. I'm due to meet the influencer at 1pm. I'll accompany her to the Dior show, filming as she bustles past banks of paparazzi, waiting to take her photograph. My team, Paris Fashion Week virgins, have been briefed to film the drama that is the entrance of the Dior show, no matter what. I plan to interview her in the car, and also inside once she's seated – if I can get anywhere near her seat, that is.

I'm smitten with David, even if one of us (me) is miles away from being divorced. He arrives in Paris tomorrow, and will stay with me while I'm working. He gave me a bracelet from Hermès and told me he's falling in love. I can't wait to spend more than a few hours at dinner with him, even if I have a terrible headache.

The car hits fashion traffic as we approach the Dior show, a sure sign we're almost there. The video guys jump out of the car to join the thousands of people gathered outside the show. Police, paparazzi, editors, buyers, the general public, A-list actresses, children, famous musicians, poodles – you name it, the Dior show in Paris is an unbelievable scene like no other.

The driver opens the car door. I let her get out first. I am well versed in how to stay small and keep out of the shot. Walking a safe distance behind her, I note the video team has made it ahead and, despite the unpredictable madness, things are going to plan.

'Misssss! 'Scuse me miss.' I look around to see who they are calling to, expecting to see a celebrity. They are, in fact, shouting at me. A wasp nest disturbed, hundreds of them swarm, forming a perfect circle around me. I lose sight of my video team and the influencer.

'What are you wearing?'

So many microphones shoved in my face, notepads scribbled upon, pens poised, photographers taking close-ups of my face.

'What's your name and what do you do?'

I finally manage to break away.

I find her sitting in the second row – a great seat, as far as the Dior show goes – and I'm told to sit down beside her by a Dior

PR. My real seat is on the opposite side of the catwalk with the British press, circa row four or five, or something.

Talk about the power of a good dress.

Seeing myself splashed across the *Vogue* website and many more best-dressed round-ups, I now understand that the long terracotta Dior dress matched perfectly with my hair, thereby offering up a striking photograph. The addition of see-through, blue-lensed GUCCI sunglasses provided the perfect splash of colour. Oh, shit. I bet they're bitching about me at the office.

My headache worsens; I ignore it. Fashion Week fatigue is normal by the time we reach Paris, the fourth week of shows. Parisian pharmacies sell the strongest painkillers. I pop Doliprane like they're M&Ms, but my chest feels wheezy, so I up my asthma-pump intake from two puffs to three.

The room is perfect: the chaotic pile of invitations neatly stored away, my clothes – mostly borrowed – hung up for a change, as opposed to draped across the back of a chair. The air smells of expensive perfume, the one I know he likes.

I'm keen to show David Paris during this crazy week, so we head out for a walk. Accustomed to the beautiful people – the models, the agents, the photographers, the editors, the best-dressed people on the planet – who walk the streets at this time, and congregate within the same square mile, filling restaurants, cafés and bars for one week only, I no longer notice them.

I take him to Hôtel Costes: not the coolest, but definitely the best zoo during Fashion Week.

'You OK?' I ask. I'm enjoying being seated at one of the best tables in the restaurant – thanks to, I am convinced, the Rejina Pyo beige linen shorts suit I'm wearing.

Not answering, his eyes continue to scan the room. Eventually, he asks, 'Are they models?' flapping his menu towards a table of young women I know.

'No, they're influencers.'

'Do you know them?' he asks, his tone making me uncomfortable.

'Why? Do you find them attractive?' I say, immediately wishing I could shove the words back into my mouth.

'They're cute, but too skinny. I like my women with more meat on their bones.'

'More *meat*?'

'Yeah, like you. Curvy.'

'I'm curvy?'

'Yes, you have an ass, a tummy, tits.'

'Do I?'

I leave it there, knowing a conversation about my body – or any woman's body, for that matter – will end in an argument.

You would never say such a thing to me. You are too classy.

'Let's go shopping, I'm in the mood to blow money,' he says. 'Wish I'd driven the Bugatti to Paris. The girls here would love it!'

Christ. I don't.

'Where do you want to go shopping?' I ask, hopeful he might suggest Chanel.

'Saint Laurent,' he replies, before quickly adding, 'Not for you, darlin', for me.'

Watching him blow €18,000 on himself in the space of two hours makes me feel deeply insecure. And feeling anxiety around a man is the proverbial nail in the coffin – every woman knows that.

David departs the following morning, leaving my stomach in a tangle. I'm no longer the bold, argumentative, distant woman he chased for four months.

He's pulling away.

Maybe I'm imagining it.

I'm tired. I'm sick.

37

Moving Mayhem

I set fire to my future and fan
the flames into an inferno

March 2020

I'm moving into a cute little house opposite the kids' school this month. Not a cute price, at £4,000 per month, but – shock, horror – I can't find anything in the area that's cheaper. I can just about afford it on my salary, but it leaves barely any wiggle room. I've driven this separation. I am the one who should move out.

21 March 2020

'Sit down, kids,' I say.

Sitting on the long bench that runs across the length of the wall, they look at us in anticipation. Little elbows resting on the table bought before one of them was born. I pause to take them both in. Before us sit two children whose parents are still together. Not long from now, they'll be told we're separating. It's like a gone-wrong before-and-after photograph. I imagine they'll never look the same again. Two portraits I'd rather not paint.

I plough on, regardless.

It's a sunny morning. All the books suggest telling children their lives are about to change for ever on a Saturday morning, giving them time to digest the news before school on Monday. 'Prepare for the weekend under duvets watching favourite cartoons,' a friend had advised.

Did you and I discuss that, too?

He is eight and she is six, and in my mind it feels like now or never. I'm turning forty-six in May. Going by the fact Mum met Mike aged forty-nine, there's plenty of time for me, for you, to start again. Otherwise, what's the alternative? Stay together until they leave home, by which time I'll be fifty-seven?

I wish I had a crystal ball. I wish I didn't have to look at my children's faces lit by sunshine before the darkest storm.

Do you speak first? Or do I?

The words come out in a tumble. 'Mummy and Daddy are splitting up.'

Our son grows immediately angry; she is silent. Eventually, her face crumples. An indescribable pain sketches across it in indelible ink, stained for ever. I realise they are too young to handle the words I've been so desperate to say out loud.

She moves off the bench on to your lap, snuggling up close for comfort. Four hearts broken. Our son screams.

The relief I'd assumed I'd feel is nowhere to be seen.

The books I've read – well, the paragraphs – say our own relationship will model how our children see and view love. Our marriage will be the major influence on the type of relationships they seek out in the future. Yet you and I haven't actively participated in healthy communication since – when? Since the birth of our second child? What chance do our kids stand if the theory is that a son will look to his mother for a role model for a future partner, and a girl to her father? Reading that finished me off. I've been living in the spare room for six months; we've been sitting at dinner in silence. There must be a happier way to live. I don't wish to be a passive passenger in my own life.

'Mum is moving out.'

The room fills with deafening agony. Their world has twisted, a childhood blown apart. A twisted stomach. I'm taken back to when I was three. Their faces, yours, all the hopes and dreams of having a family unit – two parents, two kids, one house, for ever.

I can't remember what happens next. Everything goes dark.

38

Mayhem Settles In

I can't eat, I can't sleep, I can't work, I can't . . .

3 July 2020, 9am

It's finally moving day. I feel numb, yet excited. I feel as if I'm on the run, but also moving in the right direction. I feel as though whatever is around the corner will be better than this lonely relationship we've ended up in. I feel the kids need to see their parents happy. I feel I have no choice but to move out.

Due to the pandemic and lockdown, four months have passed since I was supposed to move out, and yet somehow, instead, we found ourselves locked down together. It was the chapter we were never supposed to write. A final chapter of a book that needed closure. Living together under the same roof for months, unable to leave or go out, you and I calmly got on with the job in hand: no rows, no fuss, no stress. I worked full-time while you did all the home-schooling; it felt borderline serene.

The barbecue I bought from John Lewis; the peppers we figured out how to roast and flavour with white wine vinegar; the kids darting around in swimsuits. It was boiling hot for April, so

I ordered a paddling pool. It was too big for the garden. Of course I ordered a pool too big for the garden.

We drank a lot of very nice wine.

Work was and still is fucking hideous: mass meetings on Zoom mean I can't read anyone's faces, so in order to speak at least one coherent sentence, I can't look at the screen. Looking at people's faces when I can't read them makes me so upset that when I hang up the call, I have to take a deep breath. I can't understand what they're doing – looking down, looking away? A dozen or so faces, judging my every word.

I think a lot about the lovely house opposite the kids' school that I was meant to move into in March. Slightly ramshackle, it was the opposite of our perfect home. I've begun to fantasise about all the things I'll do when I live alone, especially on days when I feel trapped. I'm insecure about the home we bought together. I feel the need to describe the house as 'architecturally designed'. I suppose it neatly illustrates that my life is a million miles from Ashton-under-Lyne. Deep down, I know it's not my house. Having contributed a smaller amount of money to the home we poured so much love into, along with expensive concrete floors, I joke I only own the downstairs loo. I know I will be happier leaving it all behind.

We dismantled it brick by brick; we rebuilt it room by room. Every detail was considered, no stone was left unturned. You and I were going to live there for ever, with our two children, my dog and that bad-tempered cat of yours.

In my head, this move isn't permanent. Do you feel it is? I'm moving out so I can catch my breath, so we can figure out what to do next. I suggest the kids should stay in the house, after reading somewhere it's called 'nesting'. The idea is the parents fly back and forth like birds, while the baby chicks stay put. I don't want to disturb the nest: the well-built, secure nest we both made happen. I wish they could remain here, but I understand they should move between houses. That's what you want.

I've found another gorgeous little place, cheaper than the other house. The new rental is all whitewashed floorboards and clean white walls, and I'm viewing it like an art gallery that I can dress up and make my own. I say 'viewing' – not that I've *seen* it, thanks to the Covid lockdown, but it looks fantastic on the estate agent's website.

I'm in search of my identity. I need to unearth the reasons why I'm on this planet. I have to; there has to be more to life than this.

My therapist pointed out recently how I've split myself in two. Since becoming a mother, I've pushed away the wild woman inside, and in doing so, I've locked away the essence of who I am. I don't mean the old 'old' me, the pill-popping, three-day-bender me – no thanks, no more raving at the Hacienda. It's a block of flats now, anyway. I mean the wild, restless spirit that felt too much, too extra, too dangerous to unleash during early motherhood. I didn't like myself; still don't. I still carry shame around in my handbag. The therapist sure has her work cut out.

Scared to unleash the wild woman within, scared I'd be a bad mother. Terrified the kids would be taken away from me, I hid that wild woman away.

I want a house filled with friends, dogs and kids, as noisy as hell. I've never enjoyed the uncomfortable silence of our family home. Perhaps I'll finally be able to parent in the way I'd like: no more Victorian rules or self-judgement when I keep the kids up too late. Freaky Fridays will become a thing in our home. Kids will hang out and beg to stay for sleepovers, and the house will be a mad mess filled with love and laughter. That's the example I want to show my kids. Love your friends and live life to the fullest. What more could we want?

I've been to John Lewis and bought new bed sheets. Goodbye white sheets, hello pink everything. Yee-haw. Hope David likes them. I've started running again, as it helps to clear my mind. I run over to David's new flat, a rental that's so pristine it looks as though he doesn't actually live there. On his bed, he has ten or so cushions, all neatly lined up in a row, making it look like a hotel room. It's the oddest thing. I run there whenever we hang out. We have coffee, sex, then I run back home.

The dream-list of things I intend to achieve at the first whiff of freedom is extensive. For starters, there'll be no more football droning from the telly. SWEET RELIEF! No more Talksport blaring from the kitchen and car radio. Just listening to that shite makes me want to chuck the radio out the window/crash into a tree. It'll be Classic FM in the mornings, KISS FM at night, Radio 4 on Saturday afternoons . . .

I can do whatever I damn well like.

'HONEY!' I shout upstairs to the youngest child. 'Want to come with me to see our new house?'

'OK!' she shouts, slowly pottering downstairs in squeaky neon-pink Crocs. Dressed in a white cotton sundress, she looks like an angel.

'Here, wear your hat. It's going to be warm later, and we have a new garden to check out.'

We set off holding hands. Mother and daughter, giggling along the road, heading to Gail's for an expensive bun and oat milk flat white. She scoops the froth off my coffee.

'Come on! Time to see this flat!'

Six thousand pounds transferred to an estate agent; the completion of contracts; an exchange of hopes and dreams of a new life. I hope the past will disappear, and I'll feel whole again.

Right now, in this moment, wearing denim cut-offs, Nikes, a bright orange sweater bought in Ibiza – this is what happiness feels like.

'Happy moving day!' chirps the estate agent, grinning rather too widely.

My six-year-old daughter's sweaty little hand wraps itself

tightly around mine. She's excited by our new start, too, my marshmallow girl with blonde fluffy curls reflecting the sun like a halo.

He hands over the keys and we head off in the morning sunshine. Off to start a new life.

10am

With lockdown easing, I've spent the past few weeks walking past my new world, my future happiness – as in, the house I'm about to enter for the first time. On my walks past, I've been slowing down, gazing into windows, dreaming of a home destined to be filled with Freaky Fridays and fun. I've stood outside the house many times, fantasising about the life ahead of me.

Unlike our family home, which perches on the edge of a posh park like a three-storey wedding cake, the houses on our new street feel shrunken and apologetic. I've been diverting my dog walks along our new road for weeks; how strange that I'm only noticing the slight sagginess of it all now.

'Here we are!' I say to the youngest, her sweaty little hand still holding mine. As I push aside the front garden gate, it falls off its hinges. Making light, I laugh, roll my eyes in a way that says, *Silly Mummy, breaking the gate!*

My stomach flips.

The Victorian black-and-white chequered path is uneven, the tiles dislodged, cracked, broken. A once-straight path, wrecked by an overgrown front garden left to grow wild.

I'm leaving an unattended-to marriage and walking towards an unattended-to home. The brown front door hasn't been painted for decades. I rummage in my handbag for the key, before tentatively opening the door to take a peek inside.

Then the smell hits.

Mice droppings hang in the air like death. Keeping a firm hold of my daughter's hand, we make our way down a narrow hallway. The whitewashed 'art gallery' floors are so scuffed and filthy, there's no point in taking off our shoes. I can't look at my daughter.

At the end of the hallway, we turn left into the kitchen. In the photos on the website, it looked so pretty. Not any more. There's a sofa beneath the window, an unwanted, sagging, discarded, dirty, huge, misshapen thing that's not supposed to be here. There's no way I'll fit all my stuff in here when the removal van turns up at noon.

Chips, so many chips, mar the Tiffany-blue kitchen work surface. Victorian gloom meets the nineties; this is a house with neglected vintage features, uncared for for decades. The blackened fireplace in the kitchen is stuffed with black bin bags. There's a free-standing fridge, lumbering and old, so filthy I can't hide my horror.

'Go and see the garden!' I say to my daughter, to get her out of the room. 'There'll be roses and lovely flowers, I bet. Let me know what you find!'

Managing to locate the source of the smell, I open the oven.

'Oh God, fuck, that's disgusting!'

'What, Mum?'

'Nothing! Just a stupid photo on my phone!'

The oven is revolting inside, swimming in grease. It's like a scene from *Breaking Bad*. One thing's for fucking sure, the only thing the previous tenants cooked was clearly crack cocaine.

A familiar feeling I know so well but have no name for swells in the pit of my stomach.

When you disappeared into work. When Steve left me alone in the hotel room. When David went cold in Paris. Destabilised, helpless, frozen, panicked, silent, overwhelmed, on fire, numb, cold, dizzy, racing heart, no focus, panic, dissociation.

The old fridge, the dirty windows, the crack-cocaine oven, the old chipped work surfaces, my dreams of Freaky Fridays swirling down the sink. No longer in my body.

I'm gone.

The doorbell rings. It's Claire. My daughter opens the door.

'Happy new home! Where's Mummy? I've bought her a house-warming cup of coffee.'

I'm on the floor in the front room at this point. Entering the disaster zone, Claire makes her way through the gates of Hell to find me. Placing a coffee down in front of me, she takes our youngest by the hand and escorts her out of the room.

Is this where I belong now? In this other world? I've only been here what, thirty minutes, and already a visitor appears as though she's landed from another planet. A planet where I used to live, where everything remains normal. A planet Claire shall return to within ten minutes of leaving me here. Leaving me behind.

Claire's left a balled-up tissue on the floor by the coffee. Was I crying?

Wires hanging from walls; loose, dangerous electrical sockets where our eldest will attempt to plug in his PlayStation. Hung on a badly painted wall behind me is a light in the shape of a ginormous sun. Beneath it, mice droppings litter the floor.

There are no rainbows or unicorns. Our daughter's new bedroom has a misshapen ceiling, walls bending this way and that, and a wall-to-wall seagrass matting carpet that is stained and ripped and damp. There is a brown puddle beneath a weeping radiator. Everything is cracked and wonky; the room seems to slope.

'Oh, darling! It's going to be so lovely!' Claire says, walking her downstairs. The squeak of our daughter's Crocs walking across dirty floorboards might be the thing that finally breaks me.

With her eyes filled with tears, my daughter's voice shakes. 'I showed Claire my new bedroom,' she says.

Glancing over her head, I notice Claire is crying now, too.

An animal, our daughter, makes a sound I've never heard before. At least I now know what heartbreak looks like. It is wide-eyed, pale and trembling.

Oh, what have I done?

11am

I'm still on the floor when the doorbell buzzes again. It's Nicole, a friend of Jill's I've grown close to online, as she too recently ended her long-term relationship. Claire lets Nicole in.

'Shall I take the little one back to mine?' Claire says, not really asking but instructing.

I nod. 'Yes!' I say, trying to remain upbeat. 'I'll come for you when this is all sorted, my angel. My Strawberry.'

I call our daughter Strawberry. I'm not sure if you know.

Nicole walks in. Our first real-life encounter. I should probably get up off the floor.

'Right. OK. What's the bathroom like?' she says.

'No clue,' I reply. 'I've been too scared to look.'

'Alright, let's start there. We'll make a list, see if we can sort this out,' she says. Nicole is strong, kind, motherly and determined. 'Come on, let's take notes.'

It's the worst room in the house. The bathroom floor is cracked and dangerous. A broken curtain hangs off the window, and the arm of a retractable mirror sticks out of the wall – minus its actual mirror. What the fuck?

The shower tiles are broken and dirty, the handheld shower head is barely fit for purpose, and doesn't really work. The mirror above the sink is cracked. There's no plug in the sink or bath. A large cupboard in the corner belongs to a horror show: *DIY Gone Wrong*. If such a show exists, they should film an episode in this house.

'Let's start downstairs,' Nicole says, but I've disappeared inside my head and can't hear her. Snapping her fingers in front of my face, she tells me to get out my phone.

The phone rings, then. It's Gabriele. 'Hiya, the removal van is here, just letting you know.'

Little did I know I was supposed to book out parking bays at the front of the house, and now there's nowhere for the driver to park, and they hate me.

Little did I know that for the past ten years I've leaned so heavily on you.

Noon

Nicole's on the phone to the estate agent. I hear her telling him he has to come 'right now'.

The van arrives with the bunkbed from Gabs's flat, then goes to the home of some other friends to collect the stuff I bought from them. Second-hand furniture that's already lived a full life in someone else's heart.

I can't think about the orange sofa at home.

It's still my home.

We bought the sofa when I was pregnant, using the money from the sale of my house. We went to the Conran shop in Marylebone on the tube. My belly was big and round; I remember feeling too pregnant that day.

'Try it out,' you said, which is when I couldn't get back up. Laughing made my throat burn – acid reflux, such a bugger. When I couldn't get back up again, you were laughing so much you had to walk off, leaving me to roll to the side and then on to the floor. We ordered the sofa regardless, knowing in a few weeks' time we'd be lying on it, cradling the son growing inside me.

Now our baby boy is nine and the sofa is no longer a place where I can seek comfort. No more Saturdays nestled within its soft orange glow, anime cartoons on repeat. The sofa I bought in a hurry from my friends Dan and Ali, a couple who moved back to Sydney during lockdown, will tide me over in this house. Having spent many funny days and nights at their house, I know the sofa's a bit hard and skinny. Like the influencers David seemed so enthralled by in Paris.

Shit, he's coming to say hi soon.

'Alex, who runs the estate agency, is coming over to have a look,' says Nicole, now on her third or fourth list, spectacles hanging from a colourful chain, mobile phone encased in one of those things you wear across your body. 'We need to get that *thing*, that ugly sofa, out of here. I'll talk to the van guys. We can pay them cash to get rid. I'm getting the landlord's number and will speak to her directly, just in case it's hers. Is it on the website, is it in any of the pics?' she says, glasses now pushed to the top of her nose as she searches for the property on Rightmove. 'Hmm, apparently she manages the place from Devon. Apparently ... right, nope, it's not in any of the pics, so it's going,' says Nicole – and who am I to argue?

Wherever Nicole's been hiding for the past forty-six years, I could kiss the gods, angels and deities that brought her to me today.

1pm

The van arrives. The removal men ask where I want things. No need to answer; Nicole does it for me. The second-hand stained velvet sofa disappears down the hallway. I hadn't realised it was *that* narrow, nor had I realised that furnishing a house from scratch, buying everything again, from beds to towels to potato peelers – and no, I didn't make a list – was such a huge job.

I have no plates, no cutlery, no sharp knife, no chopping board, but I did order far too many glasses from Soho Home. At least I'll drink wine out of expensive glassware tonight.

I watch the removal men bring in the furniture I've cobbled together. Dan and Ali's chairs arrive, and are placed around an Ercol table I found on eBay. I've sat on those chairs many times over the years. Then Dan and Ali's giant cheese plant totters past. I decide I'll call it 'Dan'. Like Aladdin, Nicole produces vintage lights, one after another. Apparently, she has storage units all over Kensal Rise.

I've taken nothing from our family home, for fear of upsetting the kids. I'll move my stuff out slowly. There's nothing worse than stripping a house bare without replacing photos and artwork, leaving empty walls, a bleak reminder that one parent no longer lives there. I wouldn't do such a thing. I mean, who would?

My Irish rescue dog, my clothes and endless pairs of shoes, my art books and easel, the expensive glass coffee table I'd saved up to buy. I don't want our kids to see a removal van show up at their door, to see men in overalls being directed by a woman barely holding her shit together. I worry about loading clothes and books into a lorry that says, 'Hey kids, Mummy is leaving, she doesn't care about you any more.'

I care so much it hurts.

2pm

It's aggressively hot, but Nicole shows no sign of leaving. The guys are slow, despite the minimal load. Something to do with having to move the van every few minutes to let cars pass. Shame fills my body. The kids were supposed to stay here tomorrow.

'I understand that, Alex, but the oven's a health hazard, the tiles in the bathroom are dangerously cracked, and the bulbs aren't suitable for bathroom usage.' Nicole is in the front room, arguing with the estate agent.

'We've had this house on our books for what, over five years now? And not once has a tenant complained,' says Alex, bristling in his suit, which to me looks like Reiss. I stare at his thick hair, wondering how long he spends styling it each morning to give it that kind of bounce.

'When was the last time you checked the property?' I say. I'm surprised I've managed to speak. Do all estate agents take their trousers in at the leg and shorten them to show a mono-grammed sock?

'I'll have to check,' says Alex. I notice his shoes. Bet they cost triple what he paid for his suit. Why do people do that?

'Stacey?' says Nicole. I can't hear her. I'm on a trip to Savile Row with Alex, picking out a less-shiny suit in a shade better suited to his skin tone. Next, I take him to a barber located near Jermyn Street. Don't you look chic, Alex!

'Stacey? What do you want to do?' says Nicole.

'What do you mean?' I reply, unsure I have a choice. At this moment, two weeks shy of a year since meeting Steve in the pub on Kate Spicer's birthday, I feel I have no other choice but to push forward.

'About this?' she says, shaking several pieces of paper contain-ing notes she will actually follow up on – unlike mine, written on the back of anything, lost before I can take action on one simple thing. 'This mess of a house.'

I resist the urge to tell Alex about the suit I found in my mind, plus his new haircut. 'Oh this? Oh it's fine,' I say. 'It's OK.'

'Right!' says Alex, clapping his hands. 'Here's the landlord's number. She's a very nice lady. I'm sure you'll have this place fixed up in no time.'

He leaves in a puff of Chanel ÉGOÏSTE. To ensure the pris-tine double cuffs of his shirt don't touch the dirty walls, he holds them up in an exaggerated way as he moves down the hallway. God forbid Alex should have a speck of dirt land on him.

3pm

I remember something I need from 'home', but now in full momma-disaster mode, Nicole stops me at the door.

'When was the last time you ate?' she asks.

No answer.

'Right, we're going to my favourite place.'

The removal men have left, along with the ugly sofa. Nicole didn't really give them any choice.

'An electrician's coming over to install the vintage lights at around five,' she says as we join the queue in Sonora. 'You have to eat. Come on, I'll choose for you – the veggie burrito is delicious.' In addition to ordering lunch, arranging the electrician and emailing my new landlord, she somehow manages to order a full set of cutlery, which she finds in the sale via the John Lewis app. We take our burritos back to the rental: our first meal together on the first day we've actually met. So many firsts in one day.

We move furniture, glasses, pictures, bits and bobs and crap. Nicole makes my bed – also bought from Dan and Ali – and then the cleaners (booked by Nicole, unbeknownst to me) arrive and scurry around the house like ants. Nicole calls the landlord several times, listing everything that requires replacing, including the crackhead oven.

As Nicole puts the house together, bit by bit, I can barely see one metre in front of me. On around her fifth call to my landlord, I hear Nicole manage to convince her to come to London. I hear the words, 'Great, yes, we can oversee the bathroom remodel.'

'Fuck. Does she hate me?' I say when she is off the phone, slumped on the bed.

'*Hate you?* It should be the other way round. You can't move the kids in here, Stacey.'

4pm

'Hey gorgeous, it's David, I'm coming over! I have champagne and I'm ready to go!'

Despite wading through an emotional tsunami, plus the fact I look horrific, having not seen him for a week I'm looking forward to skipping out of here to the pub for a beer.

5pm

The electricians arrive. They only have an hour, so we agree they should start on the sockets to make them safe first. Forget all about pretty lights for now – safety first. Together with the cleaners, I scrub the house. We've been cleaning for hours, and it's still filthy.

The cleaners and Nicole all leave at the same time, just as David walks down the broken path. He's carrying a hessian bag containing expensive, perfectly chilled champagne. Ironically, he's brought his own glasses.

'Sorry, I'm a mess,' I say, needlessly fluffing my hair, given it's stuck flat to my head with sweat. 'I've been at this all day and we've hardly scratched the surface.'

He opens the champagne and pours two glasses. I down mine as though it were Coca-Cola.

He's not looking at the house, he's fiddling with his flies. 'Can I have a blow job, baby?'

'What? The electricians are upstairs, fixing the sockets! NO!'

They're in my son's room as we speak, trying to make it safe enough for my child to plug in a PlayStation.

'Stop it, I'm exhausted, I'm sweaty. I need to sit down,' I say, on the verge of tears, barely able to believe this is actually happening.

'Come on, show me round, then,' he says, hard-on clearly defined in his too-tight C suite jeans. As for the Tod's trainers? Gimme a break.

'I don't want to. I can't show you around. It's a horrible, horrible mess. The place hasn't been maintained, not in years. I'd rather change and go out,' I say, walking towards the door. A quick glance in the hallway mirror Nicole magicked up from a storage unit confirms I should wear sunglasses.

'Stop it! Come on!' he says, taking me by the hand, nudging me away from the front door, edging us both upstairs instead.

'Where's your room?'

'This one. Careful, the doorknob comes off. The one next door is my son's,' I say.

'OOF,' he says, confirming that A) it's a shithole, and B) there's still a lot to do.

We look into my son's room. 'Hi guys,' I say to the electricians. Then I turn to David. 'And that one over there is ... '

I can't say her name. My beautiful baby's name is stuck in my throat.

'Oh, cute, let's see.'

In my daughter's room, he pushes and cajoles, teases, pokes, convincing me down to my knees.

'Just a quick blow job, baby.'

Another thing stuck in my throat this afternoon. I relent. Knowing the sooner I give in, the faster it will be over, I kneel down. Through David's legs, I notice Nicole has placed unicorn stickers all over the bunk bed. He puts his dick in my mouth. It's hard, but not as hard as the rotten seagrass grazing my knees.

'Let me just put it inside, just quickly. Come on baby.'

How have I ended up being fucked from behind by a man I met accidentally on a dating app, on a carpet of rotting seagrass with two electricians working to secure sockets in my son's bedroom next door, having just moved into a rental with a Chernobyl oven, a house my kids can't even visit? How have I agreed to sex on all fours, on this day, looking this bad, feeling this fragile? It is so far beyond anything I imagined my life might become, two years after walking down an aisle towards you.

'Stacey?' A knock at the door makes David jump. He pulls out without cumming (coming? – Sara, care to spellcheck?). When I open the door, the electrician, who has a nice face and a gentle manner, looks as startled as me. Hair standing on end, I look like Ken Dodd. My knees are in agony, sporting the rectangular patterns of the seagrass flooring.

'We're off now,' the electrician says. 'That's all the dangerous sockets fixed; we'll be back tomorrow to sort the rest.'

'Brilliant. Thanks for coming over at short notice.' Leaving David deflating, along with his ego, I walk downstairs after them.

'I gotta go,' David says, arriving in the kitchen, looking pissed off. 'Got to pick up the girls.'

'Hang on, wait. So you knew you were coming over just for an hour, and during those sixty minutes you planned to A) drink champagne, B) get a blow job, and C) have sex with me?' My voice is shaky. I'm crying inside. I can't let him see how hurt I am.

'I left the office, grabbed the drinks. I just wanted to say hi. But you're right. I should've had a wank before coming to see you. Should've got it out of the way.'

The door slams behind him. *Got it out of the way? He should've got it out of the way?*

6pm

I send you a WhatsApp: 'Hello, I'm still sorting out the house, best the kids don't come here tomorrow, I'll figure out how I'll see them.'

You reply: 'OK.'

Pouring a large glass of red wine into glassware from Soho Home, the only part of the Soho House lifestyle I can afford to buy into, I look around at my new life.

This is it. Everything I've been waiting for. The fun starts here! Alone at last, because that's what I wanted. To be free to pursue the happiness missing in my life.

Nicole left an atomiser from Muji plugged in by the oven. It was a welcome break from the stench at first, but having been on all day, the steam and chemicals are making my lips dry. Flicking it off, I notice the silence. Silence in the kitchen. Silence in the bedrooms. Silence in the garden. Silence, silence, silence.

Sitting at the Ercol table, I pick up my phone to call David. I plan the script in advance, like I do with the majority of conversations I have. Whether at work, with friends, with everyone, I'll rehearse lines in my head first. *Act breezy and blaze!* I tell myself. *Sound jolly – really, really happy!*

'Hi!!!' I'll say. 'The house is empty. Come on over, cowboy, let's crawl into bed!'

The pre-rehearsed script doesn't include: *Come over and lie in bed, if we can find it with all the crap in my room. I don't mind if you don't. Sorry about the grubby blackout blinds rolled up on the floor and the streetlamp streaming light directly into the room. Let's ignore it all, have a glass of wine. Come back, please. I really need you to come back. I need you to hold me tight. Please come back, hold me . . .*

None of these words are part of any script.

His phone continues to ring. Five rings, six rings, seven.

I won't mention how upset I am. Won't mention I'd had it in my head we'd pop out to the pub. Won't mention he hadn't made it clear he was just passing by for an hour. Won't mention I'm sad to be here alone, knowing he's with his girls and ex-wife at her house. Won't mention the house isn't safe for my children to come and stay, and that this was never the plan. Won't mention how degraded I feel after he dropped by for a blow job and quick sex.

He doesn't answer. I go upstairs to bed.

9pm–dawn

Restless, I try to relax.

Fuck. I'm having a heart attack. The pain across my chest is unbearable. Wave after wave. It drags me under. I'm roughed up, tumbled over. I've never felt pain like it before. It won't stop. It keeps coming. There's no one to turn to. Everyone has gone home, leaving me here on my own.

Happy now?

Five Thoughts On ... the Stages of Divorce, by Me

NOTE: I did not divorce due to domestic violence or abusive behaviour. If you're in a coercive, controlling, abusive relationship, this list will feel nothing short of trite. Perhaps skip it entirely ...

1. **MATHS!** People say, 'You'll know when you know.' You'll know when it's time to leave. You'll know when you've had enough. You'll know you can't live under these circumstances for a moment longer. For example, at Christmas lunch. It's always during Christmas lunch. You look across the table and think, *I'm done watching you lick your knife, pick your teeth, lick your lips ... whatever, several times per meal, seven days a week, four weeks a month, twelve months a year ...* As you excuse yourself from the table on account of feeling utterly murderous, you may wish to throw something at the wall. Ideally aimed at a family portrait in which they are a prominent feature. Taking yourself off for a quiet moment in the loo – just you, a strong drink and the dog who follows you everywhere – you use the calculator on your phone to work out how many times you've witnessed whatever it is that drives you up the wall.

   My biggest pet peeve is listening to people sigh after taking a small sip from a hot mug of tea. Huge, totally over-the-top sighs after sipping the smallest mouthful of tea are one of the most annoying things I've ever witnessed. I know being married to the same person can be deeply irritating, but if you're unhappy, go to couples' therapy.

Note: The same logic applies also to: using the last square of loo roll and not replacing it; leaving underwear on the floor for the magic fairy* to pick up; dropping wet towels on the bed for the same magic fairy to pick up; peeking inside the dishwasher, noting its contents are clean and yet closing the door again; finishing off the milk but putting the carton back in the fridge – and wrapping up a salad spinner on Valentine's Day so your wife thinks it's a Prada handbag.†

2. **COUPLES' THERAPY – AND MORE MATHS!**
Therapy waiting lists are long, and I know it's not cheap, but the reason I'm suggesting therapy before chatting is that unsupervised 'talking' can quickly turn sour. What might begin as a civil conversation at home may turn into the O. K. Corral within a matter of seconds,‡ which is best avoided, especially if there are kids in the house.

So, imagine you've had a few therapy sessions, or, if that wasn't possible, you've talked and talked, you've cried, you've laughed – now what? I'll tell you what, you'll keep your bloody mouth shut until you've DONE SOME MORE MATHS, that's what!

Oh, you're welcome, baby. I fucked it all so you don't have to. Right. MATHS. Please, for the love of God, the baby Jesus AND the Holy Spirit, do not mention the D-word until you've really figured stuff out. For starters, where will you live? Don't assume for a second the other party (divorce schpeak) will move out. And if the other

---

* The magic fairy is knackered. The magic fairy is not giving out blow jobs ATM, BTW.

† None of the examples in this section happened to me, but all are real – heard from friends and acquaintances along the years.

‡ Unless, of course, you go to the pub. No one fights in the pub any more. Not even my family.

party does move out, will they/you be able to afford the cost of running two homes?

Often, couples end up living together until the divorce is underway and a financial settlement has been agreed. And, of course, you have to consider what happens if there's nothing to divide. No equity, no savings, no pensions . . . And what if you or they were to lose their job? Write it all down, everything – ALL OF IT – from worst case scenarios and back again. You have to be sure you'll be able to pay the bills, the rent or the mortgage, and feed yourself and your family. Unromantic, right? I did none of this and, as a result, made myself very, very poorly (as my Manc Mammy would say).

3. **LAWYER OR DIVORCE COACH?** Alright, you've done the maths – both kinds. You've worked out if you forgo manicures, gym membership and having highlights at the expensive salon in town, you can just about get by. Check everything again, then subtract your lawyer's bills. Then beg First Direct for a £45,000 loan. The business of divorce is a racket. Your lawyer is there to secure you the best deal. Well, sure. But at a cost. And what cost are you willing to pay? And I don't only mean financial. Are you willing to go to court?

You may discover, once the gloves are off, that both of you can turn into Putin's protégé overnight. If the person you are divorcing can afford a legal team and you can't, this is what I fondly call 'being up cunt's creek without a cunting paddle'. I should know. That cunt was me. He had lawyers, but I – after hiring three and firing them all, because they kept going for the jugular of the opposing legal team, causing me unbelievable stress and worry at the thought of facing my ex at children's handovers – had none. Despite blowing a cool £30,000,

I found myself precisely nowhere. I now know, of course, the lawyer's job *is* to go for the jugular of the opposing team, thereby wreaking as much havoc as physically possible and increasing their billable hours.

The legal system isn't fair, and legal aid is non-existent. Enter, the Divorce Coach. I met Sara Davison thanks to my best friend, Instagram. She started coaching having been through the most horrendous divorce herself, during which she found herself grappling with a toxic family court system. You can read her 'Five Thoughts On . . . Preparing for a Divorce' in Chapter 32.

There is an alternative to all this, of course: you and your ex-beloved could have a jolly nice chat over a homemade chicken casserole (only applicable to non-knife-licking break-ups), and, after supper, come to an agreement to file for a no-fault divorce via the court to the tune of approximately £600. Wonderful. Bravo. Remember, though: even the most gentle 'conscious uncoupling' requires knowing what's at stake. Do you really have full exposure on what's happening money-wise? Paging Angela Lansbury . . .

4. **CHILDREN!** Decisions relating to the children must be based on *their* needs, not your wants, your ego. I agreed to fifty-fifty custody without a moment's thought because A) I'm neurodivergent and give very little actual thought to anything until I find myself swimming in shit up aforementioned creek, and B) I had a full-on full-time job. I hate to admit it, but due to financial panic, I put the job first. And there's also C) to consider: I do believe, where appropriate, two parents should have equal access to their children. However, our custodial arrangements were a shambles. Three days on, four days off, or whichever way round; by day three, I felt so lonely,

heartbroken and deranged, I couldn't see straight. After a lot of trauma and upset (both mine and the kids') my ex agreed to two days on, two days off, which looks like this:

Monday – with me
Tuesday – with me
Wednesday – with him
Thursday – with him
Friday – with me
Saturday – alternate
Sundays – with him

We did this for two years, until our daughter asked to spend Thursday evenings with me. Leaving ego at the door, he quickly agreed, and I happily took on the extra night with my daughter. Now, aged nine, she needs me. Aged fifteen, she may well hate me and want to live with her dad. By listening to our children, we've been able – minus the aforementioned initial fuck-up – to work around their needs. But my God, it's been painful.

5. **FANTASY VS REALITY!** This is a big one. In your mind's eye, your new life entails art school, lovers, new mugs (unless that's just me), nights out, yoga holidays, new interiors and wearing things your ex would've choked laughing at (pink velvet platforms). Eventually, it *might* be all of that, but not immediately, and not all at the same time. The reality of divorce is a lot of bill-paying, upheaval, crying, sadness, grief, frustration, exhaustion . . . I'll stop now.

Actually, I won't.

Because this is a crucial piece of advice, and I wish someone had shared it with me.

It's like this: the lover you're fucking, the young guy

you met on Tinder with a big willy and a penchant for older ladies and sexy time with hot wax from candles (DM me for details), and the mad night out where you snogged a hat-trick, snorted vitamin C in the DJ box, got chucked out for snorting vitamin C in the DJ box, yet still managed to get someone's number on the way out ... it's *so* much fun ... Oh ... my ... GOD! Midlife emancipation, worra riot!

What's not so fun, though, is school uniforms ending up between two houses, resulting in the youngest child wearing only one shoe and PJs on school run. In order to retrieve said uniform, youngest child has no choice but to hop down the driveway, where you await, wearing a balaclava and revving the engine like a getaway car.

The child asks, 'Mum, why are you wearing a balaclava?'

To which you answer, 'Child, you are wearing pyjamas and only one shoe – no one in middle-class Queen's Park must find out our identity. Here, stick this on.' Before screeching off down the road, you hand your youngest child a Halloween mask and a Santa hat.

'Oh, hiya, sorry – we're going to pass by and pick up some school uniform,' you type, in a hasty WhatsApp to your ex, hoping it reads in a manner that says, 'I AM A WOMAN WITH HER SHIT TOGETHER.'

Except, tragically, you're not, and therefore you end up holding a dog towel over your youngest child as she changes into her uniform in the front seat outside her dad's house. Let's just pray his new, young, hot-shot lawyer girlfriend doesn't exit the house to find his ex-wife wearing pyjamas and a balaclava, and forcing the youngest – still sporting the Santa hat, because fuck it, why not? – into her vest and pants. All because Mummy forgot to empty the washing machine.

Solo parenting is relentless. Solo parenting with a full-time job is exhausting. Solo parenting with a full-time job and yet still finding yourself broke is the reason I live with a permanent knot in my tummy. I do forget about all that shit when I head out wearing black latex (twice a year). As for the balaclava, it's Balenciaga – I shoved it on my credit card.

———————————

39

Panic Attack Mayhem

Top tip – if you think today is the day you might die, defo wear nice knickers

'It stinks in here, Mum.'
   I know, son. I know.
   'Mum, my window won't open.'
   I know, son, I know.
   'Mum, the curtains are see-through.'
   I'll change them when you're on holiday with Dad, OK?
   'I don't want to sleep in my room, Mummy.'
   Don't worry, you don't have to; you can sleep in my bed with me. Your brother is right next door. We'll all be cosy together.

Lies.

My stuff is still at the family home, housed in wardrobes that line one wall of our bedroom.
   Your bedroom.
   Ordered from Italy, my old wardrobes were a thing of wonder. Off to the side of our bedroom, we built an en suite bathroom:

large and airy, with a walk-in shower. We didn't bother with a bath.

Dark wooden floors and white walls, orange light fittings, modern wall-mounted side lights giving off a gauzy light. It was the most relaxing bedroom; I slept so well there. I don't sleep any more. I'm going to the doctor to ask for sleeping pills.

You were my home, but you disappeared. I don't know where you went, but I couldn't find you. I was scared to death, I didn't know what to do. And now this: several months of marriage counselling, a brief fling with a school friend, no more marital bed. After camping out in the spare room for months on end, piles of books and old copies of *ELLE* stacked on shelves to the ceiling, I had to leave. I couldn't cope. I've been distracted by David – is that the truth? I don't know any more.

Someone suggested the panic attacks at night could be grief.

Isn't grief what you feel when someone dies?

40

Holiday Mayhem

The kids go away on their first 'family' holiday,
I carry a sick bag in my pocket all summer

The kids left today. You're taking them to Italy, then on to America. A holiday alone, without me.

When you first proposed a three-week holiday, weeks before I moved out of the family home, it seemed the perfect plan. Three weeks alone in London to organise my new house before school term starts; three weeks to hang out with my Irish dog alone, just us; three weeks emptying wardrobes, beautifully fitted wardrobes with a retractable top rail, the perfect depth of drawers – shallow top drawers for underwear and tights, the lower drawers deeper, for storing bags and sports gear.

The flimsy wardrobe at the new house was already leaning to one side, but when I hung up a few things, it fell over and broke. Day two, no kids in the house, no rescue dog to scare, I allowed myself to fully lose it. I hadn't expected the sight of an ancient IKEA wardrobe on the floor would make me so fucking angry. Smashing the rest to pieces with a hammer, I threw it out the window. The landlord has agreed to fit an open rail in the recess by the chimney. Until then, everything is on the floor.

The pink sheets on my second-hand bed feel nice. Not as nice as waking up in my old bedroom. I miss opening the wooden blinds and looking out on to Queen's Park. I miss staring at trees like I used to, lying in bed with our baby girl. Our bed was a sort of sanctuary, all of life happened there.

I'm sorry the cupboards are still filled with my things. I thought you'd ask me to come home. I thought you'd come and find me. Did I ever mention that? What I'd say if you asked me to return? In the six or so weeks of living in this hellhole, too upset to eat or sleep, have I mentioned that I want to come home? Have I mentioned I can't take another second of living like this? Have I mentioned I'd like to come back to be with you, the kids, the dog, even the cat, if you'd only ask me?

The flood of grief is relentless. I'm bound to drown at some point soon. But I can't; I have kids, and I have to turn up at work. I'm a senior manager with a large team to lead: a team stretched to its limits, all looking to me, a walking-dead body presenting as someone with their life together, giving daily guidance over Zoom calls that drain me of all energy. I've hung a huge canvas behind me. A pastel-hued Venice Beach. Everyone remarks on how good the house looks.

Little do my colleagues know that the mug of tea in front of me is actually red wine.

Five Thoughts On . . . Grieving a Marriage (and why it's valid), by Julia Samuel

Julia Samuel is a psychotherapist and bestselling author of *Grief Works* and *This Too Shall Pass*

1. The break-up of a marriage can be what I call a living loss, where you experience the same sort of feelings of

grief as if a person had died. You can feel confused and alienated, furious, and sad and despairing, thrown onto this alien planet where you don't know yourself or the world. The level of your loss is equal to your level of emotional investment.

2. You grieve the marriage, the relationship with the person who is the father or mother of your children and what it means for you as a family: being under the same roof, being around the kitchen table, having birthdays and Christmas together and sharing the tasks, school drop-offs and all of that.

3. You are also grieving the loss of the future you expected to have. And, unfortunately, pain is the agent of change, and our brain is a learning machine and pain is the emotion that forces us to adjust to this new reality. It doesn't make a difference whether you chose the reality, or it was imposed upon you (although it can be worse if it were traumatically imposed on you), it can turn up the volume of the grief.

4. Even when you chose the new reality, psychologically it's still a massive adjustment that raises so many questions, particularly for women: who I am now, as a mother, as a woman; I'm not a wife so who am I as a sexual being? You grieve many different identities.

5. We can also grieve the loss of feeling safe. When there are two of you, even in a marriage that's not working all that well, there's a sense of being in it together. There's the protection of being able to share problems, incomes, tasks. So when one partner leaves it takes a lot of emotional recalibration in order to adjust to the new version of you.

The Divorce Diet

Calories per day – 500
Food groups – anything beige

Monday (after going on a Hinge date the night before)

Breakfast – skip on account of hangover
Mid-morning snack – 2 × cashews (organic)
Lunch – 1 tablespoon of hummus, 1 × oatcake
Mid-afternoon snack – 1 × bottle of Moretti
Dinner (fruit allowed) – half bottle of red, crisps, 1 × falafel

Tuesday (after seeing ex-husband on Tinder on the same day as receiving a lawyer's bill)

Breakfast – Toast with butter
Mid-morning snack – nothing, after receiving latest lawyer's bill
Lunch – 2 × large glasses of red wine, a couple of crisps (organic)
Dinner – 1 × beer

Wednesday (after pleading with bank manager to extend overdraft to £30,000)

Breakfast – 1 × almond, blanched (organic)
Mid-morning snack – 1 × oatcake (organic)
Lunch – 2 tablespoons of hummus
Dinner – 2 × bottles of Moretti

Thursday (child-free day + blind date)

Breakfast – Skip today
Mid-morning snack – 2 × glasses of white wine
Lunch – 3 × glasses of white wine
Dinner – 5 × glasses of white wine (don't bother eating; may ruin appetite for crying over blind date's shoulder)

Friday (meeting with lawyers)

Breakfast – zero
Mid-morning snack – zero
Lunch – zero
Dinner – 2 × bottle white wine, 1 × packet of crisps (organic)

Saturday (date with a guy from Tinder)

Breakfast – bread, as can't be bothered to use toaster
Mid-morning snack – nothing, unless someone brings it to me in bed
Lunch – as above
Dinner – The Tinder date, who looks nothing shy of mental

Sunday

Breakfast – Valium, as still out at 7am
Mid-morning snack – Xanax
Lunch – N/A (asleep)
Dinner – Antihistamine, Nurofen Plus, hummus

The Divorce Cocktail List

1. Negroni
2. Negroni
3. Negroni
4. Negroni . . . and so on.

41

Motherly Mayhem

I'm so sorry, I hadn't realised how little you are

Mid-August

Our daughter calls daily from your phone, the upset clear in her shaky voice. I should be there with her, with you all. I never set out to be a mother over FaceTime. In Italy with you, on FaceTime with me, I watch her rush around the hotel gift shop, holding the phone up high. She shows me a selection of rings. 'I'm buying one of these for you,' she says, a tinge of excitement in her otherwise shaky voice.

I try hard not to cry, to focus on my breathing, to look at the selection of rings being presented by a little girl eager to please her mother.

Her little body darting around the shop, souvenir shopping without me, a swimsuit festooned in flowers, her face so clearly filled with pain. The agony of not being able to hold her tight breaks my heart into pieces. Smiling, I choose a silver ring with a dash of white enamel. Inwardly, I'm falling apart. How mad is this, her on FaceTime, me busying myself in London, trying to make a home from ashes?

If I had curtains, I'd close them and go to bed.

42

Work Mayhem

Hanging curtains in high heels
and other outfits of deception

End of August

I only have myself to blame – for the lack of sleep, for the grief, but also for the fact the sun is blasting through a gap in my bedroom curtains, shining on my forehead like a nightclub strobe, but less fun. I used to spend hours in front of strobes, hands cutting through lines of moving colour, a matrix of light made more intense by a smoke machine. That'll be double-dropping two pills at DC10 in Ibiza for you.

What I'd give to be at DC10 right now . . .

Breaking and entering in the middle of the night, grief nudged me awake three hours earlier than my alarm was due to go off.

It flickers through my fingers and toes. It's odd how grief sometimes feels cold, like a sort of frostbite making its way up towards my heart, and yet at other times it feels hellishly hot as it pushes across my head and heart. Grief follows me around night and day, never taking a day off. It feels like grief is here to stay, and will always know where to find me.

I've never put up a pair of curtains before; couldn't be arsed, to be honest. In an act of internalised misogyny, I handed over all semblance of DIY the moment I met you. Then, after I fell pregnant with our son, the narrative became even more ingrained – cleaning out the dishwasher filter, descaling the kettle, emptying the bins, all of this made me think, *That's his job now.* It was the cause of so much frustration. No one likes to clean gunk out of a dishwasher filter; I could easily have done it.

You're not here any more. You never will be. So yesterday, I did the sensible thing and decided to hang the curtains during a busy Zoom call. Twenty-three work colleagues on an hour-long call, talking about – what? I honestly had no idea. Another call I didn't need to be on – but, because, looking back, I was boundary-free, I was emotionally unable to decline, and found myself once again trying to focus on their thumbnail faces. In the end, I turned off the camera and twirled the laptop to face the wall.

No one needs to witness a sleep-deprived woman clambering precariously up a borrowed stepladder, wearing black satin Manolos embellished with far too many crystals for daytime.

'There she is,' I imagined they'd mutter to themselves while on mute, 'all dressed up in expensive clothes, hanging a cheap pair of curtains in her crack den – LOL.'

Glaring at the cheap fabric arranged flat on the bed, with no clue how to attach the curtains to the grubby runner that edged the rattling Victorian windows, I knew YouTube would have the answer. After finding a reassuringly homely-looking woman, all round-faced and rosy-cheeked, I leaned my phone against the bedhead and watched her explain, step by step, how to attach little plastic hooks to both the curtain and the rod. First, I attached every single curtain hook upside down. I had to pause her – let's call her Deirdre – several times before eventually grasping what it was I had to do. After the fourth time watching Deirdre explain the same thing on repeat, the Zoom call going on in the corner caught my attention.

'Sorry, erm, is someone from merchandising on this call? Do we even *sell* curtain hooks? Please go on mute!'

Shit. Whoops. I don't recommend hanging curtains in heels during an important work call.

That was yesterday's news. Today, I'm in bed, arm hanging out, acrylic nails scratching the badly painted floorboards. I'm staring at the blackout curtains as if I'm Eleven from *Stranger Things*, hoping to fix them closed with my eyes, a streak of blood escaping from my nose, hand outstretched before me.

No such luck.

I'm awake three hours early, lying here, dreaming of nice curtains and strobes at DC10. The sun hits the crystally Manolos, and a pretty glitter-ball effect brings a moment of joy to the ceiling. I'd flicked the embellished Manolos off my feet circa 1am. Home from another shit date with another boring middle-aged man, another version of the same person, moaning about their ex-wife.

This one lives in Clapham, so I should've known it would be deadly boring. We went to Soho House Greek Street, where on a Thursday there's a DJ upstairs. Kicking off early, we sat outside on the terrace.

'Would you like to eat something?' he asked.

'Erm, OK, sure,' I replied, with an air of uncertainty, having just decided I didn't like his ears. They were small, coming to a small point at the top. His ears made me question the size of his penis.

I shouldn't be going on dates. Not with everything that's going on.

David, having invited me to go away for the weekend to the Fife Arms in Braemar, Scotland, sent a message detailing the cost of flights, hire car and the nightly room rate, to check 'whether I was OK with the budget'.

Modern, yes. Inelegant, very. That's a phone call situation, surely? Who knows? I'm so out of practice.

I'll wear them today, the Manolos that, despite the shitshow that is my life, somehow (at least in my mind) turn me into the type of woman who hosts catered dinner parties. In Manolos, I'm a woman who has fresh flowers delivered weekly and greets her banker husband on the checkerboard steps of her Notting Hill home with a gin and tonic. In Manolos, I eat shellfish and salad for supper and attend charity luncheons wearing dresses by Dior. The Manolos will have to work hard, playing their part in the show known as Outfits of Deception.

Clapham Dad, as I now call him, seemed to like last night. I drank a cocktail too fast on an empty stomach. Blind dates in middle age are an absolute fiasco; no wonder I'm hungover. Anyway, the curtains pretty much do the job. I mean, they close and keep most of the light out, despite the fact I attached the hooks all wrong, which means that when they're closed, one half of the right-hand curtain remains flat, while the other has too many gathers. Oh, Deirdre.

A headache.

Time to get up, can't sleep any more. Everything in life is different. I can't even eat breakfast any more. It used to be my favourite meal of the day. Just lifting a fork to my mouth makes my throat close now. Not that it closes when I lift a glass of wine – hence why I live on wine.

Wine, no food. I'm finally fashion thin, but too sad to enjoy it. Life is so cruel.

I'm due to present several videos in a studio today. Water off a duck's back before the shitstorm of divorce; not so much now.

My phone makes its first bleep of the day. It's 7am.

'Hi Stacey, there'll be a Cantonese translator with you today. To be COVID-safe, we'll provide a see-through visor for you to wear. See you at 1pm.'

I'm claustrophobic, but, given all the COVID-fear, I easily give in to the idea of presenting a video wearing a mask a welder might wear on a construction site. I can't argue, not when holding down a job I can't quite believe I managed to bag, despite the total lack of job description. Plus, there's no way I can afford to leave. After years earning peanuts in magazines, I have to wonder why this job came along just as I was falling apart?

My hangover barely registers. Not even as I board the tube, and people glance up from their phones to stare. Today, I'm dressed for my own funeral. Yves Saint Laurent knee-length dress with mega-wide shoulders (vintage, from the eighties), huge black sunglasses (always a good look in the dark tunnels of the London Underground), cycling shorts (as in the trend on Instagram this week) plus aforementioned crystal-embellished Manolos. It's a look that shouts I'm either on my way to a nightclub or returning home from one.

Dazed and tired, I glance at the tube map, realising that in order to reach my destination, a train station in Clapton (aka deepest, darkest East London), I'll need to change a couple of times. I'm annoyed I didn't pack my trainers.

I feel sick. The tube is rocking and my empty stomach sways. My bones feel dinosaur-heavy. I can't think straight. The scratchy feeling in the back of my throat is anxiety.

A rising smell of cheese and aftershave breezes through the open window that connects the carriages. From behind the darkness of my sunnies, I notice the next-door carriage is packed with stinky teens on holiday. Everyone piles on at Marylebone. Wedged between a small child and a man, whom I will to touch my arse just so I can have a fight, I fix my eyes on the middle distance. I try to calm myself with thoughts of the latest Balenciaga show, sweat gathering at the back of my neck.

'Next stop, Oxford Circus,' bleats the bored tube driver.

SHITE, I've missed my stop. The double doors open, and it takes all my strength to not vomit.

I'm all dressed up because that's what I do when I'm in 'full-meltdown mode'. I pull on my armour, my clothes: some borrowed (some permanently), mostly bought in the sales or vintage, all intended to give the appearance of a woman who has her shit together.

The grief ripping my body apart makes my heart race. I haven't seen my kids for three days, and my beloved twelve-year old rescue dog couldn't move with me to the rental.

Five Thoughts On . . . Grief, by Stacey Heale

Stacey Heale is a writer, former fashion academic
and mum of two who lost her husband to cancer

1. You will read about the Five Stages of Grief – denial, anger, bargaining, depression, acceptance – as a beautifully succinct road map, but this is nonsense. Grief is not linear, and will wander whichever way the wind blows at any given moment. I have felt all these emotions within the same five minutes, only to ricochet back to the beginning. Grief also includes bitterness, jealousy, horniness, deep joy, transformation, guilt, yearning, numbness, resentment, fear, loneliness, growth, perspective, maturity. The original five stages were written by psychiatrist Elizabeth Kübler-Ross, inspired by her work with terminally ill patients about to die. They were never meant as a template for those of us left behind.

2. Grief can be a beautiful emotion. While it will wrestle you to the ground to fight in the dirt, it will also show you the stars. To witness the death of a loved one close up will show you what is important, how short life is and how we need to make the most of our time. All the

clichés are true. Grief will change you irrevocably, and it won't all be bad.

3. As a society, we are poorly equipped to talk about grief and dying, despite them being the only real guarantee in our lives. We don't know what to say, so we don't say anything at all. Say SOMETHING – anything at all is better than a void. Silence is deafening. Don't give flowers to the grieving; it's another thing to watch wither and die. Comforting things, like cashmere socks, blankets or candles, make good gifts.

4. What has shocked me the most about grief is how everyone grieving for the same person does it in totally different ways. This can create confusion, friction and distance between people all in the same boat. I have been told so many times that I am so strong to carry on after losing my husband, but strength can be a poisoned chalice; it is the acceptable face of trauma and one that people often prefer. Resilience is more important: to be given the space to break and find ways to put yourself back together.

5. Things will change, then change again and again and again. The pain of grief will morph and alter over time. If we are lucky enough to live a long life and love many people, we will experience grief many times, so we need to make friends with what it brings to the table and the changes it creates. Breathe into that change, because there are good things on the other side.

———————————

43

Custody Mayhem

*I agree to a custodial arrangement I hate then
drink wine during the day in the bath*

Four days on, three days off. A custody agreement arranged –
erm, when, precisely? I must've agreed to it. Of course I did. Why
wouldn't I?

My days and early evenings are spent on Zoom, the kids walking
in with the unfriendly nanny I hired in desperation. They all wave.
The kids go into the living room to sit on the sofa and watch TV.

So, here we are. I've agreed to three days on, four days off.
Hang on. I don't get it. Which way round is it? And what do you
mean the days change each week?

Four days, three, it doesn't matter. By the end of the second
day without our children, spikes prick at the back of my throat.
They're seven and nine; it's a lot for them to handle. Their family
home without a mum, and their mum in a rental that's the opposite of a home.

The wine I poured myself before running her bath has helped. I
took a huge glug swigged before going upstairs to wash her hair.

I unbutton her grubby white school shirt as she stands on a towel thrown over the cracked tiles. Placing the shirt in the laundry basket beside me, I look up to find her crying.

As I gently remove her little white socks, her small body is rigid. Stepping into the bath, she looks at me, huge greeny-blue eyes filled with tears. I watch them slowly, quietly, gracefully roll down both cheeks.

'Why did you leave me?' she asks.

I hide my face behind her head. It takes a moment to gather my breath. 'Leave you?' I say, forcing a mask of exaggerated astonishment. 'I didn't leave you, my love. Dad and I agreed to split up, and we both agreed it would be me who moved out.' One of many well-rehearsed lines provided by my therapist, this particular one stored in a file marked 'emergency': the answer to the question I'd hoped she'd never ask.

I'm crying now. Silent tears dripping into bath water. 'My love, mothers don't leave their children. Dad and I split up . . . I never left you.'

I can feel a part of me break. It's located somewhere inside my chest. The sound of it snapping feels so loud, I'm convinced the whole street must've heard it.

'I mean, come on!' I say, lightening the mood, hiding my face as I wash her back for the twentieth time. 'It would be impossible to leave YOU! Hmmm. Let me think. Unless a dinosaur came back from the dead, grabbed me by the hair with its long, snaggly teeth and took me back to his house. Maybe then.'

I look at her. A small smile.

Oh, dear. What have I done? Both of us are broken.

'I'm sorry,' I whisper when she falls asleep in my bed that night, all cosy in pink bed sheets. 'I'm so very sorry.'

44

Alone in Mayhem

Please help me. Someone, please help me . . .

I wake up knowing this is the day I'll die. Possibly outside Liverpool Street station, four ambulance crew running to roll my body on to a stretcher, me opening one eye to ensure they don't rip my Saint Laurent cocktail dress (I still can't get over them dropping the 'Yves') as they prepare to use the now-fired-up defibrillator. If you're gonna go, might as well go in style. All dressed up and ready to die.

I mean, it *has* to happen today; it can't be medically possible for an adult female to survive on three falafels, eight bottles of white wine and a single salt and vinegar crisp (organic) for several days. I googled it, and apparently, by rights, I should've died yesterday. I'm 'fashion-editor thin', yet I don't feel joyful or triumphant at the sight of my shrunken waistline. I feel horrible and dirty, like my insides have been scratched out with one of those tiny nail files you get in Christmas crackers.

I have a headache; my face feels numb, and I'm in no mood to go to the office, to visit a studio, or to die publicly outside a busy tube station. At least if it *is* my last day on earth, someone else will have to sort out the HR admin. Who knew being the boss equals so much fucking admin? I assumed it meant more holiday and longer lunches.

Smashed to smithereens by my own hand.

Last night, I lay awake, hand placed across my chest, trying to soothe a broken heart. Perhaps it's not there; maybe it already left the building. I imagine it floating away from me, eyes following fragments in the dark, tiny stars heading towards the ceiling. I want to die. Today.

'Hi. I have ... food poisoning.'

'Oh, that's tough, sorry! Let's see how you feel tomorrow?'

A lame excuse, but I've used all the others: *I have a cold, I've lost the dog, I've gotta run to the vet, damn, the kids are off school.* The only other thing I can think of is a 'broken wrist thanks to a pair of new-season Prada platforms'. Too far-fetched, even for me. Surely it's impossible to be rendered bed-ridden with 'severe gastric poisoning' after devouring only one salt and vinegar crisp (organic) at the pub on Sunday. My boss and team appear to have bought it, though, and so my only plan today is to spend the day in bed, blinds closed, scrolling mindlessly through social media.

Mid-morning, I stumble across a woman I used to work with at *ELLE* magazine. Divorced, mega organised, confident and super glamorous, a ten-minute nose at her profile tells me she's rebranded from fashion editor to motivational speaker. I drop her a DM, telling her how upset I am. She responds immediately, sharing her phone number.

I run a bath and call her from there. The comfort in her voice pulls everything out of me. After two hours spent sobbing down the phone, drinking warm white wine in a cold bath, then crawling back to bed, I resist the urge to call you.

Resist sending a message: 'Please come get me, please bring me home.'

45

Mayday Mayhem

Silence is deafening

Autumn is here, meaning winter's on its way.

Cold weather. I feel it, smell it, dread it. It's 4pm on a rainy Saturday afternoon. It's been four days since I last saw the kids. I've missed their squabbling, missed their endless fights over everything and nothing. The morning race to see who can touch the Rice Krispies box first used to make me want to scream. Not any more. I even miss their loud fights over an invisible block of cheese.

The sight of their empty beds makes me feel like I might throw up, so I close their doors when they're at your house. Our family home. I can't stop calling it that.

I left.

Well, as we tell our kids, 'we both decided we were splitting up, and we both decided it would be me who moved out'.

I'm upstairs in bed, exhausted. With the cheap grey curtains closed, the room turns a reassuring pitch black.

On nights alone without the children, these four walls close in. I'm awake at my own funeral. I can only eat soft, beige food, such as hummus and buttery toast. I wash it down with too much red wine.

My friends don't get it. They don't understand how I feel. They mean well when they tell me to be alone at home as opposed to heading out for a crap date with a random met on an app.

'Hunker down,' they say.

'I shall,' I reply.

'Good! Get cosy!'

If only they knew, I'd rather be out with a random man, putting on the ritz 'n' glitz, all dressed up, pretending to be living someone else's life.

I lie on Dan and Ali's narrow sofa. I've tried to be on my own in this house: forefinger flicking the TV remote, endless trailers for TV shows with startling bright colours that manically penetrate my brain. I can't focus.

The only thing I enjoy is drinking red wine on an empty stomach. The buzz of it. I begin craving the instant hit of alcohol at around 3pm.

After an hour of scrolling back and forth between Instagram, Netflix and dating apps like a yo-yo, I decide enforced 'cosy nights in' can go fuck themselves. I'll do what I like, here, in this mess.

The stench of the house, the feeling of a hard narrow sofa beneath my back, the confusing TV. Drunk and restless I eventually head upstairs, back to bed.

I'm homeless.

I don't belong here. Not in this house, not in this body. I'm untethered, I can't find my footing. The anchor I thought I had has somehow come dislodged.

I'm in fast-churning rapids and can't remember how to swim.

Must stay alive.

I am alive, but dissociating, floating above myself, a ghost in *A Christmas Carol*. Somewhere deep inside, I know I'm dead. A part of me will never be revived.

*

Both children are now downstairs, watching a film. They mustn't see me in this state. My therapist told me it's OK to cry in front of them, 'because then they see you recover'.

Not today, there's no recovering on today's agenda.

Must not scare them.

Everything hurts.

My oesophagus is too tight to eat, reminding me of an octopus tentacle being battered against a rock on a beach.

I call Claire.

'Claire.'

'Stacey? Where are you?'

'Home. If that's what you'd call it. The kids are downstairs. I'm. I'm . . . ' Sobbing and shaking, I sound like someone trying to speak underwater. Inaudible, mouth moving, bubbles instead of words. 'I'm drowning. I'm not OK. I'm exhausted. It's just . . .'

'OK, it's OK. Try to breathe.'

'It's just this never-ending pain across my chest and in my throat. I'm so hot, but my teeth are clattering. Feels like a heart attack. H-h-h-h-hold on . . . call you back.'

Without hanging up, I hurl my phone at the bed and run towards the bathroom. Although there's nothing left in my stomach, a deep-sounding gag ricochets against the bathroom walls. I'm trying to be quiet, but the sound is horror-movie loud. This reminds me of being eight weeks pregnant. If only it were 2011. Loving partner by my side, belly round, housing a new life.

Safe.

Not unsafe.

Kneeling by the toilet, I think about my old bedroom again. Large, cool, airy and clean. Lying in bed, looking at the trees in the park across the road. I hurl again. I go to lie on the bathroom floor, needing a cold tile against my cheek, but the bathroom floor of my new home is heavily cracked, and I'm too freaked out to even step on it barefoot.

Bacteria lurk in every corner. I want to go home to my old bathroom floor. Pretty, soft grey tiles.

I go back to bed. Claire's still on the line.

'Stacey?! ANSWER ME!'

'Sorry, I'm back. Needed to throw up.'

'Have you taken something? Should I call an ambulance? Stacey, where are the kids? I'm not sure if you can hear me, but I'll be there in five minutes. DO NOT TURN OFF YOUR PHONE.'

The kids are perfectly fine downstairs. I haven't and wouldn't hurt myself. I am in pain, though, a kind that I never knew existed. It's not a heart attack – my heart is shattered into pieces, so small and broken I'm convinced it's no longer there. I no longer recognise myself. It's like looking in a mirror at a funhouse on Hastings pier.

The engine of Claire's car makes the rotting Victorian windows rattle. She knocks hard, and I can hear the kids open the door. She appears in my bedroom doorway; I feel her lay a cold flannel across my forehead.

'Everything will be OK,' she says. 'I'm taking the kids for hot chocolate.'

The door slams behind them, leaving me alone again in this hellhole. I let out a noise that sounds like foxes at night. Inside my head feels strange: it's not a whirring, but a single note, at a low pitch. Knife-sharp pains rip across my chest. I've stopped screaming.

The curtains I put up are coming away from the window. The chimney stack on the far bedroom wall gently whistles, like a jolly drunk on his way home from the pub. To keep the cold out, the landlord stuffed several black bin bags up the chimney stack, which I removed the day I moved in. Bin bags stuffed up a chimney made my bedroom look like student digs. Without them, all kinds of debris scatters, another thing to sort before winter.

From custody arrangements I can't remember agreeing to,

to the shitty rental I viewed via a video during lockdown, everything's a mess. I'm broken, I'm skint, I'm scared. I'm too stressed to work, but I can't lose my job. The room grows dark again. No longer able to focus on the crack in the curtains that lets the light in, I cry myself to sleep.

46

Enough Mayhem

I have to change the narrative

The crack den, as I 'affectionately' call it – not to the children, only to friends – is located so close to school, yet each morning, we're still magically, miraculously, messily late. So late, in fact, we have to enter by the side gate only to be faced by a member of staff who scares me witless. Me in pyjamas, socks and Birkenstocks, having walked the sum total of 500 metres; her, having set an alarm for 5am so she can beat the traffic. Nothing beats her withering look. What a start to the day.

We're not late yet.

I'm awake, but our daughter is sleeping beside me, cosy in pink bedding. She looks like an angel. As for the 'fresh start' pink bedding – how delusional was I, that day in John Lewis, still living in the family home, imagining a fun-filled life ahead?

Each morning, she and I wake up to flimsy windows streaked with a foggy steam, the sight of which reminds me of how much time we spent choosing the new double-glazed sash windows for our home. I hate this room, but recently it's been hard to get up, so I lie here, stuck to the bed as though someone has coated me with superglue overnight.

There's no excuse for being late.

I head next door to the room where our son sleeps.

'Broken radiator,' I say to myself, noticing a bite of cold in his room. 'Must fix his broken radiator.' I wake him up with a made-up song I've sung since he was a baby.

> Good morning, good morning, it's time to say hello
> Good morning, good morning, it's hard for you I know ...
> You're such a sleepy head,
> And it's cosy in your bed ...
> But good morning, good morning, that's what
> your mummy said.

Sometimes my voice cracks at the end, not that he notices my voice trailing off, croaky and on the verge of tears. I have to peel him out of bed these days, taking him gently by the shoulders, guiding him towards the loo. I've laid a towel down, as always, so they don't scratch their feet on the broken tiles.

My OCD is in overdrive. The filthy stair carpet gets me the most. It's like when I have to walk around the edge of a public swimming pool; the feeling goes through me like a knife.

I'm already dressed in head-to-toe new-season ACNE, a slouchy suit and heeled boots by Celine. I have meetings to attend, some in-person at a studio over in south London, a couple over Zoom. It's how everyone seems to prefer to operate these days.

Already late, the kids jump on their scooters. I'm angry inside, and I hear myself not being kind. I'm cross at our perpetual lateness, a lateness for which there's no excuse. My phone is already ringing. Work is already calling, and the kids in full dawdle mode. Not bothering to hide how pissed off I am, I lose my shit in the street. 'Hurry up! For God's sake! Hurry UP!'

I know I'm making our son nervous, but still, I don't stop

nagging and yelling. We get to the lights just as the pedestrian crossing is about to turn red. Red like my mood. Three ... two ... one ... 'KIDS, CROSS!'

Our son is flat on the road. He's fallen off his scooter, landing face first in a huge puddle. He's sobbing, she's sobbing, and so am I.

Raising my hand to oncoming traffic, I grab our crying children and pull them on to the pavement, where I hold them tightly to my body, giving zero fucks about the brand-new ACNE suit, now covered in mud.

'I'm so sorry,' I say, taking their scooters. 'Let's go to Gail's and have a hot chocolate.'

'Nooo, not Gail's!' they say in unison, which makes us all laugh.

'OK, Costa? Hot chocolate and cheese-and-ham toasties?'

In Costa, I email the school to tell them the kids won't be in today. At home, I put our son in the shower. I hang up my suit, take off a full face of make-up, peel off my jewellery and switch off my phone. We change into our pyjamas, and carry the super-king-size duvet from my bed downstairs. Hunkering down to watch films, we order pizza and Coca-Cola on Deliveroo.

With each passing hour, a different kind of bond begins to form. I switch my phone back on, only for a minute.

'Alex. Hi. It's Stacey. Yes, good, thanks. Work is busy, but fine. Listen, I'm moving out, and so this is me giving you, what, two weeks' notice? That's right. I know the contract states a year, with a break at six months, but the place isn't fit for purpose. I'm happy to fight this in court if you are?'

Once a family of four, now we are three. I hang up the phone, knowing I have no choice but to turn this ship around. I have to remain strong, not for me – for them.

My divorce in outfits

Day one after leaving marital home

Micro denim shorts that haven't fit for fifteen years, worn with a logo sweatshirt borrowed from my son. Assuming the style of a teenager. I'm thinner than when I was eight! Finally free of the shackles of marriage, I'll wear the tiny shorts. Fuck it, tomorrow I'll wear the tiny shorts with nipple tassels!

The weeks that follow moving to crack-den rental

The house is a mess, I feel destroyed, but I sure as hell refuse to look like it! Start working a trouser suit on the school run. Wear with low kitten heels, large black sunglasses, oversized gold hoops, and a small cross-body bag in black nylon by Prada. Accessorise, accessorise, accessorise, ladies!!

Begin walking really fast to give impression I'm late for a meeting. I'm not. I'm going to Gail's, then going home at 9.15am to get changed back into pyjamas and lie on the sofa.

Two months after leaving marital home – crack-den rental is shit, must not fall apart

Ramp up school-run lewks to include evening wear. Must NOT let anyone see I've totally lost the plot – not now, not ever. Due to exaggerated heel height, the kids take it in turns to pull me along on their scooters using a dog lead.

Months three and four after leaving marital home

It's all about funereal black. Head-to-toe black. So ill from grief I might die; might as well follow the appropriate dress-code.

Month five, exit crack den in a plume of crack cocaine, move to nice street

Apparently the woman two doors up works for Sotheby's, hence why I spent all night last night styling existing wardrobe into 'art' looks. My fave is a voluminous white Simone Rocha dress, worn, despite the cold, without tights. Paired with ankle socks and black-and-white ACNE brogues, it makes me look like an artist. I casually walk very close to her living room window so she'll notice me and want to become my best friend.

I buy a duck-egg blue bike, and look ever so Scandi-cool – until I crash into Sotheby's woman's recycling bin and fly over the handlebars.

I give up with the 'art' look, and buy a black latex catsuit, which I wear to a sex club one night.

Months six, seven, eight, nine after leaving the marital home (and for the next eighteen months, basically)

I've bought a tracksuit, which I wear with fake UGGs. Well, they're actually slippers Mum sent from her local Primark. I don't leave the house. I've cut up the catsuit. I'm dead now. Goodbye.

Two years after leaving the marital home

'Sweatpants are a sign of defeat. You lost control of your life, so you bought some sweatpants.'
– KARL LAGERFELD, *The World According to Karl*

Vow to get a grip but keep forgetting, so write 'GET A GRIP' on a Post-it Note and stick it to the bathroom mirror. The kids think I'm in a 'motivational memes' stage. Whatever. I've gained a stone and I blame the tracksuit – not the wine, not the lack of exercise, not the low-level depression, not the fact I panic-bought two guinea pigs to distract the kids from screens.

My life is shit and it's all the tracksuit's fault.

Let's skip several months due to pure misery.

Three years after leaving the marital home

Due to moving four times in three years, my clothes are located all over London: Claire's garage, Natalie's house, someone's loft. I can't be arsed to retrieve my wardrobe, so buy four pairs of the same Mango flared leggings and three black sweatshirts from COS instead. Due to more stress, I drop a stone, and instantly regret cutting up the sex catsuit. I buy a dress from Batsheva, fashioned from shiny black vinyl. It was 70 per cent off in the Net-A-Porter sale; I can't work out why no one wanted it.

Current look? American youth worker by day, sex maiden with part-time job in dungeon at night.

Five Thoughts On . . . Starting Over by Sam Baker

Sam Baker is an author, journalist and founder of The Shift, a weekly podcast and online platform that seeks to empower and give a voice to women over 40

1. It's hard to contemplate a different way of doing things when you've devoted your life to following a socially prescribed path, even if it's one that has sometimes felt like a bad fit for you. But it's important to remember there are as many different ways of doing things as there are people, and one size definitely doesn't fit all. It's never too late to try something different. In fact, I believe (later) midlife is the perfect time to make a big change. You have so much life left to live, if you're lucky, do you really want the rest of it to be a carbon copy of what went before?

2. People will tell you that you'll never work/get invited/be relevant/blah blah again if you leave London, or wherever. Ignore them. They're expressing their own fears not yours. (For every London-based job I haven't been considered for, there's another that's come out of left field.) The single most important thing is to be sure you're moving TO something, not away FROM it. There's a big difference between moving to a new life in a new city, for instance, and running away from the ashes of the old one. I had to take a long hard look at myself to make sure I wasn't doing this, but we had always wanted to live in Edinburgh and the combination of no longer being tied to London for my work and, unexpectedly, lockdown, made the time feel right to embark on something new and exciting.

3. Try not to hanker for what went before. And certainly don't spend every spare moment on Instagram reliving your old life. I was 'lucky' that our move coincided with the first lockdown because it meant everyone else was in a brave new world and had to adjust to doing things remotely, too. Would I have had FOMO if that hadn't been the case? Who knows. Quite possibly. Happily, for me, I never had to find out. Do I sometimes look at former friends on Instagram having a big night out without me and feel a pang? Of course I do, I'm human, but, on balance, I don't think I've ever been happier.

4. You don't have to change everything to start over, you might be leaving a job or a relationship, or moving to the other end of the country. It can be intellectual, educational, professional, physical, emotional. It can be big or small. Yes, we made the huge commitment of selling our house and buying a new one at the other end of the country, but the job I do is almost exactly the same. And so is my husband! I have new (and old) friends in a new city, but that's all. Timing is everything. I often wonder why we didn't do this decades earlier. We certainly talked about it often enough. But weirdly, when the time was right, the decision more or less made itself.

5. It can be difficult being 'the new girl' in a new city, especially if walking into a room of total strangers isn't your idea of fun. Double that if you don't have easy 'ins' like the school gates or a new workplace. Think of it like friend dating, have the coffee and every so often you'll encounter someone you instantly hit it off with. One of the great things about being 'middle aged' (ugh!) is that I can cut straight to the chase. So while I've had some duff coffees, I've never had two! And now I have a group of brilliant new friends who literally span thirty to seventy.

Middle-aged Disco Mayhem

Chiltern madhouse

Sara: You OK?

Me: No.

Sara: Why?

Me: Are you joking?

Sara: Go on.

Me: Oh, fuck off!

Sara: What?

Me: Shite rental, work is fucking full-on, the kids are a wreck, I'm hiring a lawyer to GREAT expense, David's a dick, I can't have Bo here, three days on my own without the kids makes me want to vomit, I can't eat, or sleep . . .

Sara: You need a night out.

Me: I think I do.

S: Let's go mad.

Thursday night, Chiltern Firehouse. Not the restaurant, the back bar where A, B and C-list celebs mingle with London faces and hotel guests. To get in, you either have to book a bedroom, be extremely famous or negotiate hard with a woman in possession of a large list and an even bigger ego. Outfits don't matter; it's not what you wear, it's who you know, who you're here to see. You can wear vegan Birkenstocks, if you're here to meet Kate Moss.

I had my hen night here, also a Thursday night. The long-sleeved, high-necked maxidress I wore then couldn't be further from what I'm 'werking' tonight. In my mid-forties, I'm channelling Paula Yates meets Joan Collins. The trenches of early motherhood are a distant memory. If the hen-night outfit was an outward expression of the married mother version of me, the Newcastle 'Big Market'-worthy micro-minidresses are a sartorial expression of whatever the fuck just happened to my libido.

I've turned into a cat. Tail up, purring as I rub my arse against lampposts/people/sofas. I don't get it. I started taking HRT last month. I'm hormonally charged with extra oestrogen – could that be the reason I'm as horny as a bonobo monkey?*

The other theory, according to Dr Google, could be that my body is having a last hurrah. My body, not me. It clearly now has a mind of its own. Or, it might be down to a surge of testosterone or progesterone. *Might*. No one seems sure. Just silly old ladies in middle age. What would we know, eh? We're deranged our entire lives thanks to being hormonally challenged. I know this much is true: if this shit, the perimenopause, were happening to men, it would be front-page news every single day.

Whatever the reason, all I know is I *have* to have sex: now, later, tomorrow, all night, in the morning. I usually channel Larry David on a night out (*Curb Your Enthusiasm* series one, not two),

---

* Please google bonobo monkeys. They fuck all day and night. They have sex as a way of communication, so instead of chatting, they mosey on up and have a fast and furious shag. Thanks! Ta-ra, nice to see you!

but I've even started to flirt – with everyone. I flirt with my salad, I flirt with barristers, I even flirt with the poor sod who has the misfortune of answering my call to First Direct. 'Well, helllll-loooooooo, how is the weather in Scotland todaaaaaay, purrrr, purrrr?' I only wanted to make an international bank transfer, not have phone sex.

I want sex. Not shit sex. Not quick, three-minute sex that, when it boils down to it, is nothing short of a bloke having a wank inside my vagina before putting his pyjamas back on and snoring. Noooooo, I want sex in a way I've never had it before. I don't know what this mythical sex looks like, but I do know I want to experiment. Not with whips and shit, that's not for me – although it's a big yes to being tied up.

Older, I feel freer. I want to be handcuffed. I want my pussy licked for hours. I want to give deep-throat blow jobs on all fours with my ankles tied together. I'd never watched porn before this year. Sara says that's bullshit, but why would I lie? I've never had an appetite for anything other than baby-making missionary position. As for the drug-fuelled one-night stands of my youth, they were utterly awful. Crap sex with crap men while high on crap drugs. No, ladies – this time round it's expensive heels, good fragrance and a decent set of undies.

Mind and body are disconnected right now, though. What with moving our kids to a shitty new home, and the deep, per-manent pain in my chest that never goes, I've never been so low. *Et voilà*, along comes sexual liberation for the ride, just to add another layer of mayhem. These months of existing here, in the darkest depths, waking up having tumbled still lower during the night, have made me understand life is fragile and precious beyond anything I could've fathomed.

Behind every dark cloud, there must be sunshine. Behind every heavily made-up eye, there's a Bobbi Brown non-smudge eyeliner.

'Let's go mad.'

Sara's last words before we decided upon Chiltern Firehouse. Deep breaths.

I've been summoned to her house early. No kids at hers or mine. I ring the doorbell. Looking at me for a couple of seconds, she makes a funny noise I shan't describe as a squeal, more of an intake of breath followed by a long, low whistle.

'What?' We're standing on the broad steps of her Georgian home. It's still warm and sunny.

'LOOK AT YOU!' she says in an Edinburgh accent that feels like family to me.

'Err, OK,' I say, with no clue what she means, given she's always so fabulously dressed, and I tend to follow her around bars and clubs feeling like a dork who only made it past the door person because my friend is really attractive.

'Look at how HOT you look! Come downstairs, I've opened a bottle of champagne. Wait, I need to take a photo of you. Divorce looks good on you!'

I'm wearing a boxy black blazer with huge diamante buttons and a pair of micro-shorts usually worn to a spin class. I totter in, wearing very high Jimmy Choo heels.

'Are you going out in those glasses?' says Sara, pointing at the light pink-tinted sunnies that I have zero intention of removing all night. 'Ha! I love them! Pure porn! Right, sit on the sofa – leg out, no, the other leg, right out, come on, there! HOT HOT HOT! Right, Chiltern first, then let's see where the night takes us?'

I'm out on the smoking bit, a small outside terrace accessed by the women's loo – not the restaurant loo, the loo used by the chosen ones whose names made it onto the guest list. Somebody gave me a dab of MDMA. I dabbed at the crystals in a plastic bag, wincing as it hit my tongue. I downed it with a nearby drink.

The thing about MDMA is how quickly it hits the system. The

lights blur golden and the previously chilly terrace feels warm and sensual. A woman wearing a skin-tight shiny black corset catches my eye. I have no idea what happened between the moment where we lock eyes and then mouths, but we've left the terrace and I'm in a cubicle with her. She dips a decorated acrylic nail into a bag of something white and puts it to my nose.

It stings. My nose hurts. We're snogging, pulling off each other's clothes, hers more difficult to remove than mine. Naked, unstable on high heels, I sit down on the toilet seat. Straddling me, she writhes around on my lap.

'STACEY!? Has anyone seen a redhead? STAAACEY!'

'Sara, I'm in here!'

'Oh.'

'Wait, I'll be out in a minute.'

Removing the woman's mouth from my nether regions, I tell her I have to go.

One minute you're eating organic muesli seated at a wooden table in the glass box extension of your architecturally designed home. The next you're getting off with a woman wearing latex. Didn't see this midlife roller coaster on the horizon.

Dear www.toyboywarehouse.com

Thank you for your recent delivery of a tall, young Frenchman. I have to say, after being alerted to the site by a couple of similarly aged girlfriends, logging on to the site for the first time was quite the eye opener.

First of all, I received more messages over the course of a day than a year's worth from Tinder, Bumble, Hinge, Inner Circle combined. Calling myself 'RED 74' – red hair, red alert, geddit? – in my photos, I decided to go for a casual look. This 'lewk', as the kids say, consisted mainly of me in an out-of-character tracksuit. Note to self, must wear tracksuits more often (sorry, Karl). Scrolling through 3,891 messages from men young enough to be my child, well, I had to lie down in a dark room for an hour. Many of the messages were themed. Cougars and their cubs, being the main one. Hilarious! One such 'cub', a snippet of a thing aged around nineteen, suggested in return for me paying his rent, he'd 'go down on me for hours'. Tempting. But no. Some of the cubs do seem a little vulnerable and I can't help but wonder if this were a site for middle-aged men looking for much younger women, perhaps you'd be policing the various messages and goings on? Then I laughed at my own motherly concern. The other way round? HAHAHAH. That's called daily life, baby!

Anyway, I happened across a lovely looking young man – let's call him Napoleon – who, from his photos, I could tell worked in fashion. WHOA! Turns out I was right, and, despite my tracksuit ensemble, he recognised me! Lol. After the lockdown restrictions were lifted, he came over to visit. Arriving at my door at the same time as my Lebanese food order from Deliveroo, I couldn't decide which one I wanted to tuck into first!

The kissing, however, was bad. Meaning I had to train young Napoleon in the ways of the slow kiss, which, to his credit, he soon picked up. Worry not, this is not me asking for my subscription back – this story has a happy ending (in every way). The first time we had sex we were both so paralytic drunk, no wonder it was a bit meh. At the time, I was forty-seven and he a mere thirty-four. I've had two children, big uns, meaning ye olde tummy is a little crepey. Not to be confused with a French crepe, btw.

I awoke the following morning to find this young man asleep beside me looking so much younger than he did the night before. Jesus, I thought to myself, this is cruel. I woke up looking like Animal from *The Muppets*, he looks like an angel. Can I be arrested, I thought, given he now looked twelve?

The point of my writing is to congratulate you. 'Toys R Us', 'Pets at Home', 'Toyboy Warehouse' – your catchy little moniker delivers exactly what is says on the tin. Continuing to have sex all day with this young French buck, by our third 'go', during which he tied my hands behind my back and gave me a thoroughly good rogering from behind, it's safe to say I had the best sex of my life.

If you'd allow me a small grievance? Just a small point. May I suggest a health warning in the form of a pop-up on your site? It could read, 'WARNING: ONCE YOU SAMPLE GOODS FROM THIS SITE, YOU WILL NEVER LOOK AT A MAN YOUR OWN AGE AGAIN'. Just a thought.

Many women like myself are looking for equal partners in life and society tells us we ought to seek out long-term relationships. Thing is, once Pandora's box is open and the younger man has infiltrated your psyche (vagina) you can kiss cosy nights on the sofa watching NETFLIX goodbye! Forget about 'mooching round farmers' markets on Sunday morning' and get ready to 'whizz dangerously around Ibiza on the back of Napoleon's motorbike'. The hem of a maxi-skirt caught in a motorbike wheel outside DC10 is an awkward way to die at almost fifty.

Anyhow, thanks for your services. I continue to 'date' said Frenchie two years on. A volatile relationship – the more he annoys me (I once hit him with a baguette), the better our sex. I'm not sure what that says about me. I'm seeking help.

Best wishes,

Stacey Duguid

Conclusion: In Pursuit of Happiness

Having never lost a parent myself, listening to my friend Mindi beautifully articulate the grief she felt in the aftermath of her mother's death made the hairs on my arms stand on end. 'Losing a parent is like living in a house with no roof. It's so weird, I can't describe it as anything else. I felt untethered,' she said. I nodded. 'Yes, sorry. I know,' I said. But I don't. I can't possibly understand how it feels to lose a parent, but I can relate to the painful feeling of living in a house without a roof. Such a powerful image.

As Mindi spoke, I imagined seeing her from above. From my bird's eye view, she looked small and fragile, white-blond hair whipped by a brutal breeze. The walls of her life remained intact, but without the protective roof that had once provided infinite love her house was slowly deteriorating due to elements she couldn't control. Roofless, the rain poured in leaving Mindi exposed and battered by grief.

I'd been living in my roofless house for a month or so when a passing tornado decided to ramp up my grief a notch or ten. A combination of crappy rental, no sleep, no food, not seeing my children for four days straight: I felt uprooted by the storm, as I was hurtled through the air at high speed. Life became a frightening blur of noise and mayhem, which for me, being neurodivergent, may have been all the more exaggerated, but I'll never know; I'm not sure how it feels to be in a neurotypical head. No escape, inside my mind became a frightening place to be. I don't like change at the best of times but this, this chaotic dismantling of a happy life in search of . . . of what? A bigger, harder, faster . . . erm, fuck? Was it attention from men I yearned for, as I swished past tables in restaurants wearing high heels, microskirts, lace body stockings (feel free to insert whatever clichéd item of 'raunchy' clothing you fancy, shall we add garter and suspender belt but leave out the Birkenstocks, maybe add a dog collar?). Showing off a newly slimmed-down body (see divorce diet for details, gotta love a beer for breakfast) – as difficult as it is to admit, it's true – I wanted to be seen as a sexual being. Confused by the appearance of this 'new me': despite what my mates might think reading this, I've never felt 'sexy' before. Funny, daft, odd, weird – yes. Sexy. Lol. No.

For years I've happily tagged along in the middle of the pack – on a night out I enjoyed playing the character of the slightly 'odd friend'. I disagree with pigeonholing women, it's unhelpful to be trapped in a box, especially as a young girl. To believe there's only one way to behave sets a too rigid confine of a perceived personality. *However*, ignoring that for just a moment, on a night out, Claire is the clever one who can destroy any person (man) in an argument in, erm, 0.3 seconds. Sara is the sexy one who can also shut a man up in 0.3 seconds via the black magic of Saint Laurent latex. Jill is the soft, seductive one – it's like being on a night out with a sultry stick of candyfloss. Kim is badass in a badass hat and no one fucks with the baddass. Stacey is, well, whatever costume I happen to have pulled on that night.

Random in bar: 'Who's yer mate?'

Sara: 'Haha, oh that's Stacey. Is she being rude, weird or funny tonight?'

Random in bar: 'Errr . . . can't tell.'
Sara: 'Better than being boring . . . bye!'

Excitement and fantasy, she says, spitting out her organic (over-priced) oat flat white. Jesus Christ, woman, why now, **why at this age**? Are you having a laugh!? I hadn't realised I was yet to be 'unlocked', as in sexually awakened and I don't mean threesomes at a hippy mushroom retreat. That is until a combination of hormonal shifts collided with feeling abandoned in my relationship set off a chain reaction involving a heady mix of Agent Provocateur and HRT, aged forty-five. I needed something 'other'.

Hang on, if all I needed was to feel sexy and seen, surely I could've found it in other ways and not dismantled the lives of my children and the life I'd been hellbent on having since Cinderella lost a glass slipper. I recently found this on my iPhone notes:

Am I a romantic fool for wanting to be loved, to be fucked, to be enjoyed? Probably. Yep. But still. That delicious feeling you sometimes get during a massage when your entire body tingles as if both body and soul are being caressed then this euphoric feeling like ecstasy wiggles through your toes. I want to curl up with another person, I want to wrap myself around them, inside them, underneath them. Full-on passionate, sensual connection in a long-term relationship is unrealistic, apparently, but I want to feel that thing people talk about at least once. Feeling the warmth of another body, devouring their touch and smell, listening to what their full lips have to say . . .

Then there's dancing. Music. Someone who will move their body with mine in bed and on the dancefloor and

The note tapers off at 'and'. I imagine a child interrupting the bad Mills & Boon with a scream, 'Muuuuuum, I really need a peanut butter bagel.' Is it greedy to want it all from a relationship – sex, love, intellectual stimulation, companionship? Is it unrealistic to yearn for a connection with a romantic partner that ignites mind, body and soul? Yes. And No. I have friends who, having been sexually 'unlocked' pre-meeting their husbands, are still, even post-kids, in happy, sexually active relationships. I'd never experienced sex on my terms before and not being medically trained, I can't say for sure whether hormonal changes, therapy, HRT, going back to a full-time job shifted me to another space, but there was an unlocking. With each passing month, I knew I wanted more. I just wish I'd gone about it differently.

Prior to and also during my marriage, I lived life on autopilot. In my mid-forties, the autopilot lever broke and I had to learn how to fly the plane. Clumsily, I crashed* and as a result, the past three years have been disastrous. I wish the past few years had never happened, but what if the autopilot lever hadn't broken, what if I was still living in autopilot?

Being interviewed for a podcast and hearing myself say the words 'sometimes I wake up and don't want to carry on', that afternoon I booked an appointment with my local GP and asked to go on antidepressants 'short term'. Why I felt the need to say 'it wouldn't be for ever', God only knows, but, right then, I knew I needed help. Alone in my roofless house, during the really bad months that followed my marital separation I lived in fear, waiting for the next round of thunderclaps. Two years of living in a house without a roof destroyed all semblance of self-esteem, and with grit and resilience all but washed away, grief accompanied me on an epic nervous breakdown. Grief is so thoughtful like that. Always with you, despite not being invited. The walls of my roofless home built on foundations of loss and grief collapsed and

---

* Imagining my jungle 'crash' looks would involve a vintage YSL safari jacket, a 'balloon' silhouette trouser in mid-khaki, Prada combat boots. Remain undecided when it comes to headwear.

during one particularly bad episode, I didn't know if I'd ever be able to find the strength to rebuild; to be the woman I once was. Whoever the woman I once was, was.

Two children, a cat, one dog, a boyfriend who eventually became a husband, until it was blown away, or rather, until I threw a hand-grenade at the beams that held the happiness of our lives together. Destroying everything I thought I'd ever wanted, I plummeted to depths I never knew existed. I hadn't noticed the shielding comfort of cohabitation until I no longer had it. I could blame my parents' divorce when I was three, their socioeconomic status, the fact that unbeknownst to me, I was very far from neurotypical, built from bricks of societal expectation, of fantasies and fairytales, of class structures, desires, wants and all the rest. Around twenty years old, I began to feel it in my body – I knew my foundations were flimsy. As for the roof, until it was replaced by grey skies and storms, I'd never bothered looking up. I also never bothered repairing the foundations, letting them rot instead.

Not once did I stop to consider that by destroying the protection provided by my marriage, the foundations of my life were not strong enough to hold me up. Built slowly over time, our family roof was constructed from quiet comfort. Not as half as sexy as pain and joy, comfort, an action not an emotion, but you get the gist, it's invisible. There's comfort in sharing 'life' anxieties, there's comfort in being able to roll a few centimetres to the left or right where another heartbeat keeps time with yours. During those middle-of-the-night panic attacks, there's comfort in knowing you can reach for someone else's hand.

Parenting is a relay race. As one parent tires from physical or emotional exhaustion (or both), the other is there (usually) to pick up the baton. Without a partner running alongside, I'm quickly outdone by two children in need of food, sleep, love, emotional support, a snack, a back tickle, FIFA points, help with homework or, more usually, help untangling school-playground politics. It's not easy, however, putting single parenting overload to one side, it's the financial pressure of keeping the lights on and the fridge full that truly sends me over the edge at night. I often think, *Oh well, you brought this on yourself,* which I know is an unhelpful thought. Buying a small, rundown house in Menorca as a pension plan – was that *really* the best idea? I wouldn't know: there's no one to ask. Well, perhaps I could've asked Claire or Nicole, but would I have listened?

The most trust I've ever had in a relationship, bar my close friends, is the trust I have for my therapist. Two years before I decided to leave, seated on her cream sofa, staring into her stormy-grey eyes, wrestling with the idea of becoming a single parent, she held me together. Through the untethered months and years that followed my marital breakdown – the hotel night, meeting a narcissist, being diagnosed ADHD, moving four times, losing a job that allowed me to live alone – by losing the plot, alongside my therapist, I've eventually been able to find myself. Not my 'old' self; I never really knew who 'she' was, more the essence of the seventeen-year-old who painted all day, that person.

There were many days I couldn't face going to therapy, but I went (well, apart from the time I went to the pub on my own at midday, proceeded to get fucking hammered, all afternoon, made Jill come to meet me so she could call my therapist to tell her I wasn't coming).

Apart from that time, I stuck with the often difficult therapeutic work and eventually, I evolved and grew. It's a massive relief to no longer approach life like an out of control child. Well, I say that. Read on.

Like all tornadoes, the mayhem slowly began to dissipate. Three years after making the decision to leave – for what? Cocktails and cock*, nights out and excitement? – I'm finally coming down to

---

* I wish we'd titled this book Cocktails, Cock and Coke: A Middle-Aged Adventure. Actually, no I don't. Imagine the awkward silence of my kids/mum/ex going into the local bookstore?

earth and, for the first time in many years, I can feel my feet on the ground. I feel present in my body and am (mostly) able to focus, albeit on ADHD meds.

As I end this tale, I'm happy to say I'm over the shock and grief, the mindless dating apps, the pointless hook-ups, and although I'd love to tell you I'm living my best life, I'm no longer a love addict and all the rest, well, meh. Sometimes life feels fantastic, sometimes not. I live in fear of the boiler breaking down or the roof collapsing. There's no magical spare pot of money and, unfortunately, money remains an issue in every way imaginable. Not having it, not earning it, or earning it and not being paid on time, not being able to save it, but mostly not respecting it.

On this, I continue to discover things about myself that shock me. For example, like a child I am prone to blithely handing over big decisions to those I deem more knowledgeable. RESCUE ME, RESCUE ME! SAVE ME SAVE ME! I'm not talking about my ADHD, autism or incoming arthritis, this doesn't apply to doctors and professionals.

So, you know that Menorca pension pot idea I discussed earlier, well . . . I hired a builder I entrusted to rebuild said pension pot when actually I should have found the strength to deal with it by myself. Falling for my ex-builder's stories pertaining to love, loss, life, sickness and divorce, I hired her 'knowing' she understood this bold, brave new life of mine. MIDDLE-AGED! DIVORCED! READY FOR A NEW CHAPTER – in my mind's eye, she was the only person able to sort out the dump of a house bought on a whim and let's face it, I had 'SAVE ME' written all over my face.

In short, sing this to the theme of Abba's 'Money, Money, Money':

Money money money,
Menorca honey

It's a builders' world
Money money money,
Menorca slummy
Bang goes Stacey's pension
OhhhhlAAAA TRaaalallalaalala
What a thing I could do
if I hadn't given all my money
To a builder
On the Balearic Island of Menorcaaaaa

Here's the thing I've recently discovered about myself: I find it hard to believe in myself. I distrust my capabilities. I assume others are more qualified to do the things I don't understand. We are not talking heart bypass surgery, we're talking a slap of paint, ordering a bathroom sink, shower and overseeing some builders.

I had to face my issues with money head on, had to take responsibility for my inability to function around budgets and bills. My hairbrain scheme of building a pension pot abroad (OK, you win Mr Suit, *ELLE* Magazine 2004) had fucked up because a blindness around money. Because I felt incapable of dealing with the Menorca house, I lost *a lot* of cash. My credit cards have now reached their limit and I owe money to friends, Mum, First Direct, American Express and the Halifax. At least that's my epitaph sorted.

When we're younger, we barely know ourselves. We don't know what we want and if we do, how to get it. Aged thirty, I wish someone had taken me to one side and told me what life has in store. Not the pension-pushing squire from *ELLE*, but someone more like me. Someone brought up in an ordinary household, who went to an ordinary school, who, despite this ordinary start in life, felt restless for extraordinary things. She would've told me true freedom lies in being financially independent. She'd point to the 'stuff' I thought I needed to buy on credit – the expensive armour I could not afford but bought in order to fit in – and say, 'This will eventually ruin you.'

This mythical woman would have told me, it's only celebrities who have babies in their late forties and fifties. Time is precious, she'd say, and your thirties is as important a decade as any you'll live through, but if you want children, crack on. This is the decade in which you'll lay the foundations for the rest of your life. Don't squander these years on debt, drugs and men who are not worthy of your attention. In order to have a decent relationship, she'd tell me I needed to first have one with myself. Had I had decent therapy aged thirty, I never would have sought validation from others. Others? No, just men.

I wanted men to love me in ways my fathers couldn't. I wanted men to save me, to rescue me, to be my safe harbour, because I didn't believe I was strong enough to save myself. Out there in the rough sea of life, if men were my life raft, what was I? Flimsy flotsam crashing around in the dark.

I wish she'd told me I wasn't flimsy and the dark was no place for a woman like me.

To be able to reflect and grow, to understand who you are, to have processed difficulties from childhood, this is what happiness means to me. Would I have left a marriage had I undergone this deep work? I don't know. Would the autopilot lever have broken? Not sure. Would I have married him in the first place? Can't tell.

Back to my mythical female mentor who would bring up, let's say on my thirtieth birthday, that when we're younger, we enter into relationships concerned only by surface issues. If I were to get married again, I wouldn't shy away from deeper questions. I'd want to know the following:

- Are we making money plans for our future independently or pooling our money?
- If together, what are our key investments – houses, ISAs, pensions – and are we in agreement as to how much we put in?

- How do we budget for bigger purchases – cars, holidays, etc.?
- How do we figure out who pays for dinner and who pays the gas bill?
- How often do you want (need) to have sex?
- What time do you want to go to bed each evening?
- What age do you plan to retire, and what does that next chapter of our lives look like?
- Do you wipe the poop from the toilet bowl? Coz if you don't, I can't do this.
- If I develop new sexual fantasies, will you be strong enough to go along with them?
- Is it OK if I take time out for myself every now and then?

'Your divorce is now complete' was the biggest anticlimax of my life but also the biggest shock. To the point, what had I expected? Balloons, streamers, glitter bombs, silly-string? 'The decree absolute has been made and you are now divorced.' Shock waves vibrated through my body. I cried so hard I couldn't breathe. Then I went to the pub on my own, where I drank a bottle of white wine too quickly. No kids around, obviously, I lay on my bed flicking through a dating app while drinking more wine.

One particularly bad day after the divorce, my therapist asked whether I'd considered I might be bipolar? I broke down in tears. Having always felt something was wrong inside my head, a few years before I tried to describe it to my ex-husband.

> It's like I can't think straight but I know the answer. I can't find the name of someone I've known for a long time. I know there's something I'm meant to be doing but there are also these three other things I've scheduled at the same time. It feels as though I have a row of 5cm thick cotton wool running from the front of my skull right across the top to the back.

When asked questions in meetings, I often couldn't think straight. But as perimenopause hit, my planning worsened, meaning I'd often arrive to meetings, either on screen or in person, totally unprepared, late and visibly shaken. Exhausted and scared, during the divorce, working full-time was both a blessing and a curse. As the hairline fractures I'd managed to keep hidden from my colleagues deepened, it was only a matter of time before the axe came down.

Cracking up, daily panic attacks became the norm. In digital meetings I'd turn off my camera and turn the computer away from me. I couldn't cope looking at so many faces, couldn't cope not being able to read their expressions.

I lost my job, and without the electronic diary (run by others) bleeping away from my kitchen table, things quickly went into a chaotic meltdown. At an appointment in central London, my phone rang. It was my neighbour telling me she'd 'just taken delivery of a very large food order'. (I never do them, but when I do I go BIG.) My phone rang again. My therapist. It was the third week in a row I'd forgotten our appointment. The same time and day for over two years, it was as if it no longer existed.

The day after my forty-seventh birthday, at 4pm on 19 May 2021, I logged onto Zoom to speak to a psychiatrist.

'OK, so you are not bipolar,' he said. 'You are high-ranking ADHD. No wonder you've not been able to grasp time, planning, etc.'

I cried and cried and I couldn't stop. Finally, an answer. It was to take another two years of therapy, however, to understand and actually believe I'm not stupid. So many years spent thinking I'm dumb – all those missed opportunities, the invitations accepted I didn't show up to. My sense of self-worth has never matched how I outwardly present. Perhaps this is why I escaped my feelings of confusion in nightclubs, shopping, recreational drugs and trying to find men who could save me.

Speaking of . . . David turned out to be a total narcissist. The term is bandied about like an Instagram hashtag, but he was the real deal. I discovered to my peril, narcissism isn't a meme, it's a serious diagnosis. The narcissist chases their target – or object of desire – and chases them hard. Flattery, empty promises, the target's boundaries eventually collapse at which point the narcissist pulls away. Boundary free, I have courted and attracted such men my entire life. Not my ex, he is not a narcissist. But many others were. I wanted David to love me, but I also wanted him to save me.

It wasn't a relationship I craved, it was security I needed. I felt destabilised in ways I can't begin to describe. At sea. Yes. Then some. I'd wake up in the middle of the night – no job, in a rental I couldn't afford, no family life. What the fuck had just happened? Dismantling my kids' lives for the sake of my own happiness, surely that's the ultimate act of selfishness, the last taboo? What kind of mother does that to her children? Two young lives blown apart so I could run at 'happiness' hard. Staying in my marriage would've been way easier and had I known what I know now I'm not sure I would've left the safe harbour of my marriage. 'Ships aren't supposed to dock in harbours for ever', a stranger messaged on Instagram. 'Go on, set sail, you'll be OK,' she continued. But will I? Ask me in a year.

I'd kept my career going through early motherhood, but, looking back, I parked a huge part of myself to one side – inevitable, I suppose. Perhaps that's how relationships are supposed to roll, both parties surrender to the business of working hard to keep a family together, neither one leaving the well-trodden path, losing hope of discovering new things not about their partners but themselves?

The role I've spent a life prepping for, a script I knew so well, is gone and three years on, I still feel unbelievably sad. From graduations to grandchildren, I imagined I'd be seated beside my ex, imagined the kids coming home to the house we built together. That future is over now. I asked a friend if the feelings of hurt, sadness, anger, grief stay with you for ever. 'Yes, but in a different way,' she said, avoiding sugar-coating the truth. The pain is easing, the tornado has buggered off to whip someone else's ass, the tight knot in the back of my throat isn't there any more, and it's been weeks since I've felt heaviness inside my chest. I'll never be the same again, but I'm no longer chasing happiness in the form of external validation and regret the mayhem I brought into our lives. But it can't be all about regret.

I don't regret being sexually unlocked by the much younger Frenchman (although I could've done without the choking-cock man, the narcissist ... you can fill in the gaps). We have the best sex I've ever had in my life and as for the last point in my earlier list: *If I develop new sexual fantasies, will you be strong enough to go along with them?* He takes me on the journey as much as he comes along on mine. Unlocked, well and truly unlocked.

It's been a full-on emotional rollercoaster writing this book and there have been many times I wanted to quit, to chuck my laptop out the window, to disappear from my agent and publishing house. POOF! I'm gone! I've disappeared. Instagram account closed down, no traces of Stacey to be found. That would've meant paying back my book advance, which is impossible, given it's been spent on the Menorcan money pit.

If only to prove to myself I could finish something properly, on time and without drama, I'm glad I carried on writing through the pain (which wasn't at all cathartic, btw). OK, OK. I filed this book very late and that distant choking is the sound of my friends laughing, given I wrote this book in their various beds, wearing head-to-toe black. I wrote this book in bed at friends' houses because it was the only place I felt safe. Knowing there'd be a knock at the door with a cup of tea, a salad offered or a glass of wine after 6pm, gave me the sense of safety to rake through the memories of my childhood and beyond.

I wish I could tell the scared to death forty-five-year-old me that although things feel horrendous right now, aged forty-nine, life starts to turn a corner. 'Sorry, love, you're still broke and the Menorca pension plan still has no bathroom or running water, but the relationship with your children, friends and family has never been stronger. Ditto your sex life, thanks to Toy Boy Warehouse Dot Com. Napoleon grew up, btw. Maturing like a delicious French wine, two years after meeting he now has a sprinkling of grey hair, which weirdly he attributes to dating me. Aged almost fifty and dating someone thirteen years younger, frankly we look pretty much the same age, unless that's all in my head. Probably.

Becoming sexually unlocked, together with a truck load of therapy, has led to the kind of body confidence and self-love I never thought I'd possess.

Days and nights no longer spent swiping between Instagram, Tinder, Twitter, Instagram, Hinge, I get my dopamine leveller from ADHD meds. Where previously I'd scroll, add to basket and buy tons of stuff on Net-A-Porter, the medication means I no longer seek out the 'highs' I once used to. As someone who has spent a lifetime seeking highs, engaging in risky behaviour and impulsive decision making, I can't begin to describe the relief at finding the peace I now feel. A tatty jigsaw puzzle always missing a piece, it turns out it was peace itself I could never access.

Being at peace has opened up a space for creativity and curiosity and a year ago, I began making stuff. During the periods when this book became too painful to write, I closed my laptop and began making the weirdest things out of whatever I could find. I buried photographs in the garden only to dig them up later and paint on top of them with latex and flour and water, turning them into wonky 3D forms. I stuck the photos and debris into sketch books and began painting and drawing, making stuff without thinking or seeking perfection as an end result. Dropping out of art school at the age of eighteen has always been a huge regret but, with space to think and create, six months ago, I took the plunge and applied for a place at art school. As this book lands in bookshops, I'll be starting a Fine Art MA at Central St Martins.

I wish I could tell you all about it, lost forty-five-year-old me – you always wanted to go to St Martins...

As for the roof, I'm fixing it myself. Not the leaking, broken one in Menorca, God only knows when that will be sorted, I'm talking about the one which exists within. Rebuilding it without precise drawings or plans, without a proper budget assigned (because why change the habit of a lifetime). I can't guarantee it will end up watertight. But is anything 100 per cent weatherproof in this life of ours? Replacing the comfort and protection of a marriage for a future unknown, had the autopilot lever not broken, had I not pursued my own happiness at the cost of dismantling the happiness of my children, three years on, would the roof of my family home be showing signs of irreparable collapse?

Possibly. Yes.

Then what? Stay until I'm sixty? Leave aged fifty? I don't have the answers. I really don't.

Happiness is fleeting, thank God. Imagine being happy all the time? For starters, I'd have fuck all to write about. Over the years, pursuing happiness has led to nothing but the opposite and now, I realise, it's contentment that feels good. The mundane, the everyday. Tending to the abandoned garden of a rundown house bought to be near the kids' schools. Seeding and planting a garden from scratch. I'll hold the cheesy metaphors and just say this: contentment is underrated. Could *In Pursuit of Contentment* be the title of the next book I vowed never to write? Hopefully there'll be no taking to bed wearing head-to-to black for six months this time, but, still, figuring out new chapters is frightening. You never know how the story will end. And maybe that's the point.

Acknowledgements

Children, I told you never to read this but if you do, don't judge. Life isn't meant to be straightforward, nor is it meant to be this messy. I love you both more than you'll ever know.

Thanks . . .

Sophie Baudrand for always checking in, even though I never call back. Per Erik Borja for your mystic counsel. Natalie Alexander for making my teenage years so special. Maurice Marshall – your ability to find me in a random field off a roundabout is second to none. Space in Ibiza for providing the most fun I've ever had in my life. DC10 for afters. Simon Bushall plus me in a blonde wig because, well, you know.

The woman who started it all, Lorraine Candy, Editor-in-Chief, who, during my time at UK *ELLE*, spotted the future writer in me.

Theo, for so many things and also styling the cover of this book. And Manuel Obadia-Wills for photographing it using film in order to make it look extra special. Apologies to the swanky retoucher in Paris who had to deal with retouching my hair extensions. And he thought the Saint Laurent campaign was a tough gig – LOL. Thank you Paul Smith for the loan of the blazer, Manolo Blahnik for the borrowed shoes, and Falke, sorry I kept the tights.

Robert Caskie, literary agent who, fourteen years ago, signed this 'future author'. Jesus mate, apologies for the longest gestation period known to womankind.

My editor Jillian Young for being so unbelievably calm and in control. And patient. And kind. And for asking to meet after you read a piece I'd written in *The Times*. Nicola Jeal for commissioning the piece that resulted in this book. Nothing like a two-hour deadline on a Monday morning.

Mike, my mum's latest and hopefully final husband: thanks Mike for the past twenty-five years of travelling to the stinky south to fix things in whichever house I happened to be living in. You're ace. As are you, Lee, little brother, ditto your wife, Jessica, who I made 'go live' with me on TikTok whilst drunk at Centre Parcs. Joan and Ralph for your endless love.

Paul Sheldon, a life cut too short. I miss you.

Tony Hull for reigniting my passion to create. Whoever invented hummus, as otherwise I'd be dead by now. Inanche for my borrowed hair – I love you. Estelle Lee for all your help. Mark Broadbent, fellow Jedi. Tara, Gabs, Kate Monro, Martin C. Anne Marie Curtis for your patience, and also ignoring that time in 2008 when I got off with a random woman at the *ELLE* Style Awards and snogged her for hours in front of the CEO. Apologies to the accounts department at *ELLE* 2004–2013. Thank you for the emergency phone calls as I wrote this book, Sam Baker. Sam Jones – you inspire me every single day. My 'girls', the women with whom I want to grow old.

Thank you First Direct for the twenty-five-year overdraft.

Love you Dad. Don't be offended. Love you Mum. I'm glad we stopped fighting. Although the fight in the back garden in the pouring rain would've made for a brilliant TikTok. Love you.